The Liberal Delusion
The roots of our current moral crisis

John Marsh was born in 1947 in Cleveleys Lancashire and educated at Blackpool Grammar School and the universities of Lancaster and Oxford. His study of history and philosophy led to a lifetime interest in these subjects and especially on the impact of Enlightenment thinking on society. He taught history briefly before working in law and commerce. In 1997 he established a property investment business in London. He is married with three grown-up boys. His book *The Liberal Delusion* examines liberalism in the light of recent scientific discoveries, and argues that liberalism's core belief in human goodness is false, unscientific and harming society. His conclusion is that society has become too liberal, and that we urgently need to reappraise liberalism and separate out the positive, such as the commitment to greater social justice, from the negative - excessive freedom and loss of morality.

The Liberal
Delusion

The roots of our current moral crisis

John Marsh

Arena Books

First published in 2012 by Arena Books

Arena Books
6 Southgate Green
Bury St. Edmunds
IP33 2BL

www.arenabooks.co.uk

Distributed in America by Ingram International, One Ingram Blvd., PO Box
3006, La Vergne, TN 37086-1985, USA.

John Marsh
   The Liberal Delusion the roots of our current moral crisis
1. Civilisation, Western – 21st century. 2. Liberalism. 3. Social ethics.
4. Politics and culture.
 I. Title
303.3'72-dc23

ISBN-13   978-1-906791-99-5

BIC classifications:- JFF, JFM, JFH, JFCX.

Printed and bound by Lightning Source UK

Cover design
By Jason Anscomb

Typeset in
Times New Roman

This book is printed on paper adhering to the Forest Stewardship Council™
(FSC®) mixed Credit FSC® C084699.

ACKNOWLEDGEMENTS

Over the last few years many people have helped me on this book: by acting as sounding boards for the arguments, reading chapters and commenting on them, proof-reading etc. However three people deserve a special mention: Gary Linney, Dr. Peter May and Dr. Stephen Wren.

Contents

"Mankind is naturally good."[1]

Jean-Jacques Rousseau

"An honest discussion of human nature has never been more timely. Throughout the twentieth century, many intellectuals tried to rest principles of decency on fragile factual claims such as that human beings are biologically indistinguishable, harbour no ignoble motives, and are utterly free in their ability to make choices. These claims are now being called into question by discoveries in the sciences of mind, brain, genes and evolution."[2]

Steven Pinker, Professor of Psychology at Harvard,

in *The Blank Slate.*

"It is the liberals who fear liberty
and the intellectuals who want to do dirt on the intellect".[3]

George Orwell in *The Freedom of the Press*

---

[1] J-J Rousseau *Seconde Lettre à Malesherbes 12 Janvier 1762* Hachette ed X pp.301-302
[2] Steven Pinker *The Blank Slate* (London Allen Lane 2002) Preface page xi
[3] George Orwell *The Freedom of the Press* (an essay originally drafted as a Preface to *Animal Farm*), The Times Literary Supplement, 15 September 1972

Foreword

This book is my attempt to answer a riddle, to solve a puzzle. Have the changes in society and culture over the last 50 years been beneficial or harmful, or a mixture of the two? I am not claiming that everything was better in the 1950s; but I believe there have been losses as well as gains since then. Many of the changes have been driven by the dominant outlook of this period: liberalism. So my journey of exploration has been in part an attempt to understand liberalism. Obviously for all of us it is our own experiences that play a key role in shaping our views. I was fortunate in many - but not all - respects in my childhood.

I was a babyboomer, born shortly after World War Two at Cleveleys on the Fylde coast of North Lancashire, and so I became conscious of the world in the late 1950s. I loved the landscape of northern England, the Lake District, the Pennines and the Lancashire Dales. We were lucky to have a caravan on the shores of Lake Windermere and would travel up to the Lakes through pretty villages like Yealand Redmayne and Yealand Conyers. We would stop on the way at a second-hand bookshop in Kendal to buy holiday reading such as Sherlock Holmes stories. Once arrived we used to canoe on the lake and go across to one of the islands for BBQs. In this setting I read Wordsworth's poetry and each year my school, Blackpool Grammar School put on a Shakespeare play. Life was also enriched by being part of a large extended family with aunts, uncles, cousins and grandparents. My paternal grandfather, Arthur Marsh, was my mentor.

I remember an era of optimism and growing prosperity, coupled with a feeling of fraternity born of the hardships and comradeship of wartime. I have fond memories of Lancashire folk, who were - to use a Lancashire dialect word - jannock: fair, straightforward and warm, people who today some sections of the media demonise. It was an era of stability with a sense of common purpose. The Labour Party had created the National Health Service and helped make society more equal, and the Conservative Party in the 1950s had embarked on a vast council house building programme. I can just remember the coronation of Queen Elizabeth - an occasion for national rejoicing. We took a pride in British achievements, including standing alone against Hitler. At that time Britain was a world leader in computing, nuclear power and aerospace. So in many respects life for me was rich in terms of nature, society, family, history and culture. Yet it was not a good time for minorities: poor Alan Turing, having brilliantly helped to solve the Enigma code during the war and pioneered computing, was chemically castrated for being homosexual; class divisions were still too wide and ethnic minorities suffered discrimination. Also women did not enjoy the greater equality we have today.

Later as a student at Lancaster and Oxford universities I met many self-styled progressives, but found their arguments unconvincing: Marxists hoping for the dictatorship of the proletariat, blithely ignorant of the horrors of Stalin's Soviet Union or Mao's China. I had studied Marx as part of my degree and knew his theory was deeply flawed. I had doubts about the progressive prospectus; yet doubters like me were in a distinct minority. Later I discovered fellow sceptics. George Orwell was furious when liberals tried to stop the publication of *Animal Farm* - a shameful episode. In response he wrote an outspoken hard-hitting preface to that book, which still burns with incandescent rage. It has been largely ignored by the people who were its targets - liberals and intellectuals. It was published after his death as the essay *The Freedom of the Press*. In it Orwell accused liberals of dishonesty and of trying to falsify history; he gave as an example - the BBC.

Sir Isaiah Berlin in a famous essay called *The Two Concepts of Liberty* explained how liberals had undergone a peculiar evolution, from a belief in freedom to an intolerant conviction that they were morally and intellectually superior, and this gave them the right to bully and coerce others. When he was Prime Minister Tony Blair wrote to Berlin challenging his arguments in that essay. Blair asserted that there was a case for a superior elite imposing its views on backward ordinary people; although he did admit that it hadn't worked terribly well in the case of the Soviet Union. Quite so. Later Rowan Williams, the Archbishop of Canterbury accused white liberals of saying things which were demonstrably untrue. Historians Simon Schama, Robert Conquest and Norman Davies have all confirmed that history has been slanted to favour a liberal viewpoint. Events which show liberals and rationalists in a bad light have been swept under the carpet. Shaun Bailey, a youth worker and pamphleteer, argues that middle class liberal values have harmed poor communities. I examine all these arguments in greater detail below.

So we need to establish whether things are getting better or worse! We are wealthier, but not happier. The riots in English cities in August 2011 showed the fragmentation of society. I have tried to disentangle the various strands of liberalism, to separate out the benign from the damaging, the positive from the negative. I believe that in many cases the initial moves in a more liberal direction were helpful, but they have been carried to excess and become harmful. It is time to take stock; are we heading in the right direction, or towards moral anarchy and social disintegration?

Introduction

Is western society based on a mistake? Fundamental to any society is its understanding of human nature. It shapes our worldview and explains other people's behaviour. It affects attitudes and practices on a whole range of issues including: interpersonal relations, the upbringing and education of children, family policy, welfare, economics and penal policy. Our understanding of human nature is crucial, yet we rarely - if ever - discuss it. Since the 1960s the dominant view of human nature in the west has been a liberal one. The word 'liberal' is hard to define - a bit like nailing jelly to a wall. Nevertheless, here goes ! The word 'liberal' comes from the Latin 'liber' meaning free. Freedom lies at the heart of liberalism: free love; freedom from rules, regulations and restraints; freedom from external authority; freedom of thought; freedom from superstition and ignorance; freedom from oppression, hierarchy and privilege; freedom from the past and tradition.

In practice it has led to: the liberalisation of the laws on drinking alcohol, gambling, divorce and abortion, a sexually promiscuous society, economic liberalism with free markets and deregulation, and the ending of censorship. I hope it is clear that I am not using the word 'liberal' in any party political sense, but rather indicating a mindset and worldview. In other words 'liberalism' with a small 'l', not a capital 'L'. Most liberals are decent well-meaning people, who are rightly concerned about fairness and social justice. Also in the past liberals played a positive role in fighting social and racial prejudices. However these positive aspects should not prevent criticism of liberal ideas in the present.

The belief in freedom rests on an unspoken assumption – the goodness of human nature. If we are good, it makes sense to increase freedom, because we do not need restrictions, rules, morality or religion. Freedom will not be abused; our natural goodness will prevent this. Therefore we can liberalise laws and adopt liberal attitudes, and no harm will come. So maximising freedom assumes human nature is essentially good. I believe this assumption is mistaken. In this book I aim to show that it is contradicted by recent scientific discoveries, by the insights of Freud and Jung, by the evidence of history and by the experience of social workers.

Our view of human nature has changed over time. For thousands of years Judeo-Christian societies were based on the Bible. In the story of the Garden of Eden God forewarned Adam and Eve not to eat the fruit of the Tree of the Knowledge of Good and Evil. They ignored the warning and ate the forbidden fruit. As a result, they were driven out of the Garden. This *allegory* stands for the imperfection of human nature and the reality of evil. In religious jargon - we are sinners. This does not mean we are wholly bad – in the Middle Ages the word 'sinner' was used in archery for an arrow that fell short of its target. We are imperfect - not totally depraved. On this understanding children are sinners too and need to be disciplined and socialised by parents and the community, so they can become productive members of society. Also parents are wiser and more experienced than children, and so should be respected. In the words of Thomas Sowell, the leading African American philosopher, "Each new generation born is in effect an invasion of little barbarians, who must be civilised before it is too late."[4] In this tradition stands the 17th century English thinker Thomas Hobbes, who regarded human beings as self-centred, and saw conflict as endemic in social life.

This Biblical view of a flawed human nature was challenged around 300 years ago in the Enlightenment, which turned traditional notions upside down. For example Rousseau claimed children are born wholly good, but later their families and society warp them. In his own words, "Man is born happy and good, but society corrupts him and makes him unhappy."[5] On his theory children are pure and innocent, whereas parents and society have been corrupted, so children are morally superior to adults. It follows that parents should respect their children who are leading us to a better world. These Enlightenment ideas partly explains our present reluctance to discipline children. Child-rearing and education have fundamentally altered over the last hundred years. We have gone from a strict, authoritarian approach, to 'progressive' ideas and child-centred learning. One contributor to this trend was the founder of Summerhill school - A. S. Neill, who believed children are "naturally wise and good."[6] So they should be given the maximum amount of freedom, and never be disciplined. He represents an extreme form of liberalism, but his and other 'progressive' ideas have seeped into the educational system, resulting in some secondary schools that are marked by ill-discipline and anarchy. In Britain today school councils of pupils have been set up, which in some cases have even appointed teachers. A friend of ours teaches 4 and 5 years olds at a local primary school. She has found recently that more and more of the children starting at the school are aggressive, assertive, disobedient and very difficult to control.

In 2010 Frank Furedi, Professor of Sociology at Kent University, wrote "A substantial group of parents have given up disciplining their kids altogether.... Powerful cultural pressures are making parents uncomfortable disciplining their children."[7] Parents have abandoned 'tough love' and try instead to be friends with their children. These ideas have empowered children and enfeebled teachers and parents, whose authority has been called into question. Their confidence in disciplining children has been undermined. Parents no longer feel able or willing to tell their children what to do. It seems now that children teach parents, rather that being taught by parents. As a result many children grow up knowing few

---

[4] Thomas Sowell *A Conflict of Visions* (USA Basic Books 2002) p. 162.
[5] "Que la nature a fait l'homme heureux et bon, mais que la société le deprave et le rend misérable." Troisième Dialogue (Hachette ed IX 287) cited by E. Cassirer *The Question of Jean-Jacques Rousseau* (USA Columbia University Press 1963) p. 18.
[6] A. S. Neill *Summerhill* (London Pelican Books 1968) p. 20
[7] Frank Furedi interview in The Sunday Times 21/2/2010

boundaries, which often leads to unruly youths and anti-social behaviour. The riots in English cities in August 2011 are a stark illustration of this.

Also on this theory, criminals are essentially good, but have been warped by society, and so should be seen as victims of society, rather than offenders. This has affected our penal policies and the treatment of criminals. I helped run Victim Awareness courses in a local prison. At the end of one session, a group leader said that one of her group had been born very poor in Jamaica and wanted to make money – not unreasonably. He figured the best way was to run drugs into England. He did not have a British passport, so he had to use a fake one – not unreasonably. As a result he was now serving time for drug running. The group leader said we should think of him as a victim, not a wrongdoer. Additionally the prisoners in their cells have televisions, set-top boxes, computers and game consoles. They wear their own clothes; cook their own food; and a new block is being built with en-suite showers. One prisoner said to me - with no prompting on my part - "It's like Butlins in here mate."

However the liberal understanding of human nature has been contradicted by science, according to Steven Pinker, who is Professor of Psychology at Harvard. He argues that recent scientific discoveries relating to evolutionary psychology and genetics - including the Human Genome Project - have undermined the belief in inborn goodness. They have revealed a flawed human nature. He wrote, "Genetics and neuroscience show that a heart of darkness cannot always be blamed on parents and society."[8] In other words: the human capacity for evil is inborn. Pinker claims these discoveries undermine the worldview of many intellectuals. In his own words, "They eat away at the cherished assumptions of modern intellectual life."[9] Pinker rejects the idea of Richard Dawkins and others that the end-product of evolution is altruistic and unselfish human beings. Dawkins argues that blackbirds feed a cuckoo chick in their nest, because they are programmed to feed their own chicks, but their brains 'misfire' so they feed other chicks in their nest as well. He believes human brains misfire in a similar way, and as a result we love everyone, not just our kin. Pinker rejects this as nonsense. His stark conclusion is: "In a nutshell: Hobbes was right, Rousseau was wrong."[10] Far from mankind being innately good, Pinker gives a list of inherited human defects, including: the primacy of kinship; limited sharing within human groups; universality of violence, dominance and ethnocentrism; self-deception about our own wisdom and fairness; and a moral sense warped by kinship and friendship.[11] If Pinker is right, then the idea that men and women are born good is unscientific and mistaken.

Liberal thinking was also rejected by Freud, who saw the mind as an arena of conflict between our conscious and unconscious minds, and between the

---

[8] Steven Pinker *The Blank Slate* (London Allen Lane 2002) p. 51
[9] Pinker p. 58
[10] Pinker p. 56
[11] Pinker p. 294

superego (the conscience) and the id (the instincts such as the sex drive). Powerful forces in our unconscious minds have an influence on our thinking and behaviour of which we are unaware. Jung went further. He dismissed the notion of inborn goodness as nonsense. He held that an understanding of our flawed nature was necessary for us, but we are resistant to the truth. He wrote: "The jungle is in us, in our unconscious, and the psychologist who tries to expose the blind spot faces a thankless task. The human mind carefully refrains from looking into itself."[12] And "All that nonsense about man's inborn goodness, which has addled so many brains after the dogma of Original Sin was no longer understood, was blown to the winds by Freud, and the little that remains will, let us hope, be driven out for good by the barbarism of the twentieth century."[13] [Original sin is religious jargon for the idea that we are born imperfect and sinful, rather than innately wise and good.]

Criticism of liberal values has also come from the youth worker and pamphleteer Shaun Bailey. He grew up in a deprived inner city part of London and set up a charity called MyGeneration, which works with disadvantaged youngsters. His background is in the West Indian community of west London, where he was brought up by a single mother on a council estate. He claims liberalism harms the poor, "The more liberal we have become, the more the poor have suffered."[14] He describes the outcome of liberal policies as: a lack of discipline in schools; the erosion of marriage; the subversion of parental authority; encouraging free love and casual sex; fostering dependency; and the relaxation of the laws governing drugs and alcohol. He accuses the middle-class liberals of living their lovely lives in leafy suburbs unaware of the damage their policies cause to working class communities.

History too provides plenty of evidence of human evil. The 20th century showed the ugly side of mankind: the slaughter in the trenches in World War One; the deaths of over 120 million under communism - 50 million in the Soviet Union between 1917 and 1953, 70 million peacetime deaths under Mao, plus those who died in the killing fields of Cambodia and elsewhere.[15] These deaths are in addition to the 6 million victims of the Holocaust. Everyday there are news stories of murder, violence and war. Anthropologists have found that most primitive societies are violent and conflict-ridden, thus confirming human nature is flawed. So the evidence against the belief in innate human goodness comes from science, psychology, history, anthropology and social workers.

---

[12] C G Jung *Jung Letters* (London: Routledge & Kegan Paul 1976) Vol II p. 608 Letter to Mr. Leo P. Holliday dated 6 November 1960

[13] C G Jung *Psychological Reflections* (London Routledge and Kegan Paul 1971) p. 277

[14] Shaun Bailey *No Man's Land* (London Centre for Policy Studies) 2 May 2007

[15] The figure of 51million in the case of the Soviet Union and Soviet Russia see Norman Davies book *Europe(London Pimlico 1997)* based on the work of Robert Conquest and Roy Medvedev (Appendix III) and the figure of 70 million under Mao see *Mao: the Unknown Story* by Jung Chang and Jon Halliday (London Jonathan Cape 2005)

Despite all this evidence liberalism has not merely survived, it has become dominant in western societies. This is a puzzle. Why does it persist in the face of so many objections, and the evidence of human evil in history? The answer, I believe, lies in its emotional appeal. In his book *The God Delusion* Richard Dawkins exemplifies this, writing, "I dearly want to believe we do not need policing - whether by God or each other – in order to stop us behaving in a selfish or criminal manner."[16] This is sentimental and unscientific. It is based on ignorance of human psychology and history. It may be easy to think mankind is good, if you have been brought up by loving parents in a nice area and led a sheltered life. Your fundamental assumption is - unselfishness and kindness are normal. You may be surprised by reports of child abuse, domestic violence and murder, as well as bloodshed in other parts of the world, but you regard these as exceptions. One self-styled liberal said to me, "To be frank I live in a middle-class bubble. I'm not really aware of what goes on in poor communities."

Many people are deeply wedded to their utopian worldview. They resist any questioning of it. We prefer to think of ourselves as wise, rational and virtuous, rather than flawed, self-centred and fallible. It is nice to think that other human beings are essentially good. I remember discussing the topic with a nice old lady, who lived in a village in the Chilterns. She told me she would be depressed if she thought other people were unkind and bad; she preferred to believe in human goodness. She said to me, "I don't *want* to believe that mankind is flawed." Was she a seeker after truth or someone who had found her comfort blanket? T. S. Eliot wrote, "Humankind cannot bear very much reality."[17] However there is a problem with the rose-tinted and optimistic view of human nature: it can lead, for example, to a failure to socialise and discipline children, and then the outcome can be anti-social behaviour. Whereas if you accept reality, you can take steps to deal with the problems. But haven't some societies been too strict and disciplined? Yes, that is true. However the abuse does not remove the use. Just because some societies have been too disciplinarian, does not mean there is no place for discipline.

It was in the 1960s that a liberal and progressive consensus came to dominate British society. The Labour Home Secretary Roy Jenkins claimed a liberal society was a civilised one. However, looking round Britain today, 'civilised' is not always the word that comes to mind. Our society is marked by binge drinking, broken families, a growth in violent crime and a decline in trust. We have taken sexual liberation too far and have the highest rate of teenage pregnancies in Europe. As Jung observed, humanity only thrives when spirit and instinct are in harmony, "Too much of the animal distorts the civilised man, too much civilisation makes sick animals."[18] We have gone from the Victorian society's denial of sex, to one that is obsessed by sex: from the dominance of the superego, to the triumph of the id. Our phoney understanding of Freud believes

---

[16] Richard Dawkins *The God Delusion* (London Transworld Publishers 2006) p. 260

[17] T S Eliot *Burnt Norton* (The Four Quartets)

[18] C. G. Jung *Psychological Reflections* (London: Routledge and Kegan Paul 1971) p. 105

that we should never deny our sexual urges, and that any thwarting of our sexual instincts will result in neurosis.

My attempts to discuss these ideas with liberal friends have met with very limited success. In his book *Liberalism and its Discontents*, the distinguished American historian Alan Brinkley wrote of, "An unwillingness or inability of many liberals to look sceptically or critically at their own values and assumptions."[19] I have often met a refusal to engage with the evidence and the arguments. Steven Pinker has also encountered opposition and personal abuse. Those who challenge the liberal hegemony have been called 'fascist' or 'Nazi'. Pinker wrote, "Part of the responsibility of intellectuals is not to trivialise the horror of Nazism by exploiting it for rhetorical clout in academic cat-fights. Linking people you disagree with to Nazism does nothing for the memory of Hitler's victims, or for the effort to prevent other genocides."[20]

So is this book a straight-forward attack on liberalism? No. It is not as simple as that. There are some areas where I believe liberals are right. I acknowledge that some liberalism is necessary and beneficial. Few would want to go back to the restrictions of the Victorian era or live under a despot. There was also a need to free us from a negative attitude to sex. Liberals are right to be concerned about inequality and to fight for social justice. There still remain great inequalities and their campaign for greater fairness deserves support. I welcome the undermining of the class system, the greater opportunities open to women, and the improved treatment of racial and sexual minorities – the decriminalising of homosexuality is an obvious example. However some liberals seem to think that they have a monopoly of caring. Thomas Sowell, the leading African-American philosopher, commented "Liberals assume that if you don't accept their policies, then you don't care about the people they want to help."[21]

There is, I believe, a downside to liberalism. Freedom has often turned into selfish hedonism. We have neglected other values: the importance of social cohesion, of duties, obligations and responsibilities to others. We have lost ideals of self-restraint and self-discipline. So my argument is not that all liberalism is bad, but rather that in many areas we have become too liberal; that the liberal pendulum has swung too far. Liberty has become licence. Liberalism is like cholesterol: there are good and bad sorts. Therefore we urgently need to evaluate the positive and negative aspects of liberalism, and to discard those which harm society. In the next chapter I present the evidence against the belief in the goodness of human nature from science, anthropology, psychology and history.

---

[19] Alan Brinkley *Liberalism and its Discontents* (Cambridge Massachusetts Harvard University Press 1998) p. xi
[20] Pinker p.154
[21] Thomas Sowell widely attributed but unsourced

CHAPTER 1

The Liberal Delusions:
Human Nature is Good and Rational

There is no original evil in the human heart. There is not a single vice to be found of which it cannot be said how and when it entered.[22]

Jean-Jacques Rousseau

My belief in the goodness of the child has never wavered. ... a child is innately wise.[23]

A. S. Neill founder of Summerhill School

Why are we so good to each other?[24]

Richard Dawkins

The seemingly airy ideas of Enlightenment philosophers have entrenched themselves in modern consciousness, and recent discoveries are casting those ideas in doubt.[25]

Steven Pinker

One of liberalism's core beliefs is that human nature is essentially good. In this chapter I present the evidence against this belief, but that does not mean I believe in the opposite - the total depravity of mankind. I believe we are a mixture of good and bad.

Rousseau maintained children are wholly good, so there is no need to discipline them. How did he come to his conclusion? From years of close observation of children? He fathered five children by an illiterate servant girl. After each birth he at once took the baby down to the local orphanage, left it there, and had no later dealings with any of them. So his theories were not based on personal experience. Perhaps it is easier to believe that children are innately wise and good, if you have as little contact with your own children as Rousseau. The British educationalist A. S. Neill, was a follower of Rousseau. He was headmaster of Summerhill School and his book on it sold over one million copies; it was on the syllabus of 600 American universities. In it he wrote, "I cannot believe that evil is inborn or that there is original sin."[26] He maintained human beings are good and want to do good. He thought that all crimes were frustrated attempts to be good and claimed that a burglar, who leaves a turd on the carpet after burgling a house, is leaving something he values, as recompense

---

[22] Jean-Jacques Rousseau *Emile* (New York Basic Books 1979) p. 92
[23] A. S. Neill *Summerhill* (London Penguin 1968) p.20
[24] Richard Dawkins *The God Delusion* (London Transworld Publishers 2006) p. 252
[25] Steven Pinker *The Blank Slate* (London Allen Lane 2002) p. 13
[26] Neill p. 12

for the theft! [27] He summed up his approach as follows, "We set out to make a school where children were free to be themselves. In order to do this we had to renounce all discipline, all direction, all suggestion, all moral training, all religious instruction. ... We had a complete belief in the child as a good, not an evil, being. For over forty years this belief in the goodness of the child has never wavered."[28]

These ideas can be traced back three hundred years to the Enlightenment, which brought a new understanding of human nature. Lord Shaftesbury argued mankind is innately benevolent and Morelly dismissed the view that, "Man is born vicious and wicked."[29] The French thinker Condorcet wrote, "Is there any vicious habit, any practice contrary to good faith, any crime, whose origin cannot be traced back to the institutions and prejudices of the country."[30] Sir Isaiah Berlin wrote, "What the entire Enlightenment had in common is the denial of central Christian doctrine of Original Sin, believing instead that man is born either innocent or good, or malleable by education, or capable of radical improvement by education."[31] The German historian Ernst Cassirer observed, "Original Sin is the common opponent against which all the different trends of the Enlightenment join forces."[32] And in the words of the English historian Lesslie Newbigin, "It [Original Sin] was regarded as the most dangerous and destructive of dogmas, which had perverted human reason. The first essential for liberating human reason was to destroy the dogma."[33]

Rousseau also thought that in primitive communities, uncorrupted by civilisation, natural man lived in harmony with nature, with others and with himself - a contented being. This gave the theory of inborn human goodness its name – 'The Noble Savage'. Bougainville's account of Tahiti in his *Voyage Autour du Monde* of 1771 portrayed life on the Pacific Islands as one of blissful harmony, and helped to spread the gospel of the Noble Savage. In reality, he had fled from various islands whose inhabitants were violent. Later Margaret Mead in her book *Coming of Age in Samoa* depicted an idyll in the Pacific. The Samoans, she claimed, were naturally good: at peace with themselves, with others and with nature. However later anthropologists, such as Derek Freeman, studying the same Samoan society, found that daughters were beaten or killed if

---

[27] Neill p. 159

[28] Neill p. 20

[29] Étienne-Gabriel Morelly *Code de la Nature* Premiere Partie. "L'homme est naît vicieux et méchant."

[30] Antoine-Nicolas de Condorcet Sketch for a Historical Picture of Progress of the Human Mind (USA Westport Conn Hyperion Press 1955) p. 193

[31] Sir Isaiah Berlin *Against the Current* (Oxford University Press 1981) p. 20

[32] Ernst Cassirer *The Philosophy of the Enlightenment* (USA Boston Beacon Press 1966) p. 141

[33] Lesslie Newbigin *The Other Side of 1984.* Cited in Paul Weston *Lesslie Newbigin: a Reader* (UK Cambridge Eerdmans 2006) p. 194

they were not virgins on their wedding night and that rape was commonplace.[34] The young girls, whose accounts had been the basis of Mead's book, when interviewed again later by Freeman, said that her version was untrue. She had simply projected onto Samoan society her preconceived image. Rowan Williams, the Archbishop of Canterbury, commented that "white liberals" have a "sentimental reverence" for the culture of native peoples before the arrival of Europeans.[35] It is part of what he calls the "mythology of the goodness of the inner self."[36]

So is the Noble Savage true or a myth? Are we innately good and rational, or flawed and irrational? My wife and I organised a birthday party at a local swimming pool for one of our boys. Afterwards in a nearby room there was food and drink. The boys arrived at different times after changing. A large chocolate cake had been cut up rather quickly with the pieces of different sizes. The boys were invited to help themselves. Each in turn looked at the various pieces and took the largest. Our human nature is self-centred. Babies are selfish and this is necessary for their survival. Civilisation is a veneer beneath which lurks a selfish human nature. In the words of Thomas Sowell, the leading African-American philosopher, "If you have ever seen a four-year-old trying to lord it over a two-year-old, then you know what the basic problem of human nature is."[37]

Moreover, if mankind is wholly good, why is there so much evil in the world? If the answer is that mankind was corrupted by society, where did that evil come from? In the last century it is estimated that over one hundred and twenty million died under communism and six million in the Holocaust. Recent atrocities include: the Tutsi genocide in Rwanda, the Serbian atrocities in former Yugoslavia, the current slaughter, pillage and rape in the Congo and Sudan. To-day there are an estimated twenty-seven million slaves around the world: more than all the slaves taken from Africa in the transatlantic slave trade. The newspapers and TV news bulletins record numberless examples of human greed, cruelty, violence and selfishness. Domestic violence and cruelty to children also reveal a dark side to humanity. So the belief in innate human goodness is contradicted by plenty of evidence of evil. Yet the idea persists and the evidence to the contrary is ignored.

Steven Pinker and the Noble Savage

Steven Pinker, author of *The Blank Slate* and Professor of Psychology at Harvard, lost his faith in humanity as a teenager in Montreal in the 1960s. A

---

[34] Derek Freeman *Margaret Mead and Samoa* (Cambridge Mass. Harvard University Press 1983)
[35] Rowan Williams *Resurrection* (London Darton Longman and Todd 1982) p. 11
[36] Rowan Williams *Lost Icons* (London Continuum 2000) p. 8
[37] John Petrie *Collection of Thomas Sowell Quotes* http://jpetrie.myweb.uga.edu/sowell.html

police strike was planned. At the time he was young, idealistic and liberal, confident that human beings were good and so it would be a normal day. By contrast his parents forecast bedlam and anarchy. He wrote "I laughed off my parents' argument that if the government ever laid down its arms all hell would break loose. Our competing predictions were put to the test on 17th October 1969 when the Montreal police went on strike."[38] The outcome: 100 shops were looted; 6 banks robbed; 12 fires started; 40 shop windows smashed; $3,000,000 worth of damage to property; most downtown stores forced to close because of looting; taxi drivers burned down a rival cab firm; a rooftop sniper killed a policemen; rioters broke into hotels and restaurants; and at the end of the day the army had to be called in to restore order. Pinker described his loss of faith in liberalism in these words, "This decisive empirical test left my politics in tatters".[39] [Incidentally Richard Dawkins comments on this story in his book *The God Delusion*; he thinks more of the looting and arson would have been carried out by believers rather than by atheists. He admits he has no evidence![40]]

Pinker refers to the popularity of the Noble Savage theory: "Many intellectuals embraced the image of peaceable, egalitarian and ecology-loving natives."[41] But he argues it has been undermined by scientific discoveries: especially modern genetics and evolution. Evolutionary psychology points to a human nature shaped by the evolutionary struggle. Pinker wrote, "It is the doctrine of the Noble Savage that has been most mercilessly debunked by the new evolutionary thinking. A thoroughly noble anything is an unlikely product of natural selection, because noble guys tend to finish last. Nice guys get eaten. Conflicts are ubiquitous, since no two animals can eat the same fish, or monopolise the same mate. Social motivations are adaptations to maximise copies of the genes and one way to prevail is to neutralise the competition."[42]

Modern genetics has shown how genes influence - but do not totally determine - our behaviour, including our defects. So our flaws are partly hard-wired. There is a nasty and ugly side to our natures. Pinker wrote, "Many of the personality traits affected by genes are far from noble. ... including such sins and flaws as being rude, selfish, uncooperative and undependable. ... Study after study has shown that a willingness to commit anti-social behaviour, including lying, stealing, starting fights and destroying property is partly heritable."[43] Many psychopaths are anti-social from birth and bully other

---

[38] Pinker p. 331
[39] Pinker p. 331
[40] Richard Dawkins *The God Delusion* (London Transworld Publishers 2006) p. 261
[41] Pinker p. 56
[42] Pinker p. 55
[43] Pinker p. 50. Pinker cites research by G. R. Bock and J. A. Goode *The Genetics of Criminal and Anti-social Behaviour* (New York, Wiley 1996); D.T. Lykken *The Anti-social Personalities* (USA, N.J. Mahwah Erlbaum 1995); L. Mealy *The Sociobiology of Sociopathy* (Behavioral and Brain Sciences, 18, 523-541 1995)

children and torture animals, even when they come from good homes. Pinker goes on to say that a person who is "introverted, neurotic, narrow, selfish and untrustworthy is probably that way partly because of his genes."[44] His conclusion is, "Genetics and neuroscience are showing that the heart of darkness cannot always be blamed on parents and society."[45]

The discoveries of anthropologists have also undermined the myth of the 'Noble Savage'. They have found primitive societies more violent and blood-thirsty than our own. Lawrence Keely compared the death rates from violence of different societies where there is available data. Some South American tribes like the Jivaro have death rates from violence of 59%, the Yanomamo 39% and most tribes between 20% to 30%. For example a tribe would slaughter an entire village – men, women and children - in revenge for the death of a member of their own tribe. Tribes with plenty to eat and plenty of land and women, will attack other tribes unprovoked. However the Noble Savage lives on in the media: e.g. BBC programmes such as Bruce Parry's *Tribe* and *Tribal Wives* portray the lives of primitive tribes as a peaceful idyll.

Pinker claims these scientific discoveries have undermined the worldview of many intellectuals, who have propagated falsehoods in order to protect primitive societies.[46] To those who are shocked by the cruel, selfish and nasty side of human nature, Pinker answers, what do you expect after millions of years of evolution? We are the outcome of millions of successful slaughters. However the picture Pinker paints is not wholly bleak: as well as the nasty and selfish side of human nature, we have a kinder side, especially in relation to our kin group.

Pinker's conclusion is that a liberal view of human nature is inconsistent with modern science: in particular genetics, evolutionary psychology and some aspects of the cognitive neuroscience.[47] Liberal humanism - the creed of our intelligentsia - has been undermined by science; and what they devalue - the family, religion and moral codes – in fact play an important role in dealing with our defects. In Pinker's words, "Traditions such as religion, the family, social customs, sexual mores and political institutions are a distillation of time-tested techniques that let us work around the short-comings of human nature."[48] And "Some traditional institutions, like families and the rule of law, may be adapted to eternal features of human psychology."[49] He cites in support the philosopher Peter Singer, who believes those on the left, like himself, must abandon their liberal views and admit that human nature is self-centred. Singer wrote, "It is time for the left to take seriously that we are evolved animals, and that we bear

---

[44] Pinker p. 50
[45] Pinker p. 51
[46] Pinker p. 58
[47] Pinker p. 284
[48] Pinker p. 288
[49] Pinker p. 299

the evidence of our inheritance."[50] The romantic view of mankind which has been dominant over the last 40 years is false. Science has upset the apple cart.

Reviewing Pinker's book, John Morrish wrote that in evolution "No prizes were awarded for good behaviour. ... We are not stardust. We are not golden. And we are not going to get back to the Garden of Eden. Now get used to it. ...The point Pinker is making, is that morality, fairness, sex equality, racial tolerance and nice table manners don't come easily to a species with genes like ours. This is dynamite among Western liberals, but it wouldn't raise an eyebrow in most of the world."[51] It is only in the West that a misty-eyed sentimentalism prevails. Morrish also notes that the weaker the theory, the more fiercely people fight for it. Hence liberals' intolerance of non-liberal opinions and their bullying of opponents.

In contrast to Pinker, Richard Dawkins thinks we emerged unselfish and philanthropic out of the long bloody struggle for survival in evolution. He offers - what he calls - a fourfold Darwinian explanation of our goodness: firstly, kin share genes and so support other members of the kin group; secondly, reciprocal altruism, 'you scratch my back, I'll scratch yours'; thirdly, seeking a good reputation; fourthly, demonstrating your superiority. He wrote, "We now have four good Darwinian reasons for individuals to be altruistic, generous and moral to each other."[52] Dawkins believes that our brains 'misfire'. So human beings love everyone, not just their kin. Is there any scientific evidence for his theory that human brains misfire to produce unselfish behaviour? Dawkins admits, "Perhaps I am a Pollyanna."[53] (The Oxford English Dictionary defines 'Pollyanna' as "naively cheerful and optimistic".) He has led the life of a don in the groves of academia, and lives in North Oxford. Perhaps his conviction that human beings are naturally good needs to be put to an empirical test – as Pinker's was. Maybe he should experience more of the ugly side of life - spend a day answering the phone at Childline, where children suffering abuse and bullying ring in for help; or with the NSPCC, which deals with cruelty to children; or with case workers dealing with domestic violence; or stay for a week in Mogadishu.

Incidentally, although Pinker is not religious, he claims that the Biblical understanding of human nature has been vindicated by science. He wrote, "The theory of human nature coming out of the cognitive revolution has more in common with the Judeo-Christian theory of human nature and with the psychological theory proposed by Sigmund Freud, than with behaviourism, social constructionism and other versions of the Blank Slate."[54]

---

[50] Peter Singer *A Darwinian Left: Policies Evolution and Co-operation* (New Haven Conn. Yale University Press 1999) p. 6
[51] John Morrish inThe Independent on Sunday Sept. 29, 2002
[52] Dawkins p. 251
[53] Dawkins p. 261
[54] Pinker p. 40

Human nature is flawed: Freud and Jung

Freud and Jung challenged the belief in inborn goodness and rationality. Freud wrote: "No one who, like me, conjures up the most evil of those half-tamed demons that inhabit the human beast, and seeks to wrestle with them, can expect to come through the struggle unscathed."[55] And "The ego is not master in its own house."[56] In other words the conscious mind is unaware of the powerful influence of the unconscious. According to Jung: "My experience with human beings taught me anything but a belief in man's original goodness. I knew I was only gradually distinguishing myself from an animal."[57] Jung maintained man is less good than he thinks he is.[58]

Freud's standing is not as high as it was, nevertheless some of his insights remain important in our understanding of the human psyche. He analysed the psyche into three parts: the ego (the self), the superego (the conscience) and the id (the instincts). Before him the mind was understood as wholly conscious, rational and integrated. He discovered in treating patients suffering from hysteria (a functional disturbance of the nervous system), that consciousness is only a part of the mind. He observed, "We found to our great surprise that each individual symptom immediately and permanently disappeared when we had succeeded in bringing the memory of the event clearly to light ... and when the patient had described that event in as much detail as possible."[59] This revealed an unconscious mind which exerts a powerful influence on people's lives and of which they were totally unaware. So our minds are not totally rational. Experiences, which are emotionally charged and threatening, are repressed; and what Freud called 'half-tamed demons' lurk in our unconscious minds. The superego and the id fight for control of the ego. So conflict lies at the heart of our psyches. Far from being good and rational, Freud saw mankind as aggressive, irrational, suffering from illusions and with an urge to dominate. As the English psychiatrist David Stafford-Clark commented, "Freud had struggled to help man find a way to elevate himself above the savage beast, which through no fault of his own, is always part of him. The doctrine of Original Sin found no opposition from Freud, though his explanation of it was biological rather than religious."[60]

Freud's discoveries helped to undermine the belief in the goodness of human nature and the notion that the mind was wholly rational. Jung declared the idea of inborn human goodness nonsense; rationalism a disease; idealism an

---

[55] S. Freud *Complete Psychological Works*, Dora (1905)
[56] S. Freud *A Difficulty in the Path of Psycho-Analysis* (1917)
[57] C. G. Jung *Memories, Dreams, Reflections* (London Random House 1963) p. 88
[58] C. G. Jung *Psychological Reflections* p. 240
[59] S. Freud *Studies in Hysteria* 1893-5 (London Hogarth Press) Standard Edition p. 6
D. Stafford-Clark *What Freud Really Said* (London Penguin 1967) p. 29
[60] D. Stafford-Clark p. 201

addiction; and science partly diabolic. He said the dark side of man, which he called his shadow, had been ignored. Evil is real. We must learn to deal with it. Jung set out to liberate western man from arid rationalism. The intellect had tried to dominate, but life is more than the rational. Jung wrote, "Rationalism is the disease of our times; it pretends to have all the answers."[61] In his view modern man feels uprooted and alienated because he has been cut off from his historical and spiritual roots.

The American psychiatrist Scott Peck, who wrote the best-seller *The Road Less Travelled*, came to the conclusion that some people are evil. This was contrary to his training as a psychologist, which had taught him evil did not exist. Peck concluded that some of the patients he encountered were not simply muddled, or misguided, or confused by their upbringing, but were in the grip of a powerful force of evil. His book, *The People of the Lie* argued that our conventional thinking refuses to acknowledge the reality of evil, and the fact that some people are taken over by it.

Are we altruistic?

In his book *The Price of Altruism* Oren Harman asked whether human nature displays altruism. Bees and ants are social insects, and both deer and wolves show mutual aid. However animals help for each other depends on the closeness of the genetic link. So their apparent altruism is self-interested. The more remote the genetic connection the less altruism applies. In short, altruism depends on kinship. So we can't turn to nature for evidence of inborn human goodness. But aren't some people good? I believe most of us are socialised out of some of our selfish behaviour by parents, aunts, uncles, grandparents and society. In this way our self-centred behaviour can be modified. We do not remember all the moral instructions in the past, but we internalise them; they become our values. The mistake is to think that we are *naturally* unselfish and kind.

I was struck recently when helping out at a summer fair by the barrage of moral urgings, cajolings and tellings-off given to young children: "No, it's Susan's turn", "Remember to share", "That's good", "Don't snatch". Rather than children naturally acting in an unselfish way, they were constantly being prompted to act in a social way. The outcome is that some adults, who as children were socialised by loving and strict parents, find it second nature to lead unselfish lives, and wrongly conclude that this behaviour was inborn. They have forgotten the thousands of moral commands they were subjected to as children. Richard Dawkins was brought up in a Christian home and sent to an Anglican school. Perhaps the moral values of his parents and school were

---

[61] C. G. Jung *Memories, Dreams, Reflections* (London: Random House 1963) p. 330

internalised. Maybe he no longer remembers what he was told as a young child, and so he assumes his values were inborn.

The reaction against the belief in human goodness

World War Two led to a reaction against the rosy view of human nature and faith in progress. After Auschwitz it was hard to believe in human goodness, and amid the rubble of post-war Germany the idea of progress seemed a sick joke. Two German thinkers, Horkheimer and Adorno, asked how Europe could have behaved in this way after the Enlightenment? How could the belief in human goodness and reason have led to National Socialism in Germany? The Enlightenment had promised to free mankind from darkness, superstition and ignorance, but had led to a world where millions died in genocides and where science devised weapons of mass destruction. The authors blamed the idea that human beings were entirely rational, "For the Enlightenment anything that cannot be resolved into numbers is illusion."[62] They wrote, "On their way toward modern science human beings have discarded meaning."[63] Any deviation from the scientific paradigm was punished, "and carried a heavy price for the offender."[64] The great British scientist Lord Kelvin said, "If you cannot express your knowledge in numbers, it is of a meagre and unsatisfactory kind."[65] The non-rational aspects of life – beauty, tradition, the arts and the spiritual have been neglected and this led to "the disenchantment of the world."[66]

Postmodernists also challenge the optimistic humanism of liberals. They reject faith in science and regard the liberal view of man as naïve, holding that all truth is subjective and fallible. They note that it was a rationalist and secular ideology – Marxism, which committed so many atrocities in the twentieth century. Postmodernists argue that we all impose our worldview on reality, especially, if we believe master narratives like 'progress'. Those who claim there is only one truth are trying to coerce others. We can however free ourselves from master narratives by deconstructing them. Christopher Butler, Professor of English at Oxford, in his book *Postmodernism* wrote, "The Enlightenment reliance on universal principle and reason is always incipiently totalitarian."[67]

---

[62] M Horkheimer and T W Adorno *The Dialectic of Enlightenment* (USA Stanford University Press 2002) p. 4
[63] Horkheimer and Adorno p. 3
[64] Horkheimer and Adorno p. 19
[65] Cited by Mario Livo *The Golden Ration* (London Review 2002) p 1
[66] Horkheimer and Adorno p. 1
[67] Christopher Butler *Postmodernism* (Oxford Oxford University Press) 2002 p. 46

Faith in progress

Richard Dawkins has faith in progress, "Over time the progressive trend is unmistakable and it will continue."[68] By contrast the philosopher John Gray has no faith in progress: "Humanists like to think they have a rational view of the world; but their core belief in progress is a superstition, further from the truth about the human animal than any of the world's religions. Outside of science, progress is a myth."[69] Advances in some areas are counterbalanced by regress in others. Steven Pinker in a recent book argued that we are less violent than in the past.[70] He produces a grisly catalogue showing that mankind was more violent, vicious and cruel in the past. But the atrocities under Hitler, Stalin, Mao and Pol Pot are surely too recent for us to conclude that mankind has progressed.

By comparing what life was like in England 50 years ago with today, we can evaluate whether there has been progress. George Orwell in his essay entitled, *The English People* commented, "An imaginary foreign observer would certainly be struck by our gentleness; by the orderly behaviour of English crowds, the lack of pushing and quarrelling ... there is very little crime or violence."[71] Geoffrey Gorer, a British anthropologist, wrote a book about the English called, *Exploring English Character*. He was struck by the orderly, good-natured behaviour of the English and wondered why they were so gentle, "The English are certainly among the most peaceful, gentle, courteous and orderly populations that the civilised world has ever seen ... You hardly ever see a fight (not uncommon in Europe or the USA)... Football crowds are as orderly as church meetings. This orderliness, good humour and gentleness, this absence of overt aggression calls for an explanation."[72]

My mother, as a teenager in the 1930s, used to go to concerts at Manchester's Free Trade Hall. After the concerts she and her girl friends would walk home several miles through the streets of Manchester. 'Was it safe?' I asked. She said there had never been any problems and she had never felt any danger. Would it be safe now? My step-mother, born in Huddersfield shortly after World War One, told me folk used to leave their doors unlocked and were never robbed. An old lady in Hampstead, when we lived there in the 1980s, told me that she had lived in the area all her life. She was then well into her 80s. She said that when she was a six-year old girl, she was told by her parents she could

---

[68] Dawkins p. 307
[69] John Gray *Straw Dogs* (London Granta 2003) Foreword p. xi He was Professor of European Thought at the London School of Economics
[70] Steven Pinker *The Better Angels of Our Nature* (USA Viking 2011)
[71] George Orwell Essay *The English People* Collected Essays Vol 3 (USA New Hampshire Nonpareil 2000) p. 2
[72] Geoffrey Gorer *Exploring English Character* (London Cresset 1955) p. 13

go and play on Hampstead Heath but to be back by 6 o'clock. She said that in those days it was safe to do so.

Crime figures tell the same story: in the 1950s there were about half a million crimes a year, to-day there are five million. Take robbery: there were 66 bag snatches in London in 1926, in 2003 there were 20,136.[73] In 1898 there were 4,221 violent crimes, in 1998/9 there were 733,374 and in 2004/5 the total was 1,184,702.[74] The increase in crime is much greater than the increase in population. But liberals argue there has been no decline in moral standards. It is just a moral panic. They explain the increase in violence, by saying crime is more reported now. However Professor Jose Harris says the opposite may be true, because in Edwardian England men and women were imprisoned for crimes like drunkenness and riding a bike without lights. In 1931 for every police officer there were three crimes; now there are 44.[75] According to the UN Crime and Justice Research Institute, England and Wales now tops the league table for the frequency of crime. However crime is not spread evenly throughout society. James Bartholomew in his book *The Welfare State We're In* observed, "The relatively affluent, which includes the vast majority of media people, politicians and other opinion-formers, do not experience crime as it is suffered by millions of other people. The people who suffer most from crime are the poor. The wealthy are insulated on the whole from what is going on."[76]

Those who argue that there has been moral progress point to the improved status and treatment of women and of racial and sexual minorities. It is true that the lot of minorities and women has improved and there has been an increase in tolerance. However compared with fifty years ago, we are less polite, less orderly and live with higher levels of crime, especially in poorer areas. We are more selfish and dishonest; less trusting, less socially minded. There is a cult of celebrity and an obsession with materialism and consumerism, whereas in the past people were admired for courage and unselfishness. Today there are video games where you can play at killing and stealing.[77] Progress in some areas has been offset by a decline in others, so overall there has been no moral advance, especially for those living in poor communities.

"The new sciences of human nature really do resonate with assumptions
that historically were closer to the right than the left."[78]
Steven Pinker

---

[73] Criminal Statistics England and Wales plus police records
www.met.police.uk/crimestatistics/index.htm
[74] Office for National Statistics and Home Office
www.homeoffice.gov.uk/rds/pdfs/100years.xls
[75] Quoted in James Bartholomew in *The Welfare State We're In* (London Politico 2004) p. 17
[76] James Bartholomew *The Welfare State We're In* (London Politico 2004) p 389 note 28
[77] Grand Theft Auto
[78] Pinker p. 284

CHAPTER 2

The Liberal Delusions:
The More Freedom the Better

Man is born free but everywhere is in chains.[79]
J-J Rousseau

Self-government for the pupils and the staff, freedom to go to lessons or to stay away, freedom to play for days or weeks or years if necessary, freedom from any indoctrination whether religious or moral or political, freedom from character forming.[80]
A. S. Neill headmaster of Summerhill School

There were no more external absolute rules. The supposed foundation of every ordinance, regulation, law and maxim was fake. ... I did not have to do anything that I did not want to do ever again. I would therefore be happy. ... I could behave as I wished... and claim to be virtuous.[81]
Peter Hitchens describing his life in the 1960s

Belief in freedom is another fundamental tenet of liberalism. Of course freedom is important. The world is full of tyrants and oppression. We are lucky in the west to enjoy much greater freedom than most people. However one of the arguments of this book is that in some areas we have become too free. The 1960s witnessed an explosion of freedom - the fetters of morality, the weight of tradition, the strictures of religion and the shackles of custom were all jettisoned. After the hardships of wartime and the negative Victorian attitudes to sex, there was something to be said for such a revolution, but sadly in many respects it has ended in tears. It always does. In the early days of the French Revolution Wordsworth was thrilled – "Bliss was it in that dawn to be alive/ and to be young was very heaven". But it gave way to disillusionment after the Reign of Terror and the blood-soaked fields of the Vendée. In the early days of such a revolution anything which restricts our freedom is seen as an abomination. Onto the bonfire go rules, restraints and taboos. Nothing is forbidden; everything is permitted. Untrammelled liberty is intoxicating. We are now free to enjoy ourselves and have fun. We are subservient to nothing, to no religious or cultural norms. Our possibilities are limitless. Mankind can be remade as it wills. There is no evil. Old-fashioned values of self-restraint, loyalty and commitment are junked. In the 1960s conventional morality was dismissed as bourgeois, a denial of authentic existence and a form of bad faith for the existentialists of the period.

---

[79] Jean-Jacques Rousseau *Du Contrat Social* (1762) ch 1
[80] A. S. Neill *Summerhill* (London Pelican Books 1968) p. 9
[81] Peter Hitchens *The Rage Against God* (London Zondervan 2010) p. 20

However the freedom is illusory. Today there is a new conformism. Our societies are obsessed with sex, brands and celebrity. Our young people are bombarded with advertising telling them what is the right body shape; what is the right brand; and that it is uncool to have opinions not endorsed by celebrities. We need freedom from a greedy, materialistic and individualistic society. We suffer from a cultural mediocrity and spiritual poverty, despite our material wealth. I now examine some of the areas where I believe we have become too free.

Alcohol

The laws on alcohol have been liberalised. In 1997 the Labour Party, as part of its general election campaign, sent texts to young men saying "VOTE LABOUR THEN YOU CAN DRINK ALL DAY". In 2005 it introduced 24 hours drinking with the aim of importing a continental style café culture, instead of the traditional chucking out around 11 p.m. They hoped blokes would order another bottle of Côtes du Rhone and continue their discussion of existentialism and Jean-Paul Sartre! But the British Medical Association (BMA) reported in February 2008, "There is strong evidence that increased opening hours are associated with increased alcohol consumption and alcohol related problems." It stated Britain is in the grip of an alcohol epidemic; at peak times 70% of Accident and Emergency admissions are alcohol-related. The BMA has urged cutting the licensing hours. A Home Office report in February 2008 confirmed a 25% increase in serious violent offences in the early hours. In the two years after the laws were liberalised there was a 31% increase in alcohol related admissions to hospital.[82] 530 people a day are admitted for drinking too much. One in twenty hospital admissions are caused by alcohol in some areas and that figure does not include admissions due to alcohol-related violence and accidents. We have the highest incidence of teenage alcoholism in Europe, a growing problem of drink fuelled violence and a binge drinking culture. In 2006 excessive drinking led to 6,517 deaths, a rise of 20% in five years. A report in January 2008 blamed binge drinking for a 76% increase over 10 years in the number needing a liver transplant.[83]

Professor Ian Gilmour, the President of the Royal College of Physicians, condemned the Labour Government's approach and called for a minimum price for alcohol. In January 2010 he said, "The nation's growing addiction to alcohol is putting immense strain on health services, especially hospitals, costing the NHS over £2,700,000,000 a year."[84] Department of Health statistics released in August 2009 showed a sharp increase over 5 years in alcohol related diseases: cirrhosis of the liver up by 42% and alcoholic liver failure by 41%.[85] A quarter of people in England aged over 16 are now classed as hazardous drinkers. In December 2011

---

[82] Daily Telegraph Record of hospital admissions to the NHS
[83] Independent on Sunday 13.1.2008
[84] BBC NEWS website 1.1.2010
[85] The Guardian 16.8.2009

another report, focused on North-east England, maintained there had been an increase of over 400% over the last 8 years in the number of young people in their 30s diagnosed with terminal liver failure as a result of alcohol. Two days after its publication I met a government minister. I said surely the government needed to stop the sale of low cost alcohol and curtail its promotion. He replied that he was a 19th century liberal who believed in free markets, minimal government interference and personal responsibility. So the government should do nothing. What's more, he was a Conservative MP !

Oddly the Labour Government (1997-2010) liberalised the drinking laws, but took an illiberal attitude to smoking and created a surveillance society with more CCTV cameras per head than any other country.

Sex

In the sexual revolution of the 1960s the old taboos and restraints were overthrown. It was an era of free love and the contraceptive pill. No external rules. All regulations, laws, and restrictions were treated as false. Divorce was made easier; the stigma of single motherhood and cohabitation faded; and homosexual practices were decriminalised - some of the changes e.g. on homosexuality were beneficial. The writer Peter Hitchens admits he went on a bender, indulging in debauched self-absorbed hedonism.[86] The Victorian attitudes to sex had been negative and a degree of freeing up was necessary. But has it led to erotic bliss? Or have we have thrown the baby out with the bathwater - to choose an inappropriate metaphor!

Many of the pathfinders for this new sexual freedom would be shocked by modern morals. Freud held that persistent repression of the sex drive could lead to neurosis. In the popular mind this has morphed into the notion that we must always give way to the impulse of the moment. However Freud was no advocate of promiscuity. Likewise D. H. Lawrence wanted a more natural attitude to sex, but he forewarned, "If there is one thing I don't like it is cheap and promiscuous sex. ... And if I write a book about sex relations of a man and a woman, it is not because I want all men to begin having indiscriminate lovers and love affairs. All this horrid scramble of love affairs and prostitution is only part of the funk, bravado and doing it on purpose. And bravado and doing it on purpose is just as unpleasant and hurtful as repression, just as much a sign of secret fear."[87]

We now have the highest rate of teenage pregnancy in Europe and soaring rates of sexually transmitted diseases. British men and women are the most promiscuous according to research by Professor Schmitt of Bradley University

---

[86] Peter Hitchens *The Rage Against God* (London Zondervan 2010) p. 20
[87] D H Lawrence essay *The State of Funk* in Selected Essays (London Penguin Books 1972) p. 101

Illinois.[88] Britain came out at the top, well ahead of USA, France, Germany, Holland, Italy and Australia. The researchers said one of the relevant factors was a highly sexualised popular culture. The Independent Advisory Group on Sexual Health reported that 40% of sexually active 13-14 year olds were drunk or stoned when they first had intercourse, and UNICEF reported that more children in this age-group in the UK had had sexual intercourse than in any other country; partly because they tend to get drunk younger. The Office of National Statistics released figures in October 2007 showed a 63% increase in the number of cases of sexually transmitted diseases over the past decade – syphilis up 1,607%, herpes up 31%, HIV up 300%, gonorrhoea up 46%.[89] Single motherhood has resulted in increasing numbers of fatherless children; this has harmed children in many ways and led in part to rising crime.[90] At present 44% of children are born out of marriage. Of course many single mothers have not chosen their life-style: their husband or partner may have walked out on them or died. They often do a very good job in very difficult circumstances.

When Mary Whitehouse complained that the "BBC was pouring poison ... into millions of homes"[91] she was ridiculed. However in June 2010 a *Sunday Times* article on sex included interviews with some of those who had backed the sexual liberalisation in the 1960s and are now shocked.[92] Joan Bakewell, a BBC presenter said, "Mary Whitehouse was right." Bakewell complained that sex now pervades our culture, "You see f****** on the screen; sex magazines are displayed on lower shelves – they are pushing the boundaries. Shocking things sell." Bakewell is horrified that young children watch violent porn. She was shocked to see a young girl lying drunk in the gutter with her skirt round her waist. "It's disgusting. Distressing for everyone, including the girls themselves." The article reports that Germaine Greer now believes there is a downside to the contraceptive pill and easy abortion. Maureen Lipmann now says "Of course it's gone too far." She foresees a swing back to more traditional values. Jilly Cooper reported that in the week before the interview she had met a taxi driver, who told her that he was sitting in his cab in the Strand, when two very attractive girls came by and asked him if he wanted to go dogging (casual public sex). Fay Weldon commented "Sex has lost a lot of significance. Love is very rare now". Kiki Dee commented, "Pop videos are like soft porn... Shops sell pole-dancing kits for seven year olds. I think Mary Whitehouse said some very, very sensible things".

---

[88] Published in the New Scientist. His survey interviewed 14,000 people in 48 countries and measured one-night stands, number of sexual partners, and attitudes to casual sex.
[89] Office For National Statistics report October 2007
[90] N Dennis and G Erdos *Families Without Fathers* The Institute for the Study of the Civil Society London 1992
[91] Sunday Times article *The Swingers take a swipe at their Sixties* by Daisy Goodwin 6.6.2010
[92] Sunday Times article *The Swingers take a swipe at their Sixties* by Daisy Goodwin 6.6.2010

Pornography is now widely available. Will Hutton writing in *The Observer* in 2010 lamented, "Our extreme liberal stance has seen us deluged under a wave of pornography."[93]

In June 2012 the House of Commons Home Affairs Select Committee investigated the sexual abuse of children following the case in Rochdale where nine British Asian men were found guilty of abusing white girls, many from orphanages. One witness, Sue Berelowitz the Deputy Children's Commissioner, claimed there wasn't a town, village or hamlet where children were not being sexually exploited, often by other youngsters. She claimed internet porn was changing children's ideas of what was normal sex. Often scenes from porn movies are enacted; gangs subject young girls to severe abuse. She said, "It is very sadistic, very violent, and very ugly. In parts of London children from the age of eleven have to perform oral sex on a line of boys for up to 2 hours at a time. It is common for girls to be lured, via an internet chat-room, to an arranged meeting in a park, only to be met by a group of boys and gang raped. Then another group of boys take the girl to another part of the park and gang-rape her again. Some teenagers film this on their mobile phones to entrap their victims. I wish I could say this was uncommon, but it is quite common. What is being done is terrible. People need to put aside their denial. The victims are in their thousands not in hundreds."[94] She blamed easy access to extreme pornography for enabling and fuelling abuse. She added, "Some of the boys I've spoken to who've been involved in sexual exploitation say to us 'it was like being in a porn movie'. They have watched things and then they've enacted them." Peter Davies, the chief executive of the Child Protection and Online Protection Centre, warned that children are accessing the web at ever earlier ages, and that up to one child in twenty is a victim of sexual abuse. Moreover porn can now be accessed on mobile phones.

Also in June 2012 Channel4 investigated *Habbo Hotel*, an online game where children adopt identities and create their own hotel room. Rachel Seifert a Channel4 producer played the game posing as a child on the site for over two months. She reported that the chat on the site was "very sexual, perverted, violent and pornographic. Within two minutes I was being asked to strip before a webcam." Every time she played the game she had a similar experience. John Carr, a Child Safety Officer who played the game with the producer said, "If I was the parent of an 11 year old girl I would want there to be a moral panic."[95] In addition some TV music channels are in effect soft porn. The All Party Parliamentary Group on Body Image published a report in June 2012 which stated that children as young as 5 are worrying about their appearance and there is pressure from the media to achieve an unrealistic body, causing health and relationship problems, and wreaking havoc with self-esteem. Girls are judged

---

[93] Will Hutton *We Had It All – Sex Freedom, Money Did we Throw It all Away* The Observer 22.8.2010
[94] *The Telegraph* 12.6.12
[95] *The Telegraph* 12.6.12

merely on their sex appeal. Martin Daubney, the longest serving editor of *Loaded* magazine said, "The lad's mag I edited turned a generation on to porn - and now I'm a father I bitterly regret it. By allowing children free access to pornographic images, the next generation of young men are becoming so desensitised, I genuinely fear we're storing up an emotional time-bomb."[96]

Families

The Women's Liberation movement objected to the lack of freedom for women in the traditional family. Some feminists went further and urged women to leave their husbands and pursue self-fulfilment. Some saw men as the enemy. The number of marriages has fallen from 471,000 in the 1940s to around 237,000 today. The Social Trends Report of the Office of National Statistics stated that the Divorce Reform Act of 1969 by the introduction of no fault divorce made it easier to dissolve a marriage, and contributed to a dramatic increase in the number of divorces and to the decline of the traditional family.[97] Dr Richard Woolfson, a leading family expert wrote, "The traditional nuclear family of two parents and children has become a museum piece." Each year over a third of a million children experience the divorce of their parents. Thomas Sowell, the leading African-American philosopher, maintains liberal societies promote freedom and devalue long-term commitments - preferring loose ad hoc arrangements. However some sociologists such as Norman Dennis and George Erdos in their book *Families Without Fathers* maintain there is overwhelming evidence children do best when brought up by their biological parents, who are committed to each other in a long-term relationship like marriage.[98] Fatherless children suffer in many ways; they are more likely to become criminals; to self-harm; to be poor; to suffer abuse; to achieve less at school; to have emotional and psychological problems; to end up in prison and on drugs.[99] They claim that men have felt freed from responsibilities to their children, but most academics ignore the evidence.

Parenting is another area affected. Liberal parents have allowed their children greater freedom, set few boundaries and given minimum discipline, ignoring the traditional wisdom found in sayings such as "be cruel to be kind". At the same time we have experienced a growth of anti-social behaviour and incivility. Liberal penal policy tends to see criminals as victims of society, resulting in soft policing, soft prisons and a reluctance to discipline and punish. I helped run 'Victim Awareness' courses in a local prison. One of the prisoners I got to know well was called Barry. He was aged 40 and told me that he was last in prison when he was 17. He described prison life then as hard: lots of marching, kit

---

[96] *Daily Mail* 8th June 2012
[97] Report 15.4.2009
[98] N Dennis and G Erdos *Families Without Fathers* The Institute for the Study of the Civil Society London 1992
[99] N Dennis and G Erdos

inspection, poor food, hard beds, prison clothes, no TVs, no computers, no set-top boxes, no play-stations. But, he pointed out, the re-offending rate then was 40% - half what it is now.

Education

In October 2010 Katherine Birbalsingh, a deputy head at an inner city London secondary school, described the British education system as chaotic, "full of sloppiness and sentimentality, dumbing down and deceit... bad behaviour tolerated and poor performance covered up."[100] The exams are so dumbed down that even the children realise. The approach is one of "All must have prizes, GCSEs, and all must go to university.... To let children know how they compare with other children is considered poisonous.... The system is broken; it keeps poor children poor...a culture of excuses and low standards which expects the least from the poor and disadvantaged." Discipline has been undermined, yet she argues "kids cry out for structure and discipline". She added that "Black underachievement is due in part to the chaos in our classrooms, and in part to the fear of accusations of racism. Teachers are told they are racist if they discipline a black pupil. Other black children suffer most and copy bad examples. Black children underachieve because of what the well-meaning liberal does to them." For speaking out, she was suspended and faced a disciplinary hearing. Under pressure she resigned. However the parents of the children were unimpressed by the school's response. There was a dramatic decline in those wanting to send their children to the school. The outcome is that the school has closed. It was a Church of England school, just down the road from Lambeth Palace.

A hundred years ago schools were strict and authoritarian. So some moves in a more liberal direction were beneficial. Progressive educationalists believed in greater freedom for children and strove to weaken authority, discipline and rules. These child-centred ideas influenced the Plowden Report of 1967: nothing should be taught; everything should be discovered by the child; the teacher became a mere facilitator. Progressive ideas may have been watered down, but still influence British education. Many of our secondary schools are unruly; children learn little; and teachers are frustrated. Our prevailing liberal orthodoxy has undermined respect for teachers and opposed rules, structure, discipline and authority. I was once told by a teacher, "You should never say 'No' to a child"!

An adult who attempts to discipline an unruly child in public will probably find the police question his or her behaviour rather than the child's. The police seem to believe that all children are innocent. A doctor friend of mine related how one hot summer's day at his medical centre the windows were open and an eight year old boy keep running round, sticking his head in the window,

---

[100] Report in the Sunday Times 10.10.2010.

screaming and running off. Eventually one doctor had had enough. The next time he seized the boy by the scruff of the neck and told him to clear off. Within half-an hour the police were round at the surgery wanting to interview the doctor for assaulting a child. Locally a friend intervened to stop young teenage boys from throwing golf-balls from a local golf course into people's gardens. The police came round and wanted to interview him about his actions, not those of the teenagers. In 2009 in Portsmouth a mother, who told her child that he would be smacked when he got home, was overheard by an over-zealous off-duty policeman. He trailed her home and the following week she was visited by two council social workers. She was told that she would be put on a register until her children reached adulthood – in 12 years time! The subtext is children are innocent, grown-ups are wicked – pure Rousseau.

Economic liberalism

Many liberals loathe Mrs Thatcher and the changes she made, but they fail to recognise that a central plank of her government policy was economic liberalism, which aimed to maximise freedom in the economic sphere by the removal of restrictions and regulations. Its objective is a global free market. It was thought that markets were rational, and that all would be well if the markets were left free to act as they wished. The City of London was deregulated and a hands-off approach adopted. It is true that there had been too many restrictions, and some liberalisation was beneficial in releasing the dynamism of the economy. However too little regulation led to excess lending, excessive bonuses, the credit crunch and the deepest recession since the 1930s. These events have shown that the free market is not rational and does not always know what is best. Moreover global free-market capitalism has resulted in the dislocation of communities; the brunt of which is borne by the working classes, who find downward pressure on their wages from immigration, and face competition for the limited stock of social housing. Polish plumbers, carpenters and nannies may be a boon to the middle classes, but undercut local workers. Most of the pottery manufacture in Britain has now moved abroad, making thousands unemployed. However it is easier for the middle-class managers and accountants to move to similar jobs elsewhere than it is for the shop-floor workers. The philosopher John Gray commented, "Conservative policy cast in a neo-liberal mould has been hostile to the conservation of precious cultural achievements and forms of common life."[101]

Censorship

A society that believes in maximising freedom recoils from imposing restrictions on films, television, theatre, broadcasting, music and computer games.

---

[101] John Gray *Enlightenment's Wake* (London Routledge 2007) p. 174

Lord Attenborough, the actor and director of the film *Gandhi*, interviewed in July 2008 blamed films partly for the spate of knife crimes and violence. He said, "Now violence with gun or a knife is the norm and we in the entertainment industry are partly responsible, making weapons such as knives an acceptable commonplace. So knife crime is no longer thought of as horrific and to be abhorred. It is now part of normal existence." He claimed that audiences used to be shocked by a knife or a gun. There was a collective intake of breath, but no longer.[102] In May 2009 at Norwich Crown Court three people were convicted of the murder of 17 year-old Simon Everitt: he was beaten, bundled into a car, taken to a wooded area, tied to a tree with nylon ropes, petrol was poured over him and down his throat, then he was set alight. During the trial it emerged that these were copycat actions from the film *Severance*, which had been watched by those convicted. One of whom had remarked, "Wouldn't it be wicked if you could actually do that to someone in real life."[103]

Censorship is now regarded as an unacceptable infringement of liberty. Some of the censorship of the past was misconceived – e.g. banning D. H. Lawrence's *Lady Chatterley's Lover*. However the liberal approach has been to remove virtually all censorship. The British Board of Film Classification (BBFC) - all that remains of censorship - will authorise almost anything. In 2008 it approved video nasties which it had earlier been banned, including *SS Experimentation Camp*. Sue Clarke of the BBFC said, "In to-day's climate we do not consider these films to be a concern." The BBFC now merely informs people of a film's content and sees no need to censor films. For instance, it informed the public that *Eastern Promise* contains "three scenes of extreme visceral violence, two images of throats being slit and one of a man's eye being viciously and repeatedly stabbed". A new genre of film called 'torture porn' features sadistic and graphic violence.

"You are a stylish hooligan entering a new decade of grievous bodily harm, car-jacking and general thuggery. Drive, run and shoot your way into all sorts of trouble with the law, rival gangs and civilians. Thirty-two new missions, thirty new vehicles and unlimited criminal opportunity." This is Sony's description of their game *Grand Theft Auto: London Mission* for PlayStations. Computer games have become ever more violent. Children can play at stabbing people and blowing their heads off. The purchase of these games is restricted to 18 year olds; but in practice their younger siblings play them as well. In the first six months of 2007, 17 teenagers were stabbed to death in Britain. Rap music often celebrates violence and portrays women as sex objects. Yet there are very few restrictions on lyrics which are obscene, vulgar and misogynistic. The journalist Yasmin Alibhai-Brown commented in 2003, "In the first half of 2003 the f*** word was used 1,400 times on terrestrial television. The corruption of language in public culture

---

[102] Interview : Brighton Argus reported in the Daily Telegraph 25th July 2008
[103] Daily Telegraph 29.5.2009

is just one aspect of the general coarsening of life... There are many of us today on the left, who can see something precious, possibly irrecoverable, is being destroyed."[104]

Drugs

The issue of freedom in relation to drugs is more fraught. It can be argued that making drugs illegal has not worked - just as prohibition did not work in the USA. Therefore we should legalise all drugs and tax and control them, rather than drive them underground and make rich pickings for criminals. In January 2004 the Labour government reclassified cannabis as a class C drug, instead of class B - so possession ceased to be an arrestable offence.[105] Yet stronger versions of cannabis - called 'skunk' – now comprises 90% of the cannabis available. Four years after the reclassification, Health Authority figures showed a 50% increase in the number of people needing medical treatment as a result of using cannabis.[106] The BMA said that these figures strengthened their opposition to the downgrade.[107] A survey of local Youth Offenders teams revealed an increase in cannabis use among offenders of between 25% and 75% since the downgrade.

There is growing evidence that cannabis can cause schizophrenia, psychosis and paranoia. Professor Robin Murray, Head of Psychiatry at the Institute of Psychiatry, has come to believe cannabis causes schizophrenia. According to him, "More people are going psychotic than we expected, and cannabis is one of the contributing factors. It has taken us a long time to wake up to this."[108] A report compiled by the Prime Minister's Strategy Unit in 2006 concluded: "Recent changes in the law have increased the number of people taking cannabis. The amount of hard drug abuse has also increased. It appears the two rises are connected." Between 1997 and 2006 cannabis consumption increased by 20% and drug offences by nearly 50 per cent.[109] Britain has the highest percentage of teenagers in Europe with drug abuse and alcohol problems. UNICEF reported that the UK is the third biggest cannabis user.[110] Health authority figures released in January 2008 showed the number of people needing medical treatment as a result of cannabis increased by 50% in the four years after it was reclassified.[111] In November 2008 the downgrade of cannabis was reversed.

---

[104] Daily Mail 17.7.2003
[105] later reversed under Gordon Brown
[106] The Times 11.1.09 Health Authority figures released on that date.
[107] The Times 11.1.09 Health Authority figures released on that date.
[108] The Times Jan 11th2008
[109] News Of The World 6.8.06
[110] The Independent 16.6.2007
[111] The Times 11.1.2008

Gambling

Gambling has been liberalised. The Labour Government broke with the tradition in Britain that gambling should be allowed but not encouraged. Its Gambling Act of 2005 paved the way for Las Vegas style mega-casinos; it removed the ban on advertising gambling; it raised the limit on pay-outs from slot-machines from £2,000 to £1,000,000; it increased the number of slot machines allowed at a casino from 10 to 1,250; it removed the requirement that a person become a member of a casino 24 hours before they can gamble there; it repealed the "demand test" for new casinos; it allowed payment by credit card on internet gambling sites (banned in USA and Australia); it allowed slot machines on premises that serve alcohol (so breaking the old rule that gambling and alcohol should be kept apart, to prevent people gambling when drunk); it licenced remote gambling - via internet and mobile phones.

Yet an opinion poll in 2003 found that 93% of the population felt there was no need to liberalise the law.[112] The main group to suffer will be the poor. American research shows the poorer you are, the greater the percentage of your income you spend on gambling.[113] The big winners would be large gambling companies. In December 2005 it was reported that in the five weeks after the changes were introduced, there were 100,000 more visits to casinos.[114] Problem gambling has increased fivefold and over 300,000 gambling addicts have sought help. The Gambling Commission reported in January 2009 that Britain has 250,000 problem gamblers and the NHS has opened its first clinic for gambling addiction.

Roy Hattersley, one of the leaders of the Labour Party in the 1990s, is ashamed of the changes. He wrote about gambling in February 2012 after the opening of a mega-casino in East London, which is open 24 hours a day 7 days a week, "It seems incredible that a Labour Government should actually promote gambling to the point of allowing it to be advertised on television … nurturing a 'something for nothing' culture and the belief that the good life is one of cheap alcohol, easy credit and reality shows on television."[115] He reports that education experts now maintain children need to be taught how to resist the pull of gambling and Gamcare (which helps gambling addicts) want children taught of the dangers from the age of 12. He condemns the Labour Party, which historically owed more to Methodism than Marx and was opposed to gambling. He went on, "Some freedoms are corrosive to a good society; they should be allowed but not encouraged. The decision to promote gambling - shamefully taken by the Labour Government - is an affront to the idea of Britain as it was, and as it ought to be. Once we built our greatness on engineering, shipbuilding and steel. We made

---

[112] Commissioned by the Salvation Army NOP in 2003
[113] Gambling with Our Future p. 10
[114] The Times 12.11.05
[115] Roy Hattersley *Family values 2011* Daily Mail 15.12.2011

railway engines for the world; our ships carried cargoes across every ocean. The idea that the country will benefit from encouraging people to feed money into slot machines is an affront to the memory of what we used to be. It holds back the regeneration we need."

Even those on the liberal/left now acknowledge that there has been a loss over the last 50 years. British society in the 1950s was cohesive; marriage was a lifelong commitment; the work ethic prevailed; patriotism was universal; banks were trustworthy; most workmen sought a fair price for their work not the opportunity to rip people off; there were long-established companies whose chief executives' pay was not astronomical. Although there have been gains in the past 50 years, much that was worthwhile has been lost, as society has become more liberal. Will Hutton writing in *The Observer* reflected on the changes in our society over the last fifty years and wrote, "How could we have been so destructive?"[116]

---

[116] Will Hutton *The Baby Boomers and the Price of Personal Freedom* The Observer 22.8.2010

CHAPTER 3

The Liberal Delusions:
Morality is Unnecessary

The only real concern of liberal governments is order, plurality and tolerance. They can have no views on the ethical or transcendent nature of human life. ... So the ultimate liberal society is one in which all such convictions have been eradicated. ... I take this to be unliveable, meaningless and inhuman.[117]

Bryan Appleyard in *'Understanding the Present'*

The value-free climate of much of our financial and public life has poisoned and wounded our society more deeply than we know.[118]

Rowan Williams

Morality, integrity and personal honour have been devalued. Free-wheeling capitalism has cut its moral anchors and drifted into a morass of sharp practice and greed. The Big Banks have been found guilty of selling dodgy derivatives before the financial crisis of 2008. When Barclays Bank was founded by Quakers in 1694 its principles were honesty, integrity and plain dealing. But in 2012 it was fined £290 million pounds for rigging interest rates which affected millions of people worldwide. Also in 2012 a major pharmaceutical company was fined 1.9 billion dollars for marketing drugs for unapproved uses, and for failing to report drug and safety information to the US Food and Drug Administration. In London Lord Justice Leveson is conducting an inquiry into media ethics following the phone hacking scandal at a Sunday newspaper. One executive of that paper is now facing charges of attempting to pervert the course of justice and another is charged with perjury. TV executives judge success by ratings alone, with no consideration of the impact on people's behaviour. The BBC's first Director General Lord Reith aimed to raise the moral standards of the nation; it sometimes seems as if the current aim is to lower them.

Why liberals see little need for morality

For many liberals moral values are unnecessary - apart from tolerance and not harming others. If we are naturally good, we do not need moral rules. If people turn out badly, it is not because of any evil in them, they have been corrupted by society. We are all to blame. The belief that we are essentially good made morality redundant. Secondly, liberals hold that our freedom should not be restricted: no morality, tradition, parents, church, society or religion should limit us. There should be no social pressure to behave in any particular

---

[117] Bryan Appleyard *Understanding the Present* (London Picador 1993) p. 256
[118] Rowan Williams Daily Telegraph 4.4.10

way. Thirdly, only scientific statements are true; morality is not scientific and so has no claim to be true; scientific rationalism undermined both morality and religion. For all these reasons a liberal society - like Britain's - devalues morality and its secular schools teach no moral code. The outcome is a society that is non-judgemental, value-free and amoral.

The attack on Christian morality goes back to the Enlightenment; David Hume held that Christian virtues "are everywhere rejected by men of sense, because they serve no purpose; nor render a man a more valuable member of society. We observe on the contrary that they cross all these desirable ends; stupefy the understanding, harden the heart and sour the temper. We justly transfer them to the catalogue of vices, which pervert entirely natural sentiments."[119] For Hume there is no merit in Christian teaching such as, "Love your enemies, do good to those who hate you, bless those who curse you, and pray for those who treat you badly. If a man hits you on one cheek, turn to him the other. If a man takes your coat, let him have your shirt as well. Give to everyone who asks, and if someone takes your belongings, don't ask for them back."[120]

The Marquis de Sade, best known today for giving his name to sadism, argued that after the Enlightenment, which held that science and reason alone provide the basis for truth, we are free to do whatever we like, including sexually. We should no longer be restrained by morals, but may pursue pleasure wherever it leads. Rules can be broken; everything turned upside down; the social order inverted. In his novel *Histoire de Juliette*, Sade tells us that Juliette's creed is science. She opposes worship of anything that is not entirely rational, including God and morality. Her mentor Noirceuil urges her to do anything she wants, without fear of the consequences. According to Sade, we should enjoy our freedom from the shackles of the past. Pleasure and fun are the only criteria. Instead of obeying the 'oughts' and 'shoulds' of a moral code, we should pursue hedonism and happiness.

Like Hume and Sade, Nietzsche recast virtues as vices, and vices as virtues. He wrote, "I deny morality... I also deny immorality."[121] According to him western man is burdened by the morality of Christianity. We must throw it off and become supermen (*Übermensch*), whose freedom is unfettered. Nietzsche turned Christian morality upside down, arguing that weaklings and failures should go to ruin and we should help them on their way. He despised the pity for the unsuccessful and weak in Christianity. He argued that it is natural for the strong to oppress the weak. There is no place for remorse or pity. Be ruthless and merciless. Be great, not good. Both Nietzsche and Sade admired strength, boldness and brutality. They loathed kindness, love and fellow-feeling. Christianity, they held, should be rejected because it protected the weak.

---

[119] David Hume *An Enquiry into the Principles of Morals*, section ix, part I, para 219
[120] St. Luke's Gospel Chapter 6 verse 27-30
[121] F. Nietzsche *Daybreak section 103* Tanner p. 28

Nietzsche sneered at the Christian ideal - true happiness is to be found in the service of others - calling it a slave mentality. We know now where Nietzsche's ideas led - Auschwitz.

He wrote, "Once abroad in the wilderness, they revel in the freedom from social restraint. ... They revert to the innocence of wild animals: we can imagine them returning from an orgy ... at peace with themselves as though they had carried out a prank.... Their boldness, their terrible pleasure in destruction, their taste for cruelty."[122] Nietzsche delighted in Dionysian debauchery, "an extravagant want of sexual discipline, whose waves engulfed all the venerable rules of family life. The most savage beasts of nature were here unleashed."[123] Nietzsche acknowledged that there were dangers in abandoning Christianity, writing, "When one gives up Christian faith, one pulls the right to Christian morality from under one's feet... Christianity is a system, a *whole* view of things thought out together. By breaking the main concept, faith in God, one breaks the whole: nothing is left in our hands."[124] He understood that his ideas led to nihilism, and thought it was tragic that western civilisation is based on Christianity and that without it we have no values to hold civilisation together.

Further attacks on morality

Over the last 100 years morality has been under constant attack. A century ago Edmond Holmes, who was the Chief Inspector of Schools, wrote an influential book called *What Is And What Might Be*. He rejected Judeo-Christian values and repudiated western civilisation. He damned schools as brutal, strict and dull. The British educationalist Lawrence Stenhouse argued, "Teaching must renounce the authority of the teacher. ... In short the teacher must aspire to be neutral."[125] Any moral guidance a teacher gave was seen as indoctrination. Children should be free to make up their own minds, with no input from teachers or parents, and no attempt made to pass on society's history, culture or values. It was "an explicit call to arms against western civilisation, using children as the weapon and schools as the battlefield"[126] wrote Melanie Phillips. Children were to be used to subvert traditional values, and instead liberal values and multiculturalism would be promoted. According to liberals all values are equal, so there are no grounds for criticism of anyone else's beliefs. Steven

---

[122] F. Nietzsche *The Birth of Tragedy and the Genealogy of Morals* (New York 1956) trans Francis Golffing pp 174f

[123] F. Nietzsche *The Birth of Tragedy* section 2

[124] F. Nietzsche *Twilight of the Gods Skirmishes of an Untimely Man* Section 5

[125] Lawrence Stenhouse *The Discussion of Controversial Values in the Classroom* (Schools Council/Nuffield Foundation Humanities Curriculum Project 1969)

[126] Melanie Phillips *All Must Have Prizes* (London Warner Books 1998) p. 203

Pinker condemned this non-judgmental approach, which results in the ludicrous situation where his students felt unable to criticise the Nazis.

The 20th century educationalist A. S. Neill rejected morality saying, "I believe moral instruction makes a child bad. I find that if you smash moral instruction, a bad child becomes good."[127] He encouraged stealing; went out stealing with boys; urged clergy to go out stealing with young lads; and told boys how to swindle the railways.[128] He even sought to get rid of good manners – such as saying 'please' and 'thank you' - because they were unnatural. He insisted no respect be given to teachers, because this would inhibit the child. He opposed punishing children, "I know from experience that punishing children is unnecessary. I never punish a child."[129] Punishment would lead to a loss of confidence and self-esteem, a feeling of unworthiness and inferiority. He banned religion because it taught that mankind was sinful. These 'progressive' ideas have influenced education and teacher training.

The Canadian psychiatrist C. B. Chisholm wrote of the need to "eradicate the concept of right and wrong" instead "children should be given all sides of every question so that in their own good time they may have the ability to make their own decisions. In this way we may substitute rational thinking in the place of the old certainties and free mankind from the crippling burden of good and evil."[130] This was part of a widespread attack on conventional morality and so-called 'bourgeois' values. Each child was to be wholly free to make up its own moral values, with no input from family, tradition or religion. According to Chisholm society should not attempt to pass on its values to the next generation.

In his 2003 book *The Mind Made Flesh* Nicholas Humphrey, Emeritus Professor at the LSE, argued parents should not pass on their moral values to their children. He said, "I shall probably shock you ... the purpose of my lecture is to argue in favour of censorship, against freedom of expression, and to do so in an area of life that has traditionally been regarded as sacrosanct. I am talking about religious and moral education, especially at home, where parents are allowed to determine what counts as right and wrong. Children have a right not to have their minds crippled by other people's bad ideas – no matter who these people are."[131]

In 2009 Beverley Hughes, Britain's Minister of State for Children, Young People and Families, in the Labour Government (1997-2010) issued a booklet called, *Talking to Your Teenager About Sex and Relationships*. This warned parents not to try to pass on their moral values to their children. In particular they should not say any sexual behaviour was right or wrong. It said,

---

[127] A. S. Neill *Summerehill* (London Pelican 1968) p. 221
[128] Neill p. 46
[129] Neill p. 151
[130] C. B. Chisholm cited by Melanie Phillips in *All Must Have Prizes* (London Warner Books 1998) p. 203
[131] Nicholas Humphrey*The Mind Made Flesh* (Oxford University Press 2003) p. 291

"Remember that trying to convince them [teenagers] of what is right and wrong may discourage them from being open." It advised that any discussion of values should be kept "light", and recommended children be given a choice of options and then be left free to decide for themselves what is right or wrong, with no parental guidance. This would maximise their freedom and ensure traditional moral values were not passed on to the next generation. The booklet stressed that all moral values are relative.[132]

These examples illustrate the belief that it is wrong to pass on a set of values to children. But children do not have the maturity to create a moral code for themselves; they need to be given a pattern, one that over time they may modify, but to leave them with no guidelines is a recipe for moral chaos. We cannot operate without a set of values; nor can any particular worldview be proved correct scientifically. Moreover rationalists do not think that passing on *their* set of values to children is a problem.

The undermining of traditional values

Families, which were of vital importance in the Victorian period, partly as a means of social security, have come under sustained attack. Erich Fromm held that the patriarchal family was the authoritarian state in miniature. Wilhelm Reich preached free love; he and Theodor Adorno argued that strict disciplining of children, obedience and respect for authority were all breeding grounds for fascism.[133] These attitudes have helped to undermine parents, weaken social bonds, and contribute to the disintegration of the traditional family. In 1972 a group of leading humanists contributed to the book *Objections to Humanism*, in which they criticised their own beliefs. One contributor, Kingsley Martin, an editor of the *New Statesman*, acknowledged that humanists had ignored the fact that marriage gives security to women and children. He added, "People in love with each other want to be bound to each other, not free."[134] He conceded that freedom does not always lead to happiness, and those claiming to be free have often been disillusioned. Liberals, he argued, make the mistake of thinking that people want freedom above all. He wrote, "The trap for the unwary humanist is that he may talk as if marriage is unimportant."[135]

The welfare system encourages amoral behaviour. In November 2010 *The Sunday Times* ran an article on Keith Macdonald, who has fathered 14 children

---

[132] Government pamphlet published February 22nd 2009 by Beverley Hughes Minister of State for Children Young People and Families called 'Talking to Your Teenager About sex and Relationships.'
[133] Theodor Adorno *The Authoritarian Personality*
[134] Kingsley Martin in *Objections to Humanism* edited by H. J. Blackham (London Pelican 1963) p. 91
[135] Martin p. 91

by various women.[136] He is unemployed and living on incapacity benefit, claiming a "bad back". The cost to the taxpayer in income support, housing benefit and basic allowances will be £2,000,000 by the time the children have grown up. He is only 25 so his tally of 14 children may well increase. £5 a week is taken from his benefits to pay for his children. His is not an isolated case but replicated across the country. Jill Kirby of the Centre for Policy Studies commented that the welfare system provides "incentives for feckless parenting. MacDonald's case reflects the behaviour of other men whose lives follow a similar pattern. The women are also culpable because they have made no effort to guard against having a baby."[137]

Our poor young people are the victims of our sex-obsessed society. Today if you happen to be in a city centre late on a Saturday night you can see crowds of scantily clad girls with very short skirts - even in mid-winter - tottering around drunk. Pressure to have sex comes from TV soaps, which portray casual sex and single motherhood as the norm, magazines, and pop videos resemble soft porn. It is no surprise that the age at which girls and boys have their first intercourse gets ever younger. Young teenage girls pick up the message that they are expected to be sexually active. There is no mention of abstinence: liberal values have undermined both self-restraint and marriage. In addition the poor discipline in some secondary schools results in little being learnt. Many girls are denied a decent education and see little alternative to a career as a single mother. Moreover, they know how to play the system: they know that if a girl has a baby she will be given a council flat and welfare benefits.

De-moralising society

We seem to have not merely jettisoned Victorian values, but to have abandoned morality itself. Some changes are welcome: including a more joyful attitude to sex and the repeal of laws criminalising homosexuality. However Victorian values such as - thrift, hard work, faithfulness, self-help, self-discipline, neighbourliness, sobriety, personal responsibility, patriotism, valour and the central importance of family and marriage had some merit. For example Octavia Hill, the Victorian social reformer who built good quality housing for the poor, insisted on high standards of cleanliness and promoted a work ethic on her tenants to discourage welfare dependency.

The American historian Gertrude Himmelfarb believes the wholesale rejection of morality has been a mistake: "We have so completely rejected any kind of moral principle that we have deliberately, systematically divorced welfare from moral sanctions and incentives. We are now confronting the

---

[136] Sunday Times 28th November 2010
[137] Sunday Times 28th November 2010

consequences.... Value-free social policies imperil the moral and material well-being of their intended beneficiaries. In demoralising social policy – divorcing it from any moral criteria – we have demoralised, in the more familiar meaning, both the individual and society as a whole."[138]

James Bartholomew in his book, *The Welfare State We're In,* quotes an opinion poll, which showed that 80% of the population thought that people are less moral than in the 1950s.[139] A large majority think children are given little or no moral teaching and are left to make up their own moral code. Evidence of the decline in trust is given by Richard Layard in his book *A Good Childhood.* Surveys asking whether most people can be trusted show that 56% said yes in 1959; this had fallen to 29% in 1999 - a decline of 27% in 40 years.[140] A Children's Society survey found that 66% thought children's sense of moral values was weaker today than in the past, only 7% thought it was stronger.[141]

So has liberalism brought moral progress? Or is our society more sexually promiscuous, distrustful, selfish, disfigured by alcohol, with growing numbers of dysfunctional families and with more lonely individuals than in Victorian times? Are we squandering our moral inheritance, leaving our children and grandchildren morally bankrupt? Despite the progress made in respect of sexual and racial minorities, several surveys point to a general decline in morality. Today we are wary of morality. Moral principles – or worse, moral judgements - are taboo, and seen as evidence of an intolerant frame of mind, but those who preach non-judgementalism are very judgmental themselves about other people's values.

---

[138] Gertrude Himmelfarb *The De-moralisation of Society* (London The Institute of Economic Affairs 1995) p. 240-242
[139] Daily Telegraph Gallup poll dated 5th July 1996
[140] Richard Layard *A Good Childhood* (London Penguin 2009) p. 7
[141] Survey of 1,000 adults January 2007 cited in Richard Layard *A Good Childhood* (London Penguin 2009) p. 7

CHAPTER 4

The Liberal Delusions:
The Individual is of Overriding Importance

The biggest problem with the England team players is that most are too selfish.[142]
Paul Scholes, Manchester United and England footballer

It is a fallacy that individual freedom is a collective good.[143]
A. H. Halsey, Emeritus Professor of Sociology, Oxford

The more self-centred forms of fulfilment have been gaining ground in recent
Decades. …The future seems to promise ever increasing levels of narcissism.[144]
Charles Taylor in *The Malaise of Modernity*

The culture of competitive individualism has carried the logic of individualism to the
extreme…and the pursuit of happiness to a narcissistic preoccupation with the self.[145]
Christopher Lasch in *The Culture of Narcissism*

When the negative side of individualism is considered now, it is conventionally seen
as a product of the Thatcher years. But much of it can be traced further back to the
libertarian policies of Roy Jenkins in the 1960s and earlier.[146]
Gavron, Dench and Young in *The New East End*

Our individualistic societies are hollowing out our common culture.[147]
John Gray in *Enlightenment's Wake*

P aul Scholes played 676 games for Manchester United and was capped 66
times for England. He stopped playing for England in 2004 at the age of
29. In an interview in 2011 to mark his retirement from international
football he explained why he had brought his England career to an early end.[148]
He claimed some players did not care whether they won or lost and many had a
'me-first' attitude. England's lack of success in recent years was not due to a
lack of skills, but of the right values. He said, "I got fed up. When you're going
as a team and you want to be part of the team and playing well, and there are
individuals who are after personal glory. For example, where there's a simple
pass of 10 yards, they try instead to smack the ball 80 yards to get themselves

---

[142] Paul Scholes Interview with Sunday Times 10.7.2011
[143] Norman Dennis and George Erdos *Families Without Fathers* (London IEA Health &
Welfare Unit 1992) Foreword p. xii
[144] Charles Taylor *The Malaise of Modernity* p. 76
[145] Christopher Lasch *The Culture of Narcissism* (London Sphere Books 1980) p. xv
[146] Dench Gavron and Young p 106. Young contributed to an earlier study called *Family and
Kinship in East London.*
[147] John Gray *Enlightenment's Wake* (London Routledge 2007) p. xvii or p. 127
[148] Paul Scholes Interview with Sunday Times 10.7.2011

noticed. It was a frustration. It was just selfish. If you look at the Spanish team now, they play for each other. There isn't one who would try to do something in a game that doesn't suit the team. And that could happen here. Spanish players don't have superior skills, but a different attitude." He referred to the Barcelona team, "The big thing for them is that word again – unselfishness. They play as a team, and work hard for each other. Even Lionel Messi is a team player, not an individual star." Selfishness and greed is not confined to football. In rugby, a report on England's poor performance in the 2011 Rugby World Cup concluded, 'For some players it was more about cash and caps, than about getting better.'[149] In the world of commerce selfishness also prevails - boardroom pay increases have far outstripped average earnings; some top salaries have increased by 4,000% over the last 30 years, whereas average earnings have increased threefold. Directors earnings grew by 49% in 2010, according to the High Pay Commission which reported in November 2011.[150] Bankers bonuses in the City of London total billions of pounds. Some TV executives only care about their ratings and press barons about their circulation figures.

A culture of self-fulfilment

Liberalism's overriding concern is for freedom - in particular individual freedom and personal self-fulfilment. In the past the pattern of most people's lives was set at birth, with little scope for change. The individual was under pressure to conform to the traditions, customs and beliefs of society. The goal of the Enlightenment in the past, and liberals today, is individual autonomy - unfettered freedom to choose your own beliefs and values. As a result of its influence we enjoy today much greater freedom. We are not constrained by the social standing of our parents, nor by notions of social hierarchy. We can choose our ends and shape our lives to a much greater extent. However there is a new imperative: I must discover who I am, and realise my potential. While there are positive aspects to greater freedom and the desire to fulfil ourselves, there is also a downside which has been largely overlooked. If the purpose of my life is the pursuit of my freedom and my self-fulfilment, then obligations, duties and responsibilities to others become secondary or even redundant.

It was in the 1960s that traditional values were rejected: the solidarity engendered by World War Two had faded and the influence of Christianity which warned against selfishness had waned. Instead a 'do-your-own-thing' me-generation made a bonfire of traditional mores and taboos. Germaine Greer in *The Female Eunuch* promoted selfishness, "I have another duty, just as sacred ... My duty to myself."[151] She urged women to fulfil themselves and reject the role of a wife. Her book championed freedom and individualism, and

---

[149] Report in The Times 23.11.11
[150] BBC News online 22.11.11
[151] Germaine Greer *The Female Eunuch* (London Granada 1981) p. 25

contributed to the decline in marriage. In our culture commitments have become weaker; relationships are increasingly seen as temporary alliances to be junked if circumstances provide a better alternative. Society has become increasingly a collection of isolated individuals only thinly related to others. However there are other social patterns: Japanese society is less individualistic and has maintained a greater sense of solidarity and cohesion.

Individualism has not brought happiness. Today we live more isolated lives, with less communal activity and feel less bound to our fellow citizens. Participation in social activities has declined. Individuals have become disengaged and feel less sense of obligation to their societies, which need a sense of shared endeavour if they are to flourish. Community spirit has dwindled - the outcome is greater loneliness. We are social animals who need others: our relationships are vital to our well-being and contentment. We do not thrive as atomised individuals. The focus on individual freedom and self-fulfilment has contributed to family breakdown and so harmed children. In our culture of self-centred hedonism children are often neglected. Many adults are untroubled by any thoughts that they are behaving selfishly. It is no surprise that the age at which children run away from home gets ever younger. The outcome of these changes is that for many people life today seems to have lost its enchantment; there is a loss of a sense of meaning and growing alienation.

These individualistic trends can be traced back to The Enlightenment, which replaced the duties, which had bound society together with individual rights. "We hold these truths to be self-evident, that all men are created equal, that they are endowed by their Creator with certain inalienable rights, that among these are Life, Liberty and the pursuit of Happiness" stated The US Declaration of Independence of 1776. 'The Declaration of the Rights of Man in the French Revolution likewise championed human rights - including the right to be happy. The state became the guarantor of individual happiness. I feel sad. I have a right to feel happy. Give me a pill. In France 20% of the population are on anti-depressants. Yet all human lives contain suffering, which if accepted and worked through, can lead to greater maturity and wisdom.

Individualism versus communitarianism

Liberals begin with the conviction that societies are composed of individuals endowed with rights, which give them entitlements. Whereas communitarians maintain individuals are constituted by social belonging and emphasise community. One such communitarian is the Canadian thinker Charles Taylor. While acknowledging the positive aspects of individualism, he worries that self-centred modes of self-fulfilment are increasing, "What is self-defeating in contemporary culture is the concentration on self-fulfilment in opposition to the demands of society... This shuts out the bonds of solidarity and is shallow and trivial."[152] He notes the decline in commitment to each other, "People see their relationships as more revocable. .... an abandonment of traditional ties in favour of sheer egoism."[153] As a result we now live in a "fragmented society whose members find it harder and harder to identify with their potential society as a community."[154] He rues our growing individualism, our loss of a sense of belonging, and laments our attempt to compensate by consumerism and materialism. For Heidegger too authentic personal experience requires a social context, a shared endeavour, a common past and a sense of belonging to a community. We are not merely self-centred individuals in competition with each other. He regarded a strong social dimension as essential for individual fulfilment.

Another critic of individualism is Robert Putnam, Professor of Public Policy at Harvard and a visiting Professor at Manchester University. He is one of America's best known social scientists courted by Presidents Clinton and Bush. The title of his bestseller *Bowling Alone* is taken from the fact that in the US more people are bowling on their own, not in leagues. He fears we are witnessing the ebbing of community. The membership of trade unions, clubs, choirs, churches and sports leagues have all fallen. The bonds and networks that hold societies together, which he calls social capital, are all in decline. This is shown by lower levels of trust in government and less civic participation - a key component in maintaining democracy. He holds that where social capital is high, neighbourhoods are safer, crime is lower; there is more mutual support and co-operation; people are healthier and more citizens vote. He wrote, "Most Americans today feel vaguely and uncomfortably disconnected. ... [We long for] a more civil, trustworthy, collectively caring community" and "Americans are right to feel that the bonds of community have withered and this has real costs."[155]

The Archbishop of Canterbury, Rowan Williams, paints a picture of Britain where trust has declined, "Certain styles of human self-understanding that might lead to a sense of irony or humility or trustfulness or solidarity are becoming unavailable"[156] and "We live in a diverse and increasingly distrustful environment."[157] He maintains that the bonds we do not choose - like kinship and nationality - are now weaker and maintains liberal societies are neutral about what constitutes a good life. They have nothing to say. In his own words, "The liberal project of emancipation and entitlement for those who have been deprived of voice and power - all this is a matter of means rather than ends. As

---

[152]Charles Taylor *The Malaise of Modernity* (Canada Ontario House of Anasi 1991) p. 40
[153] Taylor p. 76
[154] Taylor p. 117
[155] Robert Putnam *Bowling Alone* (New York Touchstone 2001) p. 402
[156] Rowan Williams *Lost Icons* (London T & T Clark 2000) p. ix
[157] Williams p. 103

an end in itself the liberal state is vacuous."[158] He describes western societies as "deeply preoccupied with rights" and as a result "the fragmentation [of society] becomes ever more acute."[159] The central spiritual problem in the west is individualism, which militates against community. We have exaggerated the importance of the solitary individual. Richard Rohr, a contemplative monk, wrote, "I need to recognise that I'm in a river that is bigger than I am... Rage, anger and disappointment have become widespread in western peoples. The disconnected life leaves us separate, isolated and therefore false to ourselves and others."[160]

Human Rights versus the social good

Liberals have focussed on empowering individuals and promoting human rights. This makes thankfulness and gratitude redundant. Are you given welfare, or cured of a disease? It's my right! Moreover, 'I know my rights' has become the verbal equivalent of two fingers to authority. Teachers trying to get control of unruly pupils are told, "We know our rights. No-one has the right to tell us what to do." It is hardly surprising that in such a culture secondary school teachers find discipline a problem, and that employers find youngsters are not biddable and lack a work ethic. So they prefer to recruit immigrants. If your obligations are only to yourself, then there is no place for a work ethic which recognises obligations to others.

The Human Rights Act of 1998 unleashed a tide of litigation and created a "rights culture" - a schoolboy arsonist, whose expulsion from school was reversed, because it breached his right to education; travellers, allowed to remain on unlawful sites, because of their right to family life; a convicted killer given hard-core pornography in prison because of his right to information; a convicted rapist given £4,000 compensation because his second appeal was delayed; the burglar given taxpayers' money to sue the man whose house he broke into.[161] Likewise the European Court of Human Rights has championed the rights of the individual over the well-being of society: in February 2011 the Court ruled that European Convention on Human Rights meant that a woman on benefits who failed to pay rent cannot be evicted; and in September 2011 it ruled that a Nigerian man convicted of raping a 13-year-old girl cannot be deported back to country of birth.[162] The Court ruled in 2012 that Britain could not deport to Jordan a suspected Al Qaeda terrorist lest his human rights were infringed; the potential harm he could inflict on British citizens was ignored. In Gloucester a car thief was chased by police; he stopped the car, shinned up a

---

[158] Williams p. 104
[159] Williams p. 103
[160] Richard Rohr *Everything Belongs* (New York Crossroad Publishing 1999) p. 79
[161] *The Daily Telegraph* 10 August 2005
[162] The Times 20.10.11

drainpipe and climbed onto a house roof, from where he threw bricks and tiles at people and cars below.[163] He demanded cigarettes and his favourite food and drink - a *family-size* tub of Kentucky Fried Chicken and a *two-litre* bottle of Pepsi Cola. He rejected a mere can of Pepsi as inadequate. All his precise demands were met; the food and drink were delivered to him on the roof, by a van with a special hydraulic platform. Having refreshed himself, he resumed throwing bricks and tiles at passers-by and cars. Questioned later about their actions, the police answered that they had to respect his human rights!

A culture dominated by rights also sets one group against another, with little attempt to seek the common good. Trevor Phillips, the Chairman of the Equality and Human Rights Commission, attacked the "thoroughly bonkers" misuse of the Human Rights Act and expressed his concern that the Act did not become the property of unpopular minorities - illegal immigrants, terror suspects, and criminals at the expense of the general public.[164] He gave as an example of this lunacy: militant secularists who want to prosecute town councillors for having prayers before meetings. The liberal stress on the rights of the individual and self-fulfilment has not led to utopia, but to greater self-absorbed narcissism. To live for yourself without commitments, obligations and duties to others does not bring contentment, but more loneliness and a broken society. We need to rediscover the importance of society, of shared endeavour and common purpose. It is only in such an environment that individuals actually thrive.

---

[163] 6th June 2006
[164] The Sunday Times 11.12.2011

CHAPTER 5

The Liberal Delusions:
Greater Equality is Always Beneficial

It is just not true that humans are born equal. If we treat them equally, the result must be inequality in their actual positions.[165]
Friedrich Hayek

The fear of the terrible consequences that might arise from a discovery of innate differences has led many intellectuals to insist such differences do not exist.[166]
Steven Pinker

A surprising number of intellectuals, particularly on the left, do deny that there is such a thing as inborn talent, especially intelligence. ...
I find it truly surreal to read of academics denying intelligence.[167]
Steven Pinker

All animals are equal but some are more equal than others.[168]
George Orwell

A commitment to equality is another core liberal value. There are many positive aspects to the drive for greater equality and social justice. I recognise the damaging social consequences and injustice of wide differences in wealth between – say a hospital porter and an investment banker with his massive bonuses. Great differences in wealth within the nation and across the world cannot be justified. Many conservatives have neglected the one-nation tradition, which stresses the need for greater equality, social justice and fairness. Where there are wide differences in wealth, people who are poor suffer not only a lack of social status, but also live less healthy lives and die younger. Richard Wilkinson's research found that low status caused stress for many workers and this harmed their health.[169] His conclusion is that a more equal society will be happier, healthier and its members live longer. The pathfinders of liberalism in the Enlightenment wanted a society of equal individuals and strove to weaken inherited wealth and privilege.

However there are some negative aspects to the pursuit of equality:
- Some liberals attempt to entrench equality by denying any differences exist at birth; and insist we are all born the same;

---

[165] Friedrich Hayek *The Constitution of Liberty* (Chicago University Press) 1960/1978
[166] Steven Pinker *The Blank Slate* (London Allen Lane 2002) p. 141
[167] Steven Pinker p. 149
[168] George Orwell *Animal Farm*
[169] Richard Wilkinson *Mind The Gap: Hierarchies Health and Human Evolution* (London Weidenfeld and Nicholson 2000)

- In some cases equality of outcome has replaced equality of opportunity as an objective in education and this has led to a lowering of standards, grade inflation, the dumbing down of the syllabus and the failure of gifted pupils to achieve their potential;
- the desire for equality has led to attacks on high culture as elitist;
- equality and freedom are mutually exclusive - a zero-sum game: the more freedom the less equality and the more equality the less freedom;
- well-meaning generous welfare designed to reduce inequality has encouraged dependency and undermined self-reliance;
- equality and diversity legislation has led to the persecution of those with minority views;
- egalitarian regimes have been among the most evil and blood-thirsty in history.

Denial of differences at birth

What do we mean by equality? Is it sameness or an equality of basic rights? If we differ biologically, then society could try to 'improve' its population by encouraging some groups, and discouraging others from breeding. In extreme cases this could lead to genocide of inferior groups as happened under the Nazis. Hitler was influenced by Darwin, especially natural selection and the survival of the fittest: the idea that fitter and superior races could and should eliminate weaker ones. However Pinker points out that eugenics was a popular idea on the left, not as is commonly thought on the right, "Contrary to the belief spread by radical scientists, eugenics for much of the 20th century was a favourite cause of the left not of the right."[170] As evidence of this he cites - H. G. Wells, G. B. Shaw, Harold Laski, J. M. Keynes, Sidney and Beatrice Webb and J. B. S. Haldane

The American Declaration of Independence states, "We declare these truths to be self-evident that all men are created equal" Jefferson's definition of equality did not mean sameness; and it didn't include women or African Americans. Abraham Lincoln acknowledged inborn differences, "The signatories of the Declaration of Independence did not mean to say we are all equal in colour, size, intellect or moral development, but only certain in rights."[171] We are only born equal in terms of human rights, not in our gifts and abilities. It is a mistake is to confuse equal rights with being the same.

Many intellectuals rightly react with horror to Nazism and its belief in inborn differences between different ethnic groups. They fear that acknowledging inborn differences could lead to atrocities, such as Nazism, and so deny any inborn differences. They resolve to make it impossible for such beliefs to gain currency again. So they adopt the Blank Slate theory, which states that our minds at birth are

---

[170] Pinker p. 153
[171] Seventh Lincoln-Douglas debate October 15 1858 Pinker p. 145

all blank, therefore we are all the same and equal. We inherit nothing from our parents, our heredity, or our past. Whereas if the slate is not blank i.e. at birth we inherit from our parents then we have to accept inequality. The theory seemed to offer a way to entrench equality on a scientific basis. According to Steven Pinker they have grounded equality on a mistaken understanding of biology: i.e. the notion that we are all the same at birth. He claims that intellectuals "promulgate the fiction that we are the same because it is less open to abuse."[172] They ignore the evidence of inborn differences and insist we are all identical. Pinker maintains we should reject discrimination on moral grounds, not base it on bogus science. He added, "The discovery of innate differences among individuals is not forbidden knowledge to be suppressed."[173]

Noam Chomsky finds the modern denial of heredity very odd, "Would we find the fact that height, musical ability or the 100 yard sprint was partly heritable disturbing?"[174] Most people acknowledge that a tall father is likely to have a tall son, and a clever parent will pass on intelligence to offspring. The fear is that if groups do differ, then it would be rational to take this into account. Chomsky rejects this and points out that if racial differences were proved, it would not lead to racism, except in a racist society. So the discovery of genetic differences is not the problem, but rather the attitudes of society. Pinker added, "The idea that class has anything to do with genes is treated by modern intellectuals like plutonium. Even though it is hard to imagine how it could not be true in part."[175] The truth is that differences do exist in children from birth, and some people are born with great talents: a Mozart or a Shakespeare. I can't by effort and application become a footballer like Stephen Gerrard, nor turn myself into a musical prodigy.

Equality of opportunity replaced by equality of outcome

Equality of opportunity in education aimed to eliminate advantages some children enjoy over others by the circumstances of birth. It was a meritocratic approach, which helped able children from poor backgrounds to rise in society. But it has been replaced equality of outcome, which seeks the same outcome for all pupils, regardless of the injustice this may involve for more gifted pupils. The drive for greater equality lead to comprehensive schools which have lowered standards in British education. The Grammar Schools have been replaced by comprehensive schools, which have an egalitarian ethos and this has hindered gifted pupils. In 1973 the public schoolboy, Tony Crosland, who was the Labour Secretary of State for Education, bragged "If it's the last thing I do. I'm going to destroy every f***ing Grammar School in England. And Wales. And Northern

---

[172] Pinker p. 151
[173] Pinker p. 151
[174] Noam Chomsky *Language and Thought* (Wakefield R.I. 1993) p. 362-3
[175] Pinker p. 149

Ireland."[176] Meanwhile the upper classes preserved good schools for themselves in the independent sector. But it was under a Conservative Government, when Mrs Thatcher was Secretary of State for Education, that most of the Grammar Schools were closed. Despite the fact that she had benefited from one herself. The destruction of the Grammar Schools has led to a decline in the standards. As a result the top jobs are increasingly dominated by the products of the independent schools. Another egalitarian idea - mixed ability teaching, has proved difficult for teachers, who have to cope with a wide range of abilities.

The equality of outcomes approach has led to a levelling down, rather than levelling up, and so standards have fallen. Exams and school syllabuses have been dumbed down and standards lowered. Melanie Phillips in her book *All Must Have Prizes* noted, "A fundamentalist egalitarianism has taken root."[177] She argues that many egalitarians opposes competition on the grounds that it creates winners and losers, and insist teachers should always praise the child, regardless of the quality of the work. In January 2011 Estelle Morris, who was a Minister of Education former in the Labour Government (1997-2010), addressed The Northern Conference on Education, and insisted "children who had five 'F's at GCSE should still be able to do (sic) an academic path if they want to. It's not about selection by ability." Children must feel good about themselves. This approach undermines the pursuit of excellence and the quest for high standards. However the children not fooled: telling every child that its work is good, when it isn't, in the long term fools no-one. The children don't know where they stand. Moreover gifted pupils have been held back by the egalitarian ethos which strove for equality of outcome above all.

All cultures are equal and high culture dismissed as elitist

Cultural relativism is driven by the desire to make all cultures equal. Liberals fear that if we think we are culturally superior, this could lead to an attempt to impose our culture on others. Therefore all cultures are of equal worth, merely different. No culture is superior to any other. If they were, then people's freedom could be undercut by feelings of inferiority. So no-one must criticise any one else's moral values or cultural tastes. Pinker gives the example of the genital mutilation of young girls in some cultures. We tolerate what is an abomination, he says, because we say it is cultural. If this were carried out by an individual on a young girl, we would impose a severe punishment. If it is practised by a society, we do nothing.

The French thinker Alain Finkielkraut in his book *La Defaite de la Pensée (The Defeat of Thought)* wrote "hierarchies are abolished, and all the criteria of taste are exposed as arbitrary. No rigid division between a masterpiece and ordinary works are allowed. Shakespeare is no better than anyone else. So that we can all be

---

[176] Susan Crosland *Tony Crosland* (London Jonathan Cape 1982) p. 148
[177] Melanie Phillips *All Must Have Prizes* (London) p. 28

equal." He maintains there is a "corrosive trivialisation of culture by those entrusted with preserving it."[178] and "This fraud is the dirty little secret that our cultural commissars refuse to acknowledge." Finkielkraut continued, "We are powerless against the depredations of intellectuals who have embraced nihilism."[179] This is the new treason of the intellectuals: western culture is being destroyed from within.

Some egalitarians hold that high culture is divisive. Culture is seen as elitist: in the words of Terry Eagleton the former Marxist Professor of English at Oxford, "Shakespeare and the apostrophe are just a means of separating the sheep from the goats." Everything is equal; nothing is right or wrong. Therefore there should be no corrections of a child's work. According to Professor Jean Aitchison of Oxford, in an article for *The Guardian* there is no correct English, "I deplore the words correct and incorrect in relation to language."[180] So the sentence: 'They am in those car yesterday" is not incorrect - merely different. The BBC was hugely impressed by her article, and at once invited her to give the Reith lectures.[181] Melanie Phillips commented "Education and culture have passed into the hands of philistines."[182]

Welfare creates dependency

It is right to be concerned for poorer members of society and seek a fairer and more equal society. However there are dangers with generous welfare. The Victorians understood this. A Royal Commission on the Poor Laws reported in 1834. Its spokesman, a Mr Okedon, reported the effects of generous welfare thus: "Moral character is annihilated and the poor man of twenty years, who tried to earn his money, and was thankful for it, is now an insolent discontented, surly, thoughtless pauper who talks of rights."[183] The Report urged that benefits be kept minimal to encourage low-paid workers to take jobs. The Beveridge Report of 1942 led to the expansion of the welfare state, but it recommended that benefits be fixed at subsistence level. It defined subsistence as "a standard of living barely adequate to support life."[184] Welfare was to be a bare minimum to give an incentive to work. The intention was to preserve people's self-reliance while eliminating poverty. The report insisted that anyone on benefits went for training, and it recommended benefits were short-term. It saw little need for means tested benefits or separate housing benefit. However over time welfare became ever more generous and the gap between low paid work and welfare benefits was eroded. By 1985 there was little advantage in working for low wages; you were

---

[178] Julien Benda, *The Treason of the Intellectuals,* New Brunswick Transaction (Publishers), 2000, p. xxv
[179] J Benda p. xxv
[180] The Guardian 4.7.1994
[181] Phillips p. 119
[182] Phillips p. 120
[183] James Bartholomew *The Welfare State We're In* (Politicos, London, 2006) p. 33.
[184] Bartholomew p. 45

better off claiming the dole. In May 2002 there were 2,400,000 on incapacity benefit.

James Bartholomew, in his book *The Welfare State We're In* noted, "The National Insurance Act of 1911 introduced by Lloyd George and Churchill was liberalised far beyond the original conception and became a system of benefactors."[185] It was originally based on fixed contributions and fixed benefits, which encouraged thrift and saving. He believes that today's generous welfare harms society, and contrasts the way people behave today with the decency and civility of life in the 1950s. He cites as an example the deteriorating behaviour of football players and football crowds. Bartholomew's case is that generous social security discourages work, and so leaves many of the poor poorer. It has contributed to incivility and crime, as well as a high tax and low growth economy. Furthermore means-tested benefits have discouraged saving, leading to less self-reliance and self-respect. The outcome is that thrift and self-help have been eroded.

Equality versus freedom

Sir Isaiah Berlin maintained that the two great principles of liberalism - freedom and equality - are in conflict with each other. There is a trade-off between freedom and equality. If we are given freedom, then because we have different amounts of intelligence, talent and luck, we will become unequal over time. Friedrich Hayek held that human beings are not born equal and if we treat them equally the outcome will be inequality. So paradoxically equality can only be achieved by treating people unequally. There are different answers to this fundamental conflict, but all solutions involve different trade-offs between freedom and equality, which remains a zero-sum game: the more freedom the less equality; and the more equality the less freedom. If we compare East and West Germany before reunification: West Germany had greater freedom and greater inequality, whereas in East Germany there was greater equality - except for the elite - and less freedom.

Equality and diversity legislation

The Equality and Diversity legislation of the Labour Government (1997-2010) has led in practice to the oppression of minorities. Catholic adoption agencies were forced to close when they refused to allow gay couples to adopt. At some universities Christian Unions have been targeted by secular liberals. Birmingham University Christian Union had its funding withdrawn by the student funding body because it referred to men and women but did not specifically refer to transgender persons. The Exeter University CU was banned for refusing to have non-Christians on its executive committee. Would they insist that the Vegetarian

---

[185] Bartholomew p. 13

Society have meat-eaters on their committee? Or that the Rugby Club committee include men who only play hockey? Would they threaten Muslim societies with having non-Muslims on their executive? Edinburgh University CU was banned because it ran a bible-based course on relationships, which promoted marriage.

Atrocities committed in the name of equality

There is a long history of regimes which champion equality carrying out atrocities: in the Reign of Terror during the French Revolution and Vendée genocide; communism regarded success as evidence of criminality and this led to brutal repression and mass killings. Under Lenin and Stalin wealthier peasants called kulaks were persecuted and during the Cultural Revolution in China under Mao landlords were persecuted and tortured; also in Cambodia under the Khmer Rouge. This list is not exhaustive. The Black Book of Communism gives numerous additional examples of atheistic communist regimes. I present the evidence on this in the chapter: Atrocities by Secularists and Rationalists.

CHAPTER 6

Liberal Delusions:
Science is Certain and Benign

For the Enlightenment anything that cannot be resolved into numbers is an illusion.[186]
Horkheimer and Adorno in *Dialectic of Enlightenment*

Rationalism is the disease of our time. It pretends to have all the answers....Unfortunately the mythic side of man is given short shrift nowadays.[187]
Jung in *Memories, Dreams, Reflections*

The spiritual condition of scientific liberalism ... offers no truth, no guiding light, no path; it can tell the individual nothing about his place or purpose in the world.[188]
Bryan Appleyard in *Understanding the Present*

Science has been triumphant and our liberal societies are still scientific. But we are clearly in a decadent phase and, I think, a terminal one. The decadence arises from the obvious failure of liberalism to transmit any value other than bland tolerance.[189]
Bryan Appleyard in *Understanding the Present*

When all possible scientific questions have been answered, the problems of life remain completely untouched. ... There are, indeed, things that cannot be put into words. *They make themselves manifest*. They are what is mystical.(His italics)[190]
Ludwig Wittgenstein in *Tractatus-Logico Philosophicus*

The Enlightenment

Liberal ideas can be traced back 300 years to the Enlightenment, which was a revolution in the way people thought about human nature and authority. It championed science, rationalism and secularism, and attached little importance to history, tradition and religion. The roots of the Enlightenment were in England: Francis Bacon had expounded the scientific method and in 1660 the Royal Society was founded - the first scientific society in the world. In 1685 Sir Isaac Newton amazed the world with the publication of *Principia Mathematica*, which explained the laws of gravity. The re-appearance of Halley's comet in 1758 confirmed Newton's theories. Classical

---

[186] M Horkheimer and T Adorno *Dialectic of Enlightenment* (California: Stanford University Press 2002) p. 4
[187] C G Jung *Memories, Dreams, Reflections* (London: Random House 1963) p. 330
[188] Bryan Appleyard *Understanding the Present* (London: Pan Books 1992) p. 13
[189] Appleyard p. 248
[190] Ludwig Wittgenstein *Tractatus-Logico Philosophicus* trans D.F. Pears and B. F. McGuiness (London Routledge and Keegan Paul 2001) sections 6.52 – 6.522 p. 88-89

62

science saw the universe as a gigantic machine. The Enlightenment later spread to France - partly with the help of Voltaire, who admired John Locke and Isaac Newton.[191] In 1759 the French philosopher d'Alembert caught the mood of the times when he wrote, "A very remarkable change is taking place, a change whose rapidity seems to promise a greater transformation to come. Natural sciences daily accumulate new riches."[192] Inspired by scientific discoveries and the technological advances of the Industrial Revolution, men and women felt that they were entering a new world. Science was seen as certain, objective, unchanging and benign. It was the paradigm for all knowledge and seen, especially in the French Enlightenment, as conducive to happiness and moral progress. Of course we have benefited enormously from scientific progress - life saving advances in medicine and technology which has removed much drudgery from life, and enabled man to travel to the moon.

The shattering of the scientific worldview in the 20th century

However the classical scientific worldview of the Enlightenment has been shattered: firstly, by further scientific discoveries and secondly by the moral failure of science. The 20th century discoveries of relativity, quantum mechanics and chaos theory have all shown that the notion that science can give hard, objective and unchanging facts about the world is mistaken. Einstein's theories of relativity revealed that time and space were relative, not absolute. Even Newton's theories had to be modified. Quantum Mechanics revealed the strange counter-intuitive world of sub-atomic particles - atoms are largely composed of empty spaces and particles can disappear and appear elsewhere without travelling between the two places. A world where the observer - by the act of observing - can affect the outcome, and where according to Heisenberg's Uncertainty Principle, there will never be certainty at the sub-atomic level. Niels Bohr, one of the pioneers in the field, said "If quantum mechanics has not profoundly shocked you, you have not understood it."[193] Science has had to be modified at both the sub-atomic level and at the other extreme - the very large. It changes and evolves; its truths are provisional, not immutable certainties. Moreover quantum mechanics and relativity have not been reconciled. Chaos theory arose when a meteorologist entered raw data regarding the weather to three decimal places instead of six and found that the weather forecasts changed completely. Small initial differences led to very different final outcomes. The beat of a butterfly's wing can lead to a tornado. So we will never be able to know the world in sufficient detail to make events predictable. The dream of scientists like Laplace - that in time science would be able to forecast the future precisely - have been shown to be groundless.

---

[191] Voltaire *Lettres sur les Anglais*
[192] D'Alembert *Elements de Philosophie* 1759
[193] Quoted by Karen Michelle Barad, in *Meeting the Universe Halfway* (2007) p. 254

The idea that a scientific worldview would lead to moral progress was undermined by the slaughter of the First World War, the gulags and concentration camps of totalitarian regimes, and by nuclear weapons which pose a threat to the future of mankind. The communist creed of 'scientific atheism' was brutal and barbaric and led to over 120 million deaths (see chapter on atrocities by secularists). We now know that science is as capable of facilitating genocide and eugenics, producing thalidomide, and killing millions with nuclear bombs, as curing diseases. Rachel Carson in her book *Silent Spring* showed that the use of the pesticide DDT in California had contaminated wildlife all the way up the food chain. So science can be harmful and destructive. Moreover science ignores the greed in human nature, which has led to the exploitation of nature without regard to environmental needs. It has lacked respect for nature and the notion that it brings happiness has proved an illusion. The American philosopher Allan Bloom observed that science increases man's power, but not his virtue, and the misuse of science cannot be opposed on scientific grounds.

The arrogance of science

Peter Atkins, Professor of Chemistry at Oxford, argued in his book *The Creation* "There is nothing that cannot be understood, there is nothing that cannot be explained, and everything is extraordinarily simple."[194] On another occasion he said, "Science is omnipotent.... We will be able to explain everything through science."[195] Following many wonderful discoveries and new technologies, science became overweening and arrogant. In conversation with a family friend, who is a Professor of Mathematics at London University, I asked, "Why is there a material universe at all, rather than just nothing?" He answered that the question was invalid, because there is no scientific answer. Paul Davies, one of our leading cosmologists criticised science's claim to dictate what questions can be asked and its insistence that any question it cannot answer is invalid. Interviewed by Joan Bakewell he commented: "Most physicists rather arrogantly assume their techniques are going to reveal everything .... What really matters are things like personal freedom, our feelings for other people, love and so on .... and frankly science has tried to sweep them under the carpet or tried to define them away."[196] Issues such as meaning, purpose, morality, selfishness and altruism have been ignored. Science is not the only truth, as Jung observed, "The Enlightenment operated with an inadequate rationalistic concept of truth."[197] Jung's view was that rationalism was the disease of our times (see quote at start of chapter). Men and women are more than desiccated

---

[194] Peter Atkins *The Creation* (W. H. Freeman & Co 1981) p. 3
[195] Peter Atkins in debate with William Lane Craig 1998
[196] Joan Bakewell *Belief* (London BBC 2005) p. 94
[197] C. G. Jung *Answer to Job* (London Routledge & Kegan Paul 1979) p. 148

calculating machines; they have feelings, loves, ambitions, attachments and loyalties.

As a philosophy student I attended a lecture given by Gilbert Ryle, who was Professor of Metaphysical Philosophy at Oxford, and wrote *The Concept of Mind*. At the end of the lecture, he was asked what he would say, if the glass of water on the table in front of him turned into wine. "It couldn't happen", he replied. "But what if it did?" the questioner persisted. "It couldn't happen" he replied. "But suppose tests beforehand confirmed it was water; and tests afterwards proved it was wine." "It couldn't happen", he replied. A dialogue of the deaf. Ryle believed scientific laws are unchanging, permanent and infallible. A view that belongs to the nineteenth century. If even Newton's laws needed modification, then scientific laws are provisional. If a glass of water did in fact turn into wine, science would have to adapt to the facts, not the facts to the existing scientific laws. Bryan Appleyard, the author of *Understanding the Present*, commented that Darwin would have been appalled at the intolerance, bigotry and "imperial world-conquering zealotry of Darwinian atheists."[198] One atheist scientist interviewed by the journalist Rod Liddle commented, "There's nothing wrong with being arrogant, if you know you're right."[199] By contrast Heisenberg welcomed the 20th century discoveries, because they restored humility to science, which was lost in the 19th century.[200]

The materialist fallacy

Many scientists are materialists - they think that nothing exists except matter and energy. They regard consciousness as merely the activity of the brain, and freewill as an illusion. Many are wedded to the belief that the universe is meaningless. Rupert Sheldrake, a distinguished scientist and a fellow of Clare College Cambridge, in his book *The Science Delusion,* considers these unproven assumptions of science. He commented, "The belief system that governs conventional scientific thinking is an act of faith."[201] According to Sheldrake scientists outwardly respect the taboos of the scientific worldview, but in private they feel free to doubt, "I have been struck over and over again by the contrast between public and private discussions with scientific colleagues. In public they are very aware of powerful taboos, in private they are more adventurous."[202]

---

[198] Bryan Appleyard website 6.6.07

[199] Peter Atkins interviewed on Rod Liddle's programme *The Trouble With Atheism* (Channel4 TV programme 2006)

[200] W. Heisenberg *The Physicist's Conception of Nature* 1958

[201] Rupert Sheldrake *The Science Delusion* (London Coronet 2012) p. 7

[202] Sheldrake p. 4

Charles Taylor, the philosopher, exposes the superficial reasoning that leads from science to atheism. He argues that from within the scientific paradigm, atheism appears as the ineluctable consequence of a commitment to science. Atheism becomes part of an unquestioned background which conditions the way people think. According to Taylor, "From within the picture, it just seems obvious that the order of argument proceeds from science to atheism, through a series of well-grounded steps. The critic sees all too well how ill-grounded some of these steps are."[203] He argues that atheists are held captive by a picture of reality, which they think is based on science, but which needs to be deconstructed. Their assumptions are, he argues, "largely unnoticed" and part of an "unquestioned background."[204] Science does not inevitably lead to a materialist outlook, nor entail atheism.

Some scientists regard science as a weapon to be used against religion. The eminent American biologist Richard Lewontin explained: "Our willingness to accept scientific claims that are against common sense is the key to understanding the real struggle between science and the supernatural. We take the side of science in spite of the patent absurdity of its constructs, in spite of its failure to fulfil many of its extravagant promises of health and life, in spite of the tolerance of the scientific community to unsubstantiated just-so stories, because we have a prior commitment, a commitment to materialism. ... Moreover that materialism is absolute, for we cannot allow a divine foot in the door."[205] So much for the disinterested quest for truth!

The limitations of rationalism

The emphasis on science has eroded the moral, spiritual and aesthetic aspects of life. As long ago as the 17th century Pascal warned of the dangers of an arid and arrogant rationalism: "Le coeur a ses raisons que la raison ne connaît pas." (The heart has its reasons which reason does not know.") and "There are two extremes: to base truth only on reason, and to exclude reason altogether." If only science is true, there is no basis for meaning, purpose and values, which cannot be scientifically established, and so they wither. Religious, spiritual and moral dimensions of life were devalued and much of modern art and literature became nihilistic. The meaninglessness of modern life is reflected in literature such as T. S. Eliot's *The Wasteland* and Camus' *L'Etranger* (*The Outsider*). For Camus life is absurd: Meursault, the anti-hero of his novel, is bewildered and lost; he murders a man for no apparent reason. The prestige and dominance of science influenced philosophy leading to logical positivism. This proposed the verification principle, according to which only statements that

---

[203] Charles Taylor *Secularism* (USA Belknap Press of Harvard University 2007) p. 565
[204] Taylor p. 565
[205] Richard Lewontin *New York Review of Books* January 9 1997 quoted in Charles Taylor *Secularism* (USA Belknap Press of Harvard University 2007) p. 835

could be scientifically verified and mathematics were true. Therefore morality, religion and history could be dismissed as meaningless. These ideas were set out in 1936 by A. J. Ayer in his book *Language Truth and Logic.* However the verification principle itself could not be verified, and so the principle failed its own test for truth. Ayer humbly admitted in 1978, "Nearly all of it was false"[206] and "logical positivism died a long time ago. I don't think much of *Language, Truth and Logic* is true. I think it is full of mistakes."[207]

Allan Bloom, an American academic whose book *The Closing of the American Mind* became a best-seller, felt that many of his students were bored and listless. According to Bloom, "Science, in freeing men, destroys the natural condition that makes them human. Hence for the first time in history, there is a possibility of a tyranny grounded not on ignorance but on science."[208] According to a scientific worldview, no culture is any better than any other. There is nothing worth passing on. Bloom observed that liberal attitudes had penetrated and corrupted the student mind; people thought in the past they were right and did bad things, therefore we must never believe we are right. However tolerance of others gives no meaning and purpose to an individual life. Liberal societies have nothing to live by. Without a unified set of beliefs they becomes bland and meaningless. The result is apathy, lethargy and despair.

Some of these themes were explored by Bryan Appleyard, "Liberal man lapses into a sort of spiritual fatigue, a state of apathy in which he decides such wider, grander questions are hardly worth addressing. ... The pessimism, anguish, scepticism and despair of so much twentieth-century art and literature are expressions of the fact that there is nothing 'big' worth talking about."[209] As a way of life tolerance of others fails to give us a guide or values for our own lives, and so we become apathetic and indifferent. Appleyard rejects scientific rationalism because we experience the whole of life, not just the rational elements. We need to reclaim our history which is embodied in our language. He holds that "Science and liberalism will not give us the means to defend what we are, because it will not acknowledge the possibility that we are right. ... The inhumanity of the idea is flagrant. People live their lives by making distinctions of value. But value distinctions are not allowed, so people must not live like people."[210] Our culture, our history and our language define us. We experience the whole of life. He added, "We can have irreducible affections, values and convictions, which express our kinship with our culture and that kinship will be beyond appeal. ... I am an expression of my culture, a culture that has come close to sacrificing itself on the altar of one small aspect of itself. It must clearly

---

[206] A J Ayer The Listener 2nd March 1978
[207] A. J. Ayer in R. A. Varghese (ed), *Great Thinkers on Great Questions*, (Oxford Oneworld, 1998) p 49
[208] Allan Bloom *The Closing of the American Mind* (London Penguin 1989) p. 295
[209] Appleyard p. 12
[210] Appleyard p. 238

be defended with my life, because it is my life."[211] His conclusion is that, "It is humanly impossible actually to be a liberal. Society may advocate liberal tolerance and open-mindedness, but nobody practises it. ... For a complete personal acceptance of scientific-liberalism would reduce society to passive, bestial anarchy. There would be no reason to do anything, no decisions worth taking and certainly no point in defending one position as opposed to another."[212]

One of our foremost scientists, the cosmologist Paul Davies said, "Our secular age has led many people to feel demoralised and disillusioned, alienated from nature, regarding their existence as a pointless charade in an indifferent, even hostile, universe; a meaningless three score years and ten on a remote planet wandering amid the vastness of an uncaring cosmos. Many of our social ills can be traced to the bleak world view that three hundred years of mechanistic thought have imposed on us, a worldview in which human beings are presented as irrelevant observers of nature rather than an integral part of the natural order. Among the general population there is a widespread belief that science and theology are for ever at loggerheads. Yet I would like to suggest an alternative: a universe in which the emergence of life and consciousness is seen, not as a freak set of events, but fundamental to its lawlike workings. The position I have presented to you is one that regards the universe, as a coherent, rational, elegant and harmonious expression of a deep and purposeful meaning."[213]

---

[211] Appleyard pp. 249 & 250
[212] Appleyard p. 240
[213] Paul Davies speech in acceptance of the Templeton Prize

CHAPTER 7

Liberal Delusions:
Religion is Untrue and Harmful

Atheism is so senseless and odious to mankind that it never had many professors.[214]

Isaac Newton

It seems to me absurd to doubt that a man may be an ardent theist and an evolutionist. You are right about [Charles] Kingsley. Asa Gray, the eminent botanist, is another case in point. In my most extreme fluctuations I have never been an atheist in the sense of denying the existence of a God.[215]

Charles Darwin

I am not an atheist, and I don't think I can call myself a pantheist.[216]

Albert Einstein

There is harmony in the cosmos which I, with my limited human mind, am able to recognise, yet there are people who say there is no God. But what really makes me angry is that they quote me to support such views.[217]

Albert Einstein

Some liberals are religious. Nevertheless one strand of liberalism, which comes down to us from the Enlightenment is secular, rationalist and atheistic. It holds that science alone is true. In this tradition stands Richard Dawkins, a gifted exponent of evolution. He described faith as evil, "I think a case can be made that *faith* is one of the world's great evils, comparable to the smallpox virus but harder to eradicate. Faith, being belief that isn't based on evidence, is the principal vice of any religion."[218] Yet we saw in the chapter on Human Goodness (above) that Dawkins does have faith in human goodness and progress. I suspect Dawkins is - like the rest of us - a man of faith. If he faced a major operation would he go ahead without faith in the surgeon? Does he fly without faith in the airline and its pilots? Darwin too was a man of faith. In *The Origin of Species* he was at pains to admit that the theory of evolution had difficulties he could not answer; in particular, how beneficial mutations

---

[214] Sir Isaac Newton *A Short Schem of the True Religion*
www.newtonproject.sussex.ac.uk/view/texts/normalized/THEM00007
[215] Charles Darwin Letter to John Fordyce 7 May 1879 Letter 12041
www.darwinproject.ac.uk/entry-12041
[216] G S Viereck *Glimpses of the Great* (Macaulay, New York 1936) p 186 Max Jammer, *Einstein and Religion* (Princeton, NJ: Princeton University Press. 1999 p. 48
[217] Einstein in a conversation with Prinz Hubertus zu Löwenstein, in Löwenstein's book *Towards the Further Shore* (London Victor Gollancz 1968) p 156 Jammer p. 97
[218] Richard Dawkins (January/February 1997). *Is Science a Religion?*. American Humanist Association.

were passed on. Yet he maintained it was true, though he lacked evidence. He had faith. Some of Einstein's theories of relativity were not demonstrated scientifically until years after publication. Yet Einstein had faith in them. Nor were Newton's theories established immediately. Newton, Darwin and Einstein all had faith in their theories before they were proven. It is impossible to live life without faith. Einstein believed science is based on a faith in the rationality of the universe. He said, "Ultimately the belief in the existence of fundamental all-embracing laws rests on a sort of faith."[219]

Dawkins maintains science and faith are incompatible, yet many great scientists were and are religious. Newton was deeply religious. He wrote, "Gravity explains the motions of the planets but cannot explain who set the planets in motion. God governs all things and knows all that is or can be done. This most beautiful system of the sun, planets, and comets, could only proceed from the counsel and dominion of an intelligent Being."[220] And, "It is the perfection of God's works that they are all done with the greatest simplicity. He is the God of order and not of confusion."[221] Obviously Newton poses a problem for Dawkin's claim that science and religion are in conflict. So how does Dawkins deal with Newton? First Dawkins quotes Bertrand Russell saying, "Intellectually eminent men disbelieve in the Christian religion, but hide the fact because they are afraid of losing their income." The next sentence is, "Newton was religious."[222] So Dawkins insinuates Newton was motivated by money and was insincere. This is totally false. Newton wrote to his friend Richard Bentley, "When I wrote my treatise about our system (*Principia Mathematica*), I had an eye upon such principles as might work for the belief in a deity and nothing can rejoice me more than to find it useful for that purpose."[223] If Newton was faking belief, he overdid it. He wrote many books on theology; read the Bible every day; attacked and ridiculed atheists; and wrote letters encouraging opponents of atheism.

Dawkins makes a similar insinuation against Mendel, the founder of genetics, "Gregor Mendel the founding genius of genetics was, of course, a religious man, an Augustinian monk; but that was in the nineteenth century, when becoming a monk was the easiest way to pursue science; the equivalent of a research grant."[224] So it was easy to pursue science as a monk! These slurs on great scientists are without evidence. Both Newton and Mendel believed science

[219] Einstein to P. Wright 24 January 1936. Einstein archive reel 52-337 Jammer p. 93

[220] Sir Isaac Newton cited in Tiner, J.H. *Isaac Newton: Inventor, Scientist and Teacher*. (Michigan USA Mott Media 1975)

[221] Cited in *Rules for methodizing the Apocalypse*, Rule 9, from a manuscript published in *The Religion of Isaac Newton* (1974) by Frank E. Manuel, p. 120

[222] Richard Dawkins *The God Delusion* (London Transworld 2006) p. 123

[223] Newton to Richard Bentley 10 December 1692 www.newtonproject.sussex.ac.uk /view/texts/normalized/THEM00254

[224] Richard Dawkins *The God Delusion* (London Transworld 2006) p. 125

and religion were in harmony. It was pointed out to Dawkins in a debate that many great artists were inspired by Christianity – Tallis, Byrd, Handel, Bach, Beethoven, Bruckner, Elgar etc. He replied: they faked it to get the money![225]

Did Einstein believe in God?

According to Dawkins, Einstein was an atheist, "Einstein sometimes invoked the name of God, and he is not the only atheistic scientist to do so, inviting misunderstanding by supernaturalists eager to misunderstand and claim the illustrious thinker as their own."[226] Dawkins gives a definition of atheism as believing that there is "nothing beyond the natural, physical world, no supernatural creative intelligence lurking behind the observable universe."[227] Dawkins explains that some scientists sound religious, but if you delve more deeply into their thinking, they are in fact atheists. He presents Einstein as a prime example, and describes Einstein's religion as pantheism, which he calls "sexed-up atheism."[228] According to Dawkins, "The one thing his theistic critics got right, was that Einstein was not one of them. He was repeatedly indignant at the suggestion he was a theist."[229] But the opposite is the truth. (See quote above)

It is important to get some definitions straight, because Dawkins tells us that "to deliberately confuse the two understandings of God is an act of intellectual high treason."[230] Strong words indeed. The Oxford English Dictionary gives the following definitions: "theism is the belief in a deity, or deities, as opposed to atheism; and the belief in one God, as opposed to polytheism or pantheism." It is important to note that the definition of theism does not necessarily include the notion that God is personal. Secondly, atheism is defined as "a disbelief in, or denial of, the existence of a God." Thirdly, pantheism is "a belief or philosophical theory that God is not only immanent but also identical with the universe; the doctrine that God is everything and everything is God."

Dawkins explained that in dealing with Einstein's religious views he relied on Max Jammer's book *Einstein and Religion*, "The extracts that follow are taken from Max Jammer's book (which is also my main source of quotations from Einstein himself on religious matters)."[231] However a very different picture emerges when we study what Einstein actually said, as

---

[225] Debate at Wellington College between Dawkins and Richard Harries former Bishop of Oxford 4th December 2009 reported in Daily Telegraph 5th December 2009
[226] Dawkins p. 34
[227] Dawkins p. 35
[228] Dawkins p. 40
[229] Dawkins p. 39
[230] Dawkins p. 41
[231] Dawkins p. 37

recorded by Jammer. The following quotations from Einstein are all in Jammer's book: "Behind all the discernible concatenations, there remains something subtle, intangible and inexplicable. Veneration for this force is my religion. To that extent, I am in point of fact, religious."[232] ..... "Every scientist becomes convinced that the laws of nature manifest the existence of a spirit vastly superior to that of men."[233] ..... "Everyone who is seriously involved in the pursuit of science becomes convinced that a spirit is manifest in the laws of the universe – a spirit vastly superior to that of man, and one in the face of which we must feel humble."[234] ..... "The divine reveals itself in the physical world."[235] ....."My God created laws... His universe is not ruled by wishful thinking but by immutable laws."[236] ..... "I want to know how God created this world. .... I want to know his thoughts."[237] ..... "What I am really interested in knowing is whether God could have created the world in a different way."[238] ..... "This firm belief in a superior mind that reveals itself in the world of experience, represents my conception of God."[239] ..... "My religiosity consists of a humble admiration of the infinitely superior spirit ...That superior reasoning power forms my idea of God."[240] Einstein also wrote the foreword to Lincoln Barnett's book *The Universe and Dr. Einstein*, which quotes Einstein saying, "My religion consists of a humble admiration for the illimitable superior spirit who reveals himself in the slight details we are able to perceive with our frail and feeble minds. That deeply emotional conviction of the presence of a superior reasoning power, which is revealed in this incomprehensible universe, forms my idea of God."[241]

What gives the lie to Dawkins' claim that Einstein was an atheist, is Einstein's repeated references to 'a superior spirit', 'a superior mind', 'a spirit vastly superior to men', 'a veneration for this force' etc. This is not atheism. It

---

[232] H. G. Kessler, *The Diary of a Cosmopolitan* (London: Weidenfeld and Nicolson, 1971) p. 322 quoted in Max Jammer, *Einstein and Religion* (Princeton, NJ: Princeton University Press. 1999) p. 40
[233] A Einstein to P. Wright 24 January 1936 Einstein Archive reel 52-337 Jammer p. 93
[234] Einstein quoted in H. Dukas and B. Hoffman *Albert Einstein – The Human Side* (USA Princeton University Press 1981) Jammer p. 144
[235] Z Rosenkranz Albert through the Looking Glass (Jewish National Library Jerusalem 1998 pp. xi, 80. Jammer p. 151
[236] Einstein in conversation with W. Hermann in Hermann's book *Einstein and the Poet* (USA Branden Press 1983) p 132 Jammer p. 123
[237] E. Salaman *A Talk with Einstein* The Listener 54 (1955): 370-371. Jammer p. 123
[238] E. Strauss *Assistant bei Albert Einstein* in C. Seelig Helle Zeit-Dunkle Zeit (Europa Verlag, Zurich, 1956), p 72 . Jammer p. 124
[239] Albert Einstein, *Ideas and Opinions*, (New York: Random House 1954) p. 255. Jammer p. 132
[240] Albert Einstein *The Quotable Einstein* ed. Alice Calaprice (Princeton, NJ: Princeton University Press, 2005), pp. 195-6.
[241] Lincoln Barnett *The Universe and Dr. Einstein* (New York Dover Publications 1948 - 1985) p 109

is clear Einstein believed that there is something beyond the material universe - a supernatural creative intelligence. Therefore on Dawkins' own definition, Einstein is *not* an atheist. On one point however Dawkins is correct: Einstein did not believe in a personal God who answers prayers and interferes in the universe, nor did he hold an anthropomorphic image of God. God was not for him an old man in the sky sitting on a cloud. But he did believe in an intelligent mind or spirit, which created the universe with its immutable laws. According to Dawkins, "Einstein was repeatedly indignant at the suggestion he was a theist."[242] The evidence from Jammer's book is the exact opposite. According to Jammer, "Einstein always protested against being regarded as an atheist."[243] Einstein complained about atheists, "Then there are the fanatical atheists whose intolerance is of the same kind as the intolerance of the religious fanatics and comes from the same source."[244] Does Dawkins have any evidence that Einstein was indignant at being called a theist? Dawkins argues that science and religion are incompatible. Einstein took the opposite view: "A legitimate conflict between science and religion cannot exist.... Science without religion is lame; religion without science is blind."[245]

Max Jammer was a personal friend of Einstein and Professor of Physics at Bar-Ilan University in Israel. His book is a comprehensive survey of Einstein's writing, conversations and speeches on God and religion. In the book Jammer wrote, "Einstein was neither an atheist nor an agnostic"[246] and he added, "Einstein renounced atheism because he never considered his denial of a personal God as a denial of God. This subtle but decisive distinction has long been ignored."[247] Jammer's conclusion is that Einstein believed in God, albeit not a personal God who answers prayers. Eduard Büsching sent a copy of his book 'Es gibt keinen Gott' (There is no God) to Einstein, who replied suggesting a different title: 'Es gibt keinen persönlichen Gott' (There is no personal God).[248] However in his letter to Büsching Einstein stated, "A belief in a personal God is preferable to the lack of any transcendental outlook."[249] According to Jammer, "Not only was Einstein not an atheist, but his writings have turned many away from atheism, although he did not set out to convert anyone."[250] Further confirmation that Einstein believed in a transcendent God comes from his conversations with his friends. David Ben-Gurion, the former

---

[242] Dawkins p. 39
[243] Jammer p. 150
[244] Einstein to an Unidentified addressee dated 7th August 1941. Einstein archive reel 54-927 Jammer p. 97.
[245] Albert Einstein *Science and Religion* printed in *A Einstein Ideas and Opinions* (Crown, New York 1954,) p 44-49 quote on p 46 Jammer p 31
[246] Jammer p. 96
[247] Jammer p. 150
[248] Jammer p. 50
[249] A. Einstein letter to Büsching   Jammer p. 149
[250] Jammer p. 151

Prime Minister of Israel, records Einstein saying "There must be something behind the energy."[251] And the distinguished physicist Max Born commented, "He did not think religious belief a sign of stupidity, not unbelief a sign of intelligence."[252]

On Spinoza, Einstein said in response to a telegram from a Rabbi Goldstein, "I believe in Spinoza's God, who reveals himself in the orderly harmony of what exists, not in a God who concerns himself with the fates and actions of human beings."[253] Goldstein commented, "This clearly disproves that charge of atheism made against Einstein. Spinoza saw God manifest in nature and could not be called an atheist."[254] Some – like Dawkins - think Spinoza equated God with the material universe (pantheism), but Spinoza himself made clear this is false. He wrote, "The view of certain people that I identify God with nature is a mistake."[255] The French philosopher Martial Guéroult suggested the term panentheism, rather than pantheism, to describe Spinoza's view of the relation between God and the universe. The Oxford English Dictionary defines 'panentheism' as "the theory or belief that God encompasses and interpenetrates the universe, but at the same time is greater than, and independent of it." So panentheism is similar to pantheism, but crucially in addition believes that God exists as a mind or a spirit. The idea that God is both transcendent and immanent is also a major tenet of both Christianity and Judaism.

But isn't Einstein's understanding of an impersonal God totally removed from Christian, Jewish and Muslim thinking? Max Jammer refers in his book to the leading Christian theologian Hans Küng, who pointed out that the Bible never refers to God as a person. Küng explained, "Of course in my youth I had a simple, naïve, anthropomorphic understanding of God. At the beginning of life that is normal. It is less normal for a grown man or woman to preserve his or her childlike understanding."[256] For Küng, "God is not a person as man is a person.... God transcends the concept of person."[257] Or as C. S. Lewis put it, God is not less than personal but is "beyond personality".[258] Küng explains that part of the problem here lies in the meaning of the word 'person' – derived from the Latin 'persona' – which has changed over time. It originally meant a mask used by an actor on the stage.[259] So one actor could play several parts, using different 'personae'. In this way Jesus may be seen as the 'persona' of God,

---

[251] Jammer p. 96

[252] Jammer p. 96

[253] In 1929, Einstein was asked by Rabbi Herbert S. Goldstein whether he believed in God. Einstein responded by telegram. Jammer p. 49

[254] Jammer p. 49

[255] B Spinoza *Correspondence of Benedict de Spinoza*, Wilder Publications (March 26, 2009), letter 73

[256] Hans Küng *What I believe* (London Continuum 2010) p. 102

[257] Hans Küng *Does God Exist?* (London SCM 1984) p. 631-633

[258] C. S. Lewis *Mere Christianity* (London Fontana 1955) p. 136

[259] Hans Küng *Does God Exist?* p. 631-633

entering the human stage. The original meaning of the word has been almost completely lost. Küng, as well as Christian, Jewish and Muslim mystics may be closer than some imagine to Einstein's understanding of God.

In brief: Einstein was - like Newton before him - deeply religious and a firm believer in a transcendent God. However Einstein rejected anthropomorphic and personal understandings of the word 'God'. If any intellectual high treason has been committed, it has been committed by Dawkins himself, who has failed to deal carefully with what Einstein actually said, thereby confusing two very different understandings of God. He should have paid more attention to Max Jammer's book, and to the conclusions Jammer reached after studying all the evidence. It seems Dawkins needs to be reminded of his own 'Ten New Commandments'. The seventh reads: "Test all things; always check your ideas against the facts and be ready to discard even a cherished belief if it does not conform to them."[260] There is another conclusion to be drawn from this: Dawkins has drawn attention to the attempt in America to rebrand atheists as 'brights', implying atheists are clever and theists stupid. Einstein and Newton were both theists, so this is nonsense. This realisation should help to stop the bullying of Christian children, who are told they are stupid to believe in God. One girl personally known to the author was bullied so much for being a Christian that she had to move schools. So after all of Dawkins rhetorical bluster and verbal swagger, we are left with fallacious reasoning and factual errors - a case of 'argument weak, shout louder'.

Are science and religion compatible?

Are science and faith are in conflict? The evidence of history is that they have been overwhelmingly in harmony. In the Middle Ages the Oxford Franciscan School contributed to the development of scientific methodology. Roger Bacon described a repeating cycle of observation, hypothesis, experimentation and the need for independent verification. These ideas were carried to Padua and Galileo in the 17th century. Other key figures were Copernicus, a monk; Kepler, a devout Lutheran and Francis Bacon, who refined the scientific method, and spoke of God's two books: the Book of Nature and the Bible. The conflict theory is allegedly supported by some historical incidents, such as the trial Galileo and the Huxley/Wilberforce debate at Oxford on evolution. Galileo had adopted the Copernican heliocentric theory. A church consultation found correctly that Galileo had not provided evidence for his theory. Pope Urban VIII suggested it should be described as an hypothesis. Galileo complied, but put the words into the mouth of a fool called Simplitico. The Pope was affronted. As Arthur Koestler observed, "It was not a fatal collision between opposites, but a clash of individual temperaments aggravated

---

[260] Dawkins p. 299

by unlucky circumstances."[261] The Roman Catholic Church foolishly put him on trial and he was sentenced to house arrest at his villa overlooking Florence. Yet Galileo remained a Christian and wrote, "The intention of the Holy Spirit is to teach us the way to go to heaven, not the way the heavens go."[262]

The debate between Huxley and Bishop Wilberforce at a meeting of the British Association in Oxford in 1860 allegedly shows the triumph of science over religion. However John Hedley Brooke, Professor of Science and Religion at Oxford University, notes that the story of the triumph of Huxley over Wilberforce first appeared 31 years after the event.[263] According to Brooke, Huxley was a brilliant self-publicist who claimed that there was "inextinguishable laughter at my wit" and Huxley's anecdote may be a "retrospective invention".[264] Wilberforce has been portrayed as a buffoon, but Darwin described Wilberforce's review of *The Origin of Species* as follows, "He picks out with skill the most conjectural part and brings forward well the difficulties."[265] A contemporary account of the debate from the botanist Sir Joseph Hooker shows Huxley did not carry the audience with him; and the ornithologist Henry Baker Tristram thought Huxley had lost.[266] Objections to Darwin's theory also came from eminent scientists such as Sir Richard Owen, a leading anatomist, and Lord Kelvin. The Athenaeum report said there were no winners; the debate was a draw. Brooke comments on the myth of the victory of science over religion, "The legend, once created, became part of the folklore of science."[267] It persists today, despite the lack of evidence.

In the words of Colin Russell, Professor of the History of Science at the Open University, "The common belief that the relations between religion and science over the last four centuries have been marked by a deep and enduring hostility … is historically inaccurate, a caricature so grotesque that it needs explaining, how it could possibly have achieved any degree of respectability"[268] No major historian of science today accepts it. John Lennox, Professor of Mathematics at Oxford University, explains that the conflict myth has become embedded in the popular mind, "A mythical conflict is hyped, and shamelessly used in another battle between naturalism and theism."[269] Professor David Bentley Hart states, "It is not difficult to demonstrate the absurdity of the

---

[261] Arthur Koestler *The Sleepwalkers* (New York Macmillan 1959) p. 426
[262] Galileo *Letter to Grand Duchess Christina* 1615
[263] John Hedley Brooke *Science and Religion* (Cambridge Cambridge University Press 1991) p. 41
[264] John Hedley Brooke p. 41
[265] Cited by John Lennox in *God's Undertaker* (Oxford Lion 2007) p. 25
[266] John Hedley Brooke p. 41
[267] John Hedley Brooke p. 41
[268] Colin Russell *Beliefs and Values in Science Education* (Buckingham Open University Press 1995) p. 125
[269] John Lennox *God's Undertaker* (Oxford Lion 2007) p. 27

claim that Christianity impeded the progress of science."[270] The conflict theory is grounded on ignorance of the history of science.

Is the story of The Garden of Eden an allegory?

Dawkins insists the creation stories in the Bible are science, "I pay religions the compliment of regarding them as scientific theories."[271] Compliment? According to the Bible, in the Garden of Eden there were two trees: "the tree of life and the tree of the knowledge of good and evil."[272] God told Adam and Eve not to eat the fruit of the tree of the knowledge of good and evil. Was it a real tree or part of an allegory? Can you buy such trees at a Garden Centre? 'Adam' is the Hebrew for mankind, and 'Eve' the Hebrew for life. Most people understand it is an allegory. Dawkins has made a category mistake. A recent survey showed the overwhelming majority of Christians in this country see the story as an allegory - as Jewish and Christian thinkers have for thousands of years.[273] St. Augustine's commentary on Genesis - published in 405 A.D. - described the account as figurative; as did Philo of Alexandria – a Jewish writer at the time of Christ. Origen, a Christian thinker, who lived 1800 years ago, wrote, "What man of intelligence, I ask, would think that the first, second and third day existed without a sun? And who could be found so silly as to doubt that these are figurative expressions."[274] The answer: creationists and Dawkins. He needs it to be a scientific account, so that he can argue science and the Bible are in conflict. If the account is figurative and deals with the relationship of man and God, there is no conflict. Dawkins' basic argument is: either God or evolution is true; evolution is true; therefore there is no God. The problem here is with the first premise. What is the evidence that God and evolution are in conflict? According to Charles Darwin evolution and religion are compatible. (See quote at start of chapter.) It is very odd to have the cornerstone of your argument kicked away by the very man whose theories you are supposedly defending! Dawkins also claims that theism is a meme – a mental virus. If so, has Dawkins' brain been infected with a similar virus – a meme called atheism? If his claim is scientific, there is a problem, because real viruses can be detected by cryo-electron microscopy, yet these viruses haven't been found. Also if atheism and theism are simply the results of which virus you've got, why spend time trying to persuade people? Are viruses susceptible to argument?

---

[270] David Bentley Hart *Atheist Delusions* (USA New Haven Yale University Press 2009) p. 99

[271] Dawkins R, *River out of Eden* (London Harpercollins 1995) pp. 46-47

[272] Genesis 2.9

[273] A survey for Theos showed 70% of British Christians regard the Genesis account of creation as figurative not literal.

[274] Origen First Principles, Butterworth, G (trans) (London SPCK 1936) Bk 4 ch 3.

We all have worldviews; they are an unprovable set of assumptions. For Dawkins and his ilk only science is true. However this belief cannot be proved by science, so the theory self-destructs. Peter Atkins, the Oxford chemist, claims: "There is no reason to suppose that science cannot deal with every aspect of existence. Only the religious - among whom I include not only the prejudiced but the underinformed - hope that there is a dark corner of the universe that science can never hope to illuminate."[275] However Lord Rees, the British cosmologist, is more humble, "We may never know the answers to some scientific questions because our brains are not up to it."[276] Rationalists object to faith because it is not rational. But some things in life are beyond the reason – meta-rational, not irrational. Take love. Reason and logic can take us so far, but unless at some point we commit ourselves to someone, we will never enter into a loving relationship. Moreover atheists are mistaken in thinking that science is certain; its truths are provisional. (See chapter on science)

Does science prove the existence of God?

For some scientists evolution shows that chance, not design, lies at the heart of the universe. However modern physics points to the existence of God for other scientists. The astronomer Fred Hoyle said scientific discoveries had "greatly shaken" his faith in atheism. He reflected on the energy needed to produce large quantities of carbon, "Some super-calculating intellect must have designed the properties of the carbon atom, otherwise the chance of finding such an atom through the blind forces of nature would be utterly minuscule. …A superintellect has monkeyed with physics, and with the chemistry and biology. The numbers one calculates from the facts seem to me so overwhelming as to put this conclusion almost beyond question."[277] A very small change of nuclear resonance by 1 or 2 per cent and there would be no carbon, and hence no carbon based life such as ours.[278]

There are many examples of the physical laws being fine-tuned for life: the force of gravity and electromagnetism, as well as the mass of sub-atomic particles. If they were ever so slightly different, life on earth would be impossible. If the expansion of the universe had been more even, stars and planets would not have formed. If the forces in the atomic nuclei were weaker, the universe would be made of hydrogen; if stronger, then oxygen would be the base element. The eminent astrophysicist Paul Davies explores these ideas in his book *The Goldilocks Enigma* - the universe, like the porridge Goldilocks ate, is

[275] Peter Atkins *The Limitless Power of Science* cited by John Lennox in *God's Undertaker* (Lion Oxford 2007) p. 8
[276] Melvyn Bragg *The King James Bible* BBC2 TV 12.3.2011
[277] Fred Hoyle, *The Universe: Past and Present Reflections*. In Engineering and Science, November, 1981. pp. 8–12
[278] Paul Davies *The Goldilocks Enigma* (London Allen Lane 2006) p. 157

just right. The evidence for design lies in the laws of the universe, which is a cosmos, not a chaos. Davies maintains, "Science is based on the assumption that the universe is thoroughly rational and logical. Atheists claim the laws of nature exist reasonlessly and the universe is ultimately absurd. As a scientist, I find this hard to accept. There must be an unchanging rational ground in which the logical, orderly nature of the universe is rooted."[279]

He argues that the physical laws of the universe have been fine tuned to produce life and consciousness, "The emergence of life and consciousness is written into the laws of the universe in a very basic way."[280] This does not mean designed to produce the planet Earth and human beings. If the Big Bang were re-run, it would not produce Earth and homo sapiens, but there would be life and consciousness, according to Davies. He added, "I belong to a group of scientists, who do not subscribe to a conventional religion, but nevertheless deny that the universe is a purposeless accident....There must be a deeper level of explanation. Whether one wishes to call that deeper level 'God' is a matter of taste."[281] He rejects the multiverse theory, according to which there are billions of other universes, because there is no scientific evidence whatsoever for it. He called it "The last refuge of the atheist."[282] In his book *The Grand Design* Stephen Hawking argued that the laws of physics had created the universe, without explaining how those laws came to be there in the first place first. This was dismissed by other leading scientists: Roger Penrose commented, "It enjoys no observational support whatever."[283] and Professor Frank Close of Oxford described it as like poetry or art, having no "experimental evidence"[284] to support it. The distinction between science and science fiction is becoming blurred.

The physicist Freeman Dyson commented, "The more I examine the universe and study the details of its architecture, the more evidence I find that the universe in some sense knew we were coming."[285] The astronomers Martin Rees and John Gribbin noted, "The conditions in our universe really do seem to be uniquely suitable for life forms like ourselves."[286] Roger Penrose, the leading British mathematician, stated: "There is a certain sense in which I would say the universe has a purpose. It's not there by chance. Some people take the view that we happen by accident. I think that there is something much deeper, of which

---

[279] Paul Davies, "What Happened before the Big Bang? in *God for the 21st Century*, ed Russell Stannard (Philadelphia: Templeton Foundation Press, 2000) p 12
[280] Paul Davies Templeton Lecture 1995
[281] Paul Davies *The Mind of God* (Penguin, 1992) p. 16
[282] Paul Davies lecture given in Oxford at the Oxford Playhouse attended by the author.
[283] Financial Times September 4th 2010
[284] Financial Times September 4th 2010
[285] Freeman Dyson *Disturbing the Universe* (New York: Harper & Row, 1979) p. 250
[286] John Gribbin and Martin Rees *Cosmic Coincidences* (Bantam Books 1898) p. 269

we have very little inkling at the moment."[287] Francis Collins, the leading American geneticist, headed the team of 2,400 international scientists on the Human Genome Project, which in 2003 mapped the 25,000 human genes. He was an atheist until the age of 27, when he converted to Christianity. In conversation with Richard Dawkins, Collins stated that the universe is fine tuned for life: for instance if the force of gravity differed by one part in a hundred million million life would be impossible.[288] Dawkins did not challenge this. Many eminent scientists, besides Newton and Einstein, believed/believe in God including Copernicus, Kepler, Galileo, Robert Boyle, Joseph Priestly, Michael Faraday, James Maxwell, Arthur Eddington, John Polkinghorne, Freeman Dyson, Francis Collins, Arthur Peacocke and Owen Gingerich. In addition the pioneers of quantum mechanics were all believers: Heisenberg, "I have repeatedly pondered on the relationship of science and religion, for I have never been able to deny the reality to which they point."[289] Max Planck, "There can never be any real opposition between science and religion; for the one is the complement of the other."[290] Erwin Schrödinger, "Science is reticent when it comes to a question of the great unity of which we somehow form a part. The popular name for it in our time is God."[291]

The philosopher Antony Flew was Britain's leading atheist before Richard Dawkins. By 2004 two scientific discoveries had changed his mind. First, the Big Bang theory showed the universe began at a particular point in time. This raised the question, "What caused the universe to begin?" Second, the universe appears to have been fine-tuned for life. Flew wrote, "Not merely are there are regularities in nature, but they are mathematically precise, universal and 'tied together'. How did nature come packaged in this fashion? Scientists from Newton to Einstein to Heisenberg have answered the Mind of God."[292] Stephen Jay Gould, a leading American evolutionary biologist, argued science deals with the 'how' questions, and religion with the 'why' questions. According to Gould, "Either half of my colleagues are enormously stupid, or else the science of Darwinism is fully compatible with religious belief – and equally compatible with atheism."[293] Dawkins commented, "Gould could not possibly have meant what he wrote. We have all bent over backwards to be nice

---

[287] Comments by Roger Penrose in *A Brief History of Time* a documentary by Errol Morris based on Stephen Hawking's book of the same title.
[288] organised by Time Magazine
[289] Werner Heisenberg *Across the Frontiers* trans. Peter Heath (San Francisco: Harper and Row, 1974) p. 213
[290] Max Planck *Where is Science Going?* (New York: Norton, 1977) p. 168
[291] Erwin Schrödinger *My View of the World* (Cambridge: Cambridge University Press, 1964) p. 93
[292] Antony Flew *There is a God* (London HarperOne 2007) p. 96
[293] Stephen Jay Gould *Impeaching a Self-appointed Judge* Scientific American 267, No 1. 1992, 118-121

to an unworthy but powerful opponent."[294] Dawkins likened Gould to Neville Chamberlain, the British politician who appeased Hitler! [295]

Is religion harmful or beneficial?

Einstein wrote, "The most important function of religion is to make clear fundamental ends and valuations. If one asks whence derives the authority for these ... one can only answer they exist in society as powerful traditions, which act upon the conduct and aspirations of individuals. ... The highest principles for our aspirations and judgements are given to us in the Jewish-Christian religious tradition."[296] Einstein added, "a person, who is religiously enlightened, appears to me to be one who has, to the best of his ability, liberated himself from the fetters of his selfish desires."[297] Religion helps to free us from the greedy, acquisitive self fostered by our materialistic society. It believes happiness is to be found in the service of others, not in the pursuit of selfish hedonism. It helps people handle suffering creatively. Religion also gives people a set of moral values; as well as faith and courage in difficult times. It fosters self-discipline and social cohesion. Our individualistic western societies, obsessed with sex and celebrity, are hardly contented and fulfilled. Today young people are under great pressure to conform to an image that is considered cool. Religion gives us another yardstick; thereby helping to free us from the tyranny of today's fads and fashions. Jonathan Haidt, Professor of Psychology at the University of Virginia, argues that religion, rejected by liberals as a superstition, is a key component of successful communities, by fostering trust and co-operation. He cited research showing that religious people are more generous with their time and money in helping communities than secular folk and research into 19th century American communes found that after 20 years 39% of religious communities had survived, but only 6% of secular ones.[298]

Dawkins claims "Religion is the root of all evil."[299] Are all rapes, murders, thefts and robberies caused by religion? Is all domestic violence caused by religion? Dawkins and Christopher Hitchens claim atheists are morally superior to theists. Yet history shows atheistic regimes have a record of brutality, sadism and mass murder: from the Reign of Terror and Vendée genocide in the French Revolution, to the Great Terror in the Soviet Union and the killing fields of Cambodia. The death toll of atheistic communism is over 120,000,000. (See

---

[294] Dawkins p. 81
[295] Dawkins p. 90
[296] A Einstein 'The Goal' lecture given 19th May 1939 published in *Ideas and Opinions* pp41-44; and in *Out of My Later Years* pp25-28. Jammer p. 90
[297] Albert Einstein essay *Science and Religion* in magazine *Nature* 1940
[298] Jonathan Haidt *The Righteous Mind: Why Good People Are Divided by Politics and Religion* (London Allen Lane 2012)
[299] Richard Dawkins Title of Channel4 TV Documentary January 2006

chapter on secular atrocities.) Dawkins tries to disown these atheist atrocities, "Atheists may do evil things, but they don't do evil things in the name of atheism."[300] However Lenin and Stalin hated religion. Communist regimes were avowedly atheistic and killed believers. In the USSR the state carried out torture and mass murder. The League of the Militant Godless persecuted believers. Mao launched his attack on Tibet and its Buddhist culture with the slogan "Religion is poison."[301] To claim that atheistic beliefs and deeds are unrelated is ridiculous. Would anyone claim that Hitler's hatred of the Jews and the holocaust were unrelated?

However, haven't there been religious wars? Yes, and Dawkins claims "Religious wars really are fought in the name of religion."[302] Let's take as an example the Thirty Years War, fought allegedly between Protestants and Catholics in the Holy Roman Empire between 1618 and 1648. Yet in it Roman Catholic France sided with Protestant Sweden and gave it financial support. France was eager to weaken the power of the Habsburgs, as were many of the smaller German states. It is claimed that the troubles in Northern Ireland were a religious conflict. Was the IRA really fighting for Roman Catholicism? Was their cause the doctrine of transubstantiation and Papal infallibility? In fact they had a political objective - a united Ireland. And the peace agreement – the Good Friday Agreement – makes no mention of religion. Many so-called religious conflicts are not simply fought about religion.

After the attack on the Twin Towers in New York Dawkins proposed the slogan "Science flies you to the moon. Religion flies you into buildings."[303] It is unfair to condemn all theists because there are a few fanatics. Suppose someone condemned all scientists because some of them developed the atomic bomb, mustard gas, DDT and Nazis scientists such as Josef Megele carried out vivisection on human beings. Would that be fair? We don't judge all scientists by the worst. Most people accept that the overwhelming majority of Christians, Jews and Muslims are good and decent people – as indeed are most scientists!

An overall assessment of religion is a vast topic, nevertheless a few broad-brush comments can be made. After the fall of the Roman Empire it was the church that kept western civilisation alive: it cared for the sick and needy; it provided schools and hospitals; it preserved ancient literature; and it developed the life of the mind. Kenneth Clark in his BBC series 'Civilisation' described Christianity as a humane and civilising influence. The abolition of the slave trade was led by William Wilberforce and improvements in social conditions led by Lord Shaftesbury – both Christians (and conservatives!) More recently Christians played a key role in ending apartheid in South Africa without

---

[300] Richard Dawkins *The God Delusion* p. 315
[301] Mao Zedong at press conference after the invasion of Tibet in 1950
[302] Richard Dawkins *The God Delusion* p. 316
[303] Debate at Wellington College between Dawkins and Richard Harries former Bishop of Oxford 4th December 2009 reported in Daily Telegraph 5th December 2009

violence; and the downfall of atheistic communism in Eastern Europe. A secular media is unwilling to give credit where it is due. Today there are hundreds of thousands of charities engaged in humanitarian causes inspired by religious people. Few charities have been founded by atheists.

The atheist Bertrand Russell concluded that if science alone is true, life is meaningless. He wrote, "Man is the product of causes which had no prevision of the end they were achieving; his origin, his growth, his hopes and fears, his loves and beliefs are but the outcome of the accidental collocations of atoms; no fire, no heroism, no intensity of thought and feeling can preserve an individual beyond the grave; all the labour of the ages, all the devotion, all the inspiration, all the noon-day brightness of human genius are destined for extinction in the vast death of the solar system."[304] One of the twentieth century's leading humanists, H. J. Blackham, conceded, "humanists can be put on trial for reducing human life to pointlessness."[305]

Steven Pinker in *The Blank Slate* acknowledged the positive role religion in human society, but he raised the objection to belief known as the Ghost in the Machine: if the body ceases to exist at death, how can the mind or soul survive? Rowan Williams' answer is that belief in an afterlife does not mean we think that a ghost or soul survives death, but that given the belief that the nature of God is love, and that he has entered into a loving relationship with his creatures, then it would be inconsistent for him to abandon them at death. So Williams argues that God remembers them after death, and literally re-members them.[306] They are given a new life, though we have no idea what form this could take.

Humility, arrogance and abuse

Voltaire urged humility in dealing with such questions as, "Why is there a universe?" "Is there a God?" Much is mysterious: the Big Bang, the emergence of life from inanimate matter and human consciousness. He held that certainty is an absurdity in such matters. Yet many atheists are dogmatic. Our earliest records of modern atheism are from Spain in the 17th century. Orobio de Castro, a philosophy professor, described atheists there as "full of vanity, pride and arrogance."[307] When Edward Gibbon – the author of *The Decline and Fall of the Roman Empire* – visited Paris in the mid 18th century, he complained, "I was

---

[304] Bertrand Russell *A Free Man's Worship* cited by H. J. Blackham in Objection to Humanism (London Penguin Books 1965) p. 104

[305] H. J. Blackham in *Objection to Humanism* (London Penguin Books 1965) p. 109. In the book leading humanists criticised their own beliefs.

[306] Rupert Shortt *God's Advocate* (London Darton Longman and Todd 2005) Rowan Williams was one of the interviewees

[307] Orobio de Castro, Prologue, *Epistola Invecta Contra Prado* cited in Y. Yovel *Spinoza and Other Heretics*, Vol I (Princeton NJ 1989) p53 quoted by Karen Armstrong in her book *The Case for God* (London The Bodley Head 2009) p. 184

often disgusted with the capricious tyranny and intolerant zeal of the philosophers; they preached the tenets of atheism with the bigotry of dogmatists, and damned all believers with ridicule and contempt."[308] The philosopher David Hume also found the atheists he met in Paris dogmatic.[309] By contrast great scientists such as Sir Isaac Newton were humble men. He described himself as "a small boy playing on the shore with a few pebbles, while the great ocean of truth lies before me."[310] Darwin himself was courteous, open-minded and humble, unlike many of today's scientists.

Many atheists abuse their opponents describing them as stupid, wicked, Nazi appeasers etc. Dawkins calls parents, who give their children a Christian upbringing child abusers. Does this also apply to atheist parents who pass on their beliefs to their children? How tolerant would Dawkins be if one of his children became a Christian? Many parents - theists and atheists alike - hope to pass on their beliefs to their children. So the charge of child-abuse applies equally to atheists. Dawkins in 2010 supported the setting up of atheistic schools. He financially supports children's camps called 'Camp Quest' that promote atheism. They were founded by an atheist called Edwin Kagin, who says his most uplifting moment was when an 11 year old girl told him that it was OK not to believe in God. However all is not well in the atheist camp. Mr Kagin's son has become a Christian minister and banned his children from attending Camp Quest. The most blatant example of brainwashing children was by atheistic Communist regimes. In the Soviet Union schoolchildren were forced to chant, "Science has disproved religion."

The language of atheists is often rabid. Take Lenin, "Every religious idea, every idea of God, even flirting with the idea of God, is unutterable vileness of the most dangerous kind, contagion of the most abominable kind. Millions of sins, filthy deeds, acts of violence and physical contagions are far less dangerous than the subtle, spiritual idea of God."[311] Christopher Hitchens, "Religion poisons everything"[312] and "Christianity is a wicked cult.... Its teachings are immoral ...it is totalitarian"[313] and "Organised religion is violent, irrational, intolerant, allied to racism. ... hostile to free enquiry, contemptuous of women and coercive of children."[314] Bertrand Russell, "Christianity is to blame

---

[308] Edward Gibbon *Autobiography* p. 145; Meridian Books published 1961 ed Dero A Saunders.

[309] Peter Gay *The Enlightenment* (London W. W. Norton & Co 1977) p. 401

[310] David Brewster, *Life of Sir Isaac Newton*, new edn, revised W. T. Lynn, London: Tegg, 1875, p. 303.

[311] Letter Lenin to Maxim Gorki 14 November 1913 cited by Robert Conquest in *Harvest of Sorrows* p. 199

[312] Christopher Hitchens *God is not Great: How Religion Poisons Everything* (London Atlantic Books 2007) Book Title

[313] Christopher Hichens and Douglas Adams debates on DVD called Collision

[314] Christopher Hitchens *God is not Great: How Religion Poisons Everything* Book Title (London Atlantic Books 2007) cited in Sunday Times 28.11.2010

for everything cruel, destructive and wicked since the fall of the Roman Empire."[315] Christopher Hitchens seems to think of God as an external despot who must be fought, so that the self-governing individual is free. He imagines an old man in the sky sitting on a cloud issuing edicts, so we become robotic non-entities. This childish picture of God certainly would not be recognised by those within the contemplative and mystical traditions of Judaism, Christianity and Islam. Richard Dawkins likened the distinguished astrophysicist Lord Rees to a Nazi collaborator, Quisling, for accepting the Templeton Prize in 2011. The philosopher John Gray claims it is all part of an attempt by atheists to demonise religion.

For many scientists, science points to the existence of God, not to atheism. The idea that science and religion are in conflict is a myth. Einstein wrote, "We are like a child entering a huge library filled with books. The child knows someone must have written the books. It does not know how. It suspects a mysterious order, but doesn't know what it is. That, it seems to me, is the attitude of even the most intelligent person, towards God."[316] George Orwell, who held that there was a need to revive a religious attitude,[317] wrote, "I once played a rather cruel trick on a wasp. He was sucking jam on my plate and I cut him in half. He paid no attention, merely went on with his meal, while a tiny stream of jam trickled out of his severed oesophagus. Only when he tried to fly did he grasp the dreadful thing that had happened to him. It is the same with modern man. The thing that has been cut away is his soul."[318]

Can you be a Christian and a liberal?

What a stupid question! Of course you can be a Christian and a liberal! The author must be a buffoon. I can imagine some replies. However it all depends what you mean by the word 'liberal'; if you mean caring for and helping the poor and the needy, then of course there no conflict with Christianity, indeed all Christians should be liberal in this sense. But liberals and Christians disagree about human nature, the extent of freedom, and individualism which gives primacy to individual self-fulfilment. The Enlightenment claimed problems can be solved by human goodwill and better education, etc. This ignores the reality of evil - crime, drugs, alcohol, violence, poverty, degrading rap music and violent computer games etc. Tom Wright the former Bishop of Durham and a leading Anglican theologian wrote "An older generation of liberal thinkers, alarmed at the thought that there might be such a

---

[315] Malcolm Muggerridge *Chronicles of Wasted Time* Vol 1 The Green Stick (Glasgow Fontana 1972) p. 193
[316] G S Viereck *Glimpses of the Great* (Macaulay, New York 1936) p 186 Jammer p. 48
[317] George Orwell *Essay on Arthur Koestler*
[318] George Orwell *The Collected Essays, Journalism and Letters of George Orwell* Vol 2 My Country Right or Left (New York: Penguin 1970) p. 320

thing as 'evil' which they thought had been banished by Acts of Parliament and better drains, tried to insist that nobody was evil at all, merely misguided, and that the misguiding had been done by society as a whole, so that we were all guilty."[319] He added, "Liberals stand convicted of culpable arrogance."[320] He criticised theologians for whom, "Christianity was reduced to a liberal ethic as though Jesus simply went about telling people to be nice to each other."[321]

Rowan Williams, the Archbishop of Canterbury, contrasted niceness with truth, "It is a total misreading of the Desert Fathers to think it's all about tolerance and a niceness, which is reluctant to identify any absolute rights and wrongs, truths and falsehoods. The desert is about the struggle for truth, or it is nothing."[322] On abortion he argues we focus too exclusively on the mother's right to choose and the rights of the foetus are overlooked. He calls this the right to protect your own interest at the expense of others; and sex has become separated from what he calls ordinary prosaic fidelity, which may be vital in poor communities, giving emotionally security and financial stability. Children need trustworthy parents; chaotic relationships do them a disservice. Our society no longer views the maintaining of bonds as important. He believes we do not value the stability and prosaic heroism of earlier generations and said, "The changeability of relationships and the transience of marriage may look fine if you belong to the commentating classes of North London, but you don't have to go many miles to see what the cost is for people who cannot take that sort of thing for granted."[323] Lesslie Newbigin, who went to India as a missionary later becoming Bishop of Madras wrote, "We are carried along by a tide that sweeps us towards increasing moral anarchy and social disintegration."[324] He urged Christians to address, "The manifest failures of the liberal secular state"[325] and "the multiplying signs of a descent into moral anarchy."[326] He praised Muslims for being more willing to fight against secularism and liberalism.

---

[319] N. T. Wright *Evil and the Justice of God* (London SPCK 2006) p. 80
[320] N. T. Wright *Evil and the Justice of God* (London SPCK 2006) p. 22
[321] N. T. Wright *Who Was Jesus?* (London SPCK 1992) p. 4
[322] Rowan Williams *Silence and Honeycakes* (London Lion 2004) p. 35.
[323] Interview given by Rowan Williams before the start of National Marriage Week in 2007.
[324] Lesslie Newbigin *A Reader ed. Paul Weston* (London Eerdmans 2006) p. 250
[325] Newbigin p. 255
[326] Newbigin p. 250

CHAPTER 8

Liberal Delusions:
History and Tradition are Unimportant

History is not dead and gone, history is what we are.[327]

Heidegger

Body and soul have an intensely historical character.... We have plunged down a cataract of progress which sweeps us ever further from our roots... But it is precisely the loss of connection with the past, our uprootedness which has given rise to the discontents of civilisation... We live more in the future and its promise of a golden age than in the present... We rush headlong into novelty driven by dissatisfaction and restlessness.... The less we understand our fathers and forefathers the less we understand ourselves, and thus with all our strength we rob the individual of his roots and his guiding instincts.[328]

Jung

The traditions we inherit from our forebears are not fetters on our identities, shackles which repress our self-expression, but the necessary conditions of having selves to express.[329]

John Gray

To be a self is to own a story: to act as a self, is to act out of an awareness of a particular past ....To lose one's history is to be condemned to absolute bondage to the temporal process.[330]

Rowan Williams

We are carried along by a tide that sweeps us towards increasing moral anarchy and social disintegration. We should look back on the way we have come. A society that has lost its memory, is like a ship which has lost its rudder. It can only drift with the tides. I find it alarming that history seems to have such a diminishing place in our public education. We know and do not like the symptoms of Alzheimer's disease when we find it among our friends. It sometimes looks as if a dissemination of a sort of Alzheimer's disease is part of the current agenda. If we are to get our bearings for the future, we need to pay attention to the past, not to return to it, but to learn from it.[331]

Lesslie Newbigin

---

[327] Quoted by Michael Inwood *Heidegger* (Oxford University Press 1997) p. 100
[328] C G Jung *Memories, Dreams, Reflections* (London Random House 1963) p. 263
[329] John Gray *Gray's Anatomy* (London Allen Lane 2009) p. 324
[330] Rowan Williams *Resurrection* (London Darton Longman and Todd 2002) p. 24-25
[331] Paul Weston *Lesslie Newbigin A Reader* (Cambridge UK William Eerdmans 2006) p. 250

The rejection of history, tradition and custom

The authors quoted above believe(d) that one of the reasons we are discontented today is that we have been uprooted. We do not understand ourselves, because our history has been taken from us, by those who neglect the past. However it is our history that makes us who we are. Memory establishes identity for individuals and communities. If we forget our past, we lose our identity. Human beings cannot grasp their present situation, nor decide how to act in it, unless they know how they arrived there. The writers quoted above all recognised the importance of history and having roots. They saw human beings as historical - with a need to understand their past.

However most liberals have a different attitude to history, tradition and the past. The liberal approach can be traced back to thinkers of the Enlightenment, whose aim was the overthrow of traditional authority in order to give individuals the freedom to become self-governing. They believed that the shackles from which we need to be freed include the traditions and customs of the past, which they considered ignorant and repressive. In their opinion history is merely a depressing account of our wretched lives in the past, from which we can learn nothing. We need a new beginning. Forget the past. Celebrate the new. The golden age is in the future. The accent should be on youth, not experience; parents and elders have been tainted by the past. Moreover liberals are confident that the triumph of their ideas are inevitable. We are told we must 'go with the flow', move with the times and accept change.

By contrast conservatives believe the past is the key to understanding the present and that progress is not inevitable. One reason for these contrasting attitudes to history is the different understandings of human nature. If we are essentially good, progress is achievable; the future can be better than the past. Bryan Appleyard in his book 'Understanding the Present' commented, "Liberalism offers individuals the idea of progress. .. What we do is targeted at some point in the future. Time takes on a moral dimension. Future time is good, past time is bad. The past is thinned out until it becomes a mere prologue to the future. History is a dusty archive of doubtful value. This inhuman insistence on forward movement and going with the flow deny the possibility of peace within human life. Progress and movement do not offer the individual a way of understanding his life."[332]

Jung's work as a psychotherapist led him to the conviction that individuals need to understand their history and come to terms with their past, only then can they move on and become more integrated individuals. Likewise, he argued, societies need to come to terms with their inheritance. He contrasted individuals in harmony with their past and those who reject it, "Do our inherited components find fulfilment in our lives or are they repelled? Inner peace

---

[332] Bryan Appleyard *Understanding the Present* (London Pan Books 1992) p. 236

depends on whether the historical element, which is inborn in the individual, can be harmonised with the present."[333] He believed that our uprootedness and alienation from our past is the cause of many of our problems. He wrote, "Modern Man has cast history aside. He wants to break with tradition so that he can experiment with his life and determine what value and meaning things have in themselves, apart from traditional propositions."[334] But in the process, Jung claimed, we have become uprooted and alienated from our past.

History is central to our understanding of human existence, according to Heidegger: whose masterwork is titled, *Sein und Zeit* (Being and Time). His argument is that the past lives on in the present and our lives are deeply historical. We understand our lives in terms of our past. We are embedded in our historic communities and a sense of a shared history is essential, if we are to live meaningful lives. To quote Heiddegger, "We need to win back our roots in history ... to take a creative view of tradition."[335] Without an understanding of history we can make no sense of the present. For example European history over the last 60 years has been dominated by a reaction against the horrors of Nazism and World War Two, without this understanding we can make no sense of the events in Europe over the period.

In his book *The Blank Slate* Steven Pinker contrasts the different approaches to history by liberals and conservatives. He names these opposing standpoints: the 'Utopian Vision' (liberal) and the 'Tragic Vision' (conservative). The former has optimism about the future; the latter holds that fundamental flaws in human nature will remain, so Utopia is impossible. Pinker wrote, "In the Utopian Vision human nature changes, so traditional institutions have no inherent value. That was then, this is now. Traditions are the dead hand of the past, the attempt to rule from the grave."[336] Whereas, "In the Tragic Vision human nature has not changed. Traditions such as religion, the family, social customs, sexual mores and political institutions are a distillation of time-tested techniques that let us work round the shortcomings in human nature."[337] Pinker maintains science has vindicated the conservatives, writing, "My own view is that the new sciences of human nature really do vindicate some version of the Tragic Vision, and undermine the Utopian outlook that until recently dominated large segments of intellectual life."[338] Historical awareness serves another useful purpose; it gives us a sense of detachment from the pressures of the present day. Those who lack a sense of history have no other yardstick than the present, and

---

[333] C G Jung *Memories, Dreams, Reflections* (London Random House 1963) p. 264

[334] C G Jung *Modern Man in Search of a Soul* (London Routledge and Kegan Paul 1976) p. 275

[335] Charles Guignon editor *The Cambridge Companion to Heidegger* (UK Cambridge University Press 1993) p 26 from Heidegger's Introduction to Metaphysics

[336] Steven Pinker *The Blank Slate* (London Allen Lane 2002) p. 289

[337] Pinker p. 288

[338] Pinker p. 293

so are more likely to be in thrall to the fads, whims and fashions of today. These pressures are aggravated by the advertising industry with its constant attempt to manipulate people.

Cultural bereavement

The urge to reject the past and create the world anew has led to the destruction of inherited culture. In the French Revolution, which embodied Enlightenment thinking, a new calendar was created starting again at year one; art and statues were smashed; priests butchered and churches desecrated. The historian Simon Schama records that Robespierre had "tried to stop the appalling cultural anarchy unleashed by the dechristianisers.... and the term vandalism was coined for the wanton assaults on statues, paintings and buildings."[339] Mao's Cultural Revolution in China similarly sought to obliterate traditional Chinese culture. He set out to exterminate traditional beliefs, including Confucianism; he even had the house where Confucius lived demolished. In Tibet traditional culture and religious beliefs were ruthlessly suppressed by Mao's invading army in 1950. In Cambodia the Khmer Rouge cruelly uprooted traditions; all family bonds were denied by the state. In the Soviet Union the poetess Irina Ratushinskaya was sent to the gulag where she wrote, "I have become a pitiful lump of flesh tortured by hunger and cold. ... The main objects of the regime's hatred are God, the spirit, the word and man's need to live in a cultural context."[340]

Rowan Williams, Archbishop of Canterbury, describes the effects of our cultural bereavement, "When we see societies losing or suppressing their past, we rightly conclude that they are unfree, diseased, or corrupt: either they are oppressed by an alien power intent on destroying their roots and identity... or they are engaged in an internal repression."[341] He cites the victims of the Soviet terror, who spent long years in the gulags and desperately tried to recover their history and culture once they were free. In Britain's case the repression is internal. He talks of "our present cultural bereavement"[342] and added, "Some damage to the corporate psyche seems to be taking place ... a cultural loss and a cultural crisis."[343] His view is that the weakening of British identity over the last 40 years, far from making people more tolerant and accepting of foreign peoples and cultures, has had the opposite effect. It is those who feel their identity is affirmed, rather than denied, who feel able to accept others.

---

[339] Simon Schama *Citizens* (Penguin Books London 1989) p. 829
[340] Cited by Paul Froese in *The Plot To kill God* (USA The University of California 2008) p. 8
[341] Williams *Resurrection* (London Darton Longman & Todd 1982) p. 25
[342] Rowan Williams *Lost Icons* (London T & T Clark 2003) p. 8
[343] Williams *Lost Icons* p. 58-9

After spending 30 years in India Lesslie Newbigin returned to Britain in 1974 and wrote a number of books contrasting European and Indian culture. He concluded that Europeans had lost their bearings and were adrift because they had repudiated their history. (See quote at start) Further he complained that the constant denigration of the country's past has led to a disproportionate sense of guilt and shame. George Orwell did not share the attitude of progressives to history. He was not convinced that the past was benighted and should be forgotten, "There is now a widespread idea that nostalgic feelings about the past are inherently vicious. One ought apparently to live in a continuous present, a cancellation of memory, and if one thinks of the past at all, it should merely be to thank God that we are so much better than we used to be."[344] By contrast he saw love of the past as a guarantee for the future. He understood the importance of history. In his novel *Nineteen Eighty-Four* one of Big Brother's slogans was, "He who controls the present controls the past; he who controls the past controls the future."[345] Orwell was well aware that communists had used the teaching of history to promote the idea of progress: the past was portrayed as a period of gloom and oppression, in order to convince the down-trodden populace that things were getting better. However the hero of the novel, Winston Smith, realised that things were better in the past, not worse, and rebelled against an ideology which insisted that history was progress. Instead he tried to find links to the past, to recover the memory of it, especially among the working classes, who he believed were less corrupted than the elite. Like Big Brother and the communists, liberals portray history as progress.

An anti-British version of history?

George Orwell held that British intellectuals were anti-British.[346] There were a number of reasons for this: the slaughter in the trenches of the First World War undermined faith in authority; and the class system which ensured that promotion in the army or civil service was based on class, not ability. Melanie Phillips describes the British intelligentsia as 'self-hating'[347] and maintains they think there is nothing good to perpetuate. "At some point during the 20th century the British intelligentsia turned against the culture of which they were the custodians. ... This profound atrophy of the human spirit is the belated legacy of the Enlightenment."[348] She concluded that western civilisation appears to be in terminal decline.[349] The historian of culture George Steiner lamented the current fashion for self-loathing, for morally indicting the

---

[344] George Orwell CE IV pp. 445-6
[345] George Orwell *Nineteen Eighty-four* (London Penguin 1949)
[346] George Orwell *Notes on Nationalism* in *Essays* (London Penguin 2000) p. 313
[347] Melanie Phillips *All Must Have Prizes* (London Warner Books 1996) p. 319
[348] Phillips p. 307
[349] Phillips p. 321

brilliance of the past.[350] The historian Robert Conquest, famous for his histories of the Soviet Union, commented on "The deep-seated and false idea that all empires - particularly the British one - were mere oppressors."[351] And Melanie Phillips observed, "The concept of a common culture, common bonds and a shared story that we need to tell each other as human beings in order to survive as a co-operative enterprise became synonymous with oppression."[352]

Oliver Letwin MP, when he was the Shadow Home Secretary, said British children are taught the low points of British history but not its high points. They are taught how wrong Britain's slave trade was, but not that Britain led the way in the abolition of slavery, "The prime duty of the Royal Navy for much of the 19th century was to stop the slave trade of other nations. I fear it has become unfashionable to speak of such things. I fear our children will take away a sense of shame, not pride."[353] In fact the Royal Navy was stationed off the coast of West Africa at great cost from 1805 to 1867 to stop the slave trades of other countries. This didn't suit the West African Kingdom of Dahomy which sent a delegation to London to protest at the loss of trade. It had grown very rich enslaving fellow Africans and selling them to slave traders.

John Sentamu the Ugandan-born Archbishop of York, has spoken of Britain suffering from an identity crisis because the British people no longer know who they are, and this leads them to put up barriers against outsiders. He praised the British Empire and contrasted the British respect for local cultures with the French approach of total assimilation. In his view British people need to take a more positive view of their past, "If English culture does not discover itself afresh it will lead to political extremism."[354] He also accuses the media of exaggeration and only reporting bad news, "The media give a sense of despair and hopelessness born from stories, which describe criminality, horror and cruelty."[355] The Indian Prime Minister Manmohan Singh has spoken of the positive contribution the British made to India, "Our judiciary, our legal system, our bureaucracy and our police are all great institutions derived from British-Indian administration and they have served our country exceedingly well."[356]

When Dr. Nicholas Tate was head of the School Curriculum and Assessment Authority, he proposed that education should include the transmission to the next generation of British values.[357] He wrote an article entitled, "They come not to praise England, but to bury it"[358] He was dismissed

---

[350] Steiner p. 55
[351] Robert Conquest *Dragons of Expectation* (London Duckworth 2005) p. 63
[352] Melanie Phillips *All Must Have Prizes* (London Warner Books 1996) p. 219
[353] Oliver Letwin speech entitled 'Agreeing to Differ' given at Conservative Central Office in April 2003
[354] John Sentamu The Times 22.11.2005
[355] The Sunday Times 16.3.2008
[356] Manmohan Singh FT Magazine 4.12.2005
[357] Nicholas Tate *The Sunday Times* 27.8. 2000
[358] Nicholas Tate *The Sunday Times* 27.8. 2000

as a cultural fascist. My son told me that in his class at school a pupil said to a teacher that it was a shame St. George's Day wasn't celebrated. The teacher replied "Are you a Nazi?" Tate's thesis is that we should take more pride in our achievements: the English language and literature, major sports, and scientific achievements from Newton to Darwin to the discovery of DNA. We are busy denigrating our own culture and replacing it with multiculturalism. As a result we are sleepwalking to segregation in the opinion of Trevor Phillips of the Commission for Equality.[359] Instead of passing on British culture and history, education focuses on politically correct views on ecology, equality and diversity. Large chunks of British history are ignored; the Anglo-Saxons have been largely airbrushed out.

In schools British history is taught in a fragmented and non-chronological way and was made optional from the age of 14. In March 2009 the Labour Government announced plans to eliminate most history teaching from primary schools.[360] Instead children were to study the social networking site Twitter, blogging and Wikipedia. In a recent survey of schoolchildren most thought Churchill was just an insurance company. In November 2011 Michael Gove, the Education Secretary, said he was "genuinely worried" about the teaching of history and highlighted a recent poll showing widespread ignorance of history even among *history* undergraduates - 90% of whom could not name a 19th century British Prime Minister.[361] They struggled to name the British general at Waterloo - most said Nelson, the monarch at the time of the Armada, Brunel's profession and the location of the Boer War. Schoolchildren's understanding is, he claimed, bleaker still. Gove continued, "I don't think it is propaganda to have a national curriculum broadly sympathetic to our past and our values."

Professor Niall Ferguson of Oxford and Harvard, a familiar TV historian, maintains British schools fail to teach children the main events of history and follow a 'junk history' curriculum. Standards are at an all-time low. The subject is badly taught and undervalued.[362] Another historian, Jonathan Clark maintains we are in a process of "dehistoricisation which involves the foreshortening and even the discarding of the historical dimension."[363] He describes, "An intellectual hostility to public morality, to civic humanism, to duty and to the historical sense."[364]

So how should we approach history and tradition? Liberals are right to argue that we cannot simply preserve the totality of our inheritance, but they are wrong to reject the past wholesale. We need a nuanced approach which acknowledges the past and yet is open to questioning it, one that allows us to be

---

[359] Trevor Phillips The Times 22.9.2005
[360] Daily Mail 25.3.2009
[361] Michael Gove reported in The Sunday Times 27.11.11
[362] Niall Ferguson The Telegraph 9.3.2011
[363] Jonathan Clark *Our Shadowed Present* (London Atlantic Books 2003) p 2
[364] Clark p. 5

in dialogue with our inheritance. We should acknowledge the importance of the past, but that does not mean slavishly follow every tradition, that nothing can be questioned or changed. Rather we should recognise that we are the inheritors of a particular tradition, and that we need to engage with it. So we need to recover our sense of history and find our roots. This will help to give meaning and purpose to our lives. It provides us with a longer-term perspective, so we can become less obsessed with current trivia. While acknowledging past wrongdoing, we can again become members of historic communities, which understand themselves, and take a legitimate pride in their achievements.

CHAPTER 9

Liberal Delusions:
Universalism and Multiculturalism are Beneficial

... to belong to a given community, to be connected with its members by indissoluble and impalpable ties of common language, historical memory, habit, tradition and feeling, is a basic human need, no less natural than that for food or drink or security or procreation.... Cosmopolitanism is the shedding of all that makes one most human, most oneself.[365]

Sir Isaiah Berlin

Anglo-American academics hope that human beings will shed their traditional allegiances and their local identities and unite in a universal civilisation grounded on generic humanity. They cannot even begin to grapple with the political dilemmas of an age dominated by renascent particularisms, militant religions and resurgent ethnicities.[366]

John Gray, formerly Professor of European Thought at the LSE

To be rooted is perhaps the most important and least recognised need of the human soul. ... A human being has roots by virtue of his real, active and natural participation in the life of a community which preserves in a living shape certain particular treasures of the past and certain particular expectations for the future. This participation is a natural one, in the sense that it is automatically brought about by place, by conditions of birth, profession and social surroundings. Every individual needs to have multiple roots.[367]

Simone Weil

A world culture that was a uniform culture would be no culture at all. We should have humanity de-humanised. It would be a nightmare. But on the other hand we cannot resign the idea of world culture altogether. ... So we must aspire to a common world culture, which will not diminish the particularity of its constituent parts.[368]

T. S. Eliot

Liberals believe in one universal cosmopolitan culture and generic humanity, where no-one feels French or Russian, Catholic or Muslim. The Enlightenment sought to end particular loyalties and identities so there would be no wars or conflicts. Likewise liberals today seek to weaken particular cultures, religions and national identities which divide mankind. Yet local and particular loyalties persist; and some argue that they are getting stronger. So can we reconcile universal and particular loyalties? Do liberals stress too much cosmopolitanism and diversity, and fail to recognise the need for rootedness and cohesion? Is belonging to universal mankind too remote to

---

[365] Isaiah Berlin *Against The Current* (Oxford University Press 1981) p. 12

[366] John Gray *Enlightenment's Wake* (London Routledge 2007) p. 2

[367] Simone Weil *The Need for Roots* (London Routledge 1978) p. 41

[368] T S Eliot *Notes Towards the Definition of Culture* (London Faber and Faber 1948) p. 62

have any emotional appeal? The polarity here can be described in various ways: solidarity versus diversity; rootedness versus cosmopolitanism; patriotism versus identity with universal mankind. Within living memory European nations have been at war, in part because their populations had little sense of a common European identity, let alone a universal identity. From this perspective it is clear we should welcome greater stress on universal mankind and less on particular loyalties.

The reassertion of particularity?

Belgium recently became the world-leader in political paralysis. The country's political parties tried in vain to form a government for over a year following elections in June 2010. The country is splitting along linguistic and cultural fault-lines. Scotland voted in 2011 for an SNP government committed to the break-up of the United Kingdom. According to John Gray, the former Professor of European Thought at the LSE, "Human beings individuate themselves as members of historic communities, having memories that cross generations, not as specimens of generic humanity or having a history only by accident."[369] When the Soviet Union and Yugoslavia broke up, deep-rooted religious, national and ethnic divisions re-asserted themselves. Today we are witnessing the rebirth of particularity and a rejection of universalism. Gray held that liberal ideas have become dominant and as a result, "The person has become a cipher without history or ethnicity, denuded of the special attachments that in the real human world give us the particular identities we have. Emptied of these contingencies that in truth are essential to our identities."[370] Gray argued that without a common culture societies fall apart; and where societies are both multiracial and multicultural, they will disintegrate. He criticised the attempt by intellectuals to homogenise world culture, referring to, "The professionally deformed discourse of numberless academic seminars on race and gender, with its tacit agenda of global cultural homogenisation on the US model."[371]

Sir Isaiah Berlin was one of Britain's leading thinkers in the second half of the twentieth century. His friend and biographer, Michael Ignatieff, summed up Berlin's view as follows, "It had been a mistake ... to suppose that men and women could live their lives according to abstract, cosmopolitan values and what Berlin called 'idealistic but hollow doctrinaire internationalism.'"[372] In the book *The Legacy of Isaiah Berlin* Professor Mark Lilla commented, "The good life is a life with attachments and we need to cultivate and perpetuate them

---

[369] John Gray *Enlightenment's Wake* (London Routledge 1995) p. 8
[370] Gray p. 6
[371] Gray p. 190
[372] Michael Ignatieff *Isaiah Berlin* (London Chatto & Windus 1998) p. 292

because liberalism, or modernity perhaps, threatens it."[373] Berlin, who was Jewish and a Zionist, wrote, "The rejection of natural ties seems to me to be noble but misguided. ... to be understood is to share a common past, common feelings and language, common assumptions, the possibility of intimate communications – in short to share common forms of life."[374]

Events in Britain

The capture of the Labour Party in 1994 by Blair, Mandelson and Brown led to the creation of New Labour. Having successfully rebranded the Labour Party and won a handsome election victory in 1997, their thoughts turned to rebranding Britain. The Millennium Dome was turned into a celebration of this New Britain with no history and no religion traditional aspects of Britain were out of favour. Support for rebranding Britain came from the liberal media. The aim was to transform Britain by mass immigration and impose multiculturalism. Andrew Neather was a key speechwriter for Tony Blair, Jack Straw and David Blunkett and was present at discussions on immigration policy in No 10 Downing St. He drafted the keynote speech for Immigration Minister Barbara Roche in September 2001. In October 2009 he wrote that "It had been the deliberate policy of the government to open up the UK to mass immigration"[375] And to "rub the right's nose in diversity."[376] As a result there was a net increase in population of over 3 million, which has led inevitably to a housing shortage and high house prices. Yet in the General Election of 2010 the Labour Party denied that this had been its policy.

After the London bombings of July 7, 2005 the Labour Government began to question multiculturalism and commissioned the distinguished educationalist Sir Keith Ajegbo to investigate and report on diversity within the school curriculum. His report stated, "Many indigenous white pupils have negative perceptions of their own identity. In the case of white working class boys, their sense of linkage with a tangible history is often absent. We spoke to one white British pupil in Year 3 who said after hearing in a class discussion how the rest of the class came from the Congo, Portugal, Trinidad and Poland that she came from nowhere. The report quoted another girl who said, "I do feel sometimes that there is no white history. There's black history month or they do Muslims or Sikhs. We learn about that, but we don't learn about white people, so we feel a bit left out."[377] The Ajegbo report concluded, "White children in

[373] Edited by Ronald Dworkin, Mark Lilla and Robert Silvers *The Legacy of Isaiah Berlin* (USA New York Review Books 2001) p. 182

[374] Ignatieff   p. 292

[375] Andrew Neather Daily Telegraph   23.10.2009

[376] Andrew Neather Daily Telegraph   23.10.2009

[377] Sir Keith Ajegbo *Diversity and Citizenship Review* (London Department of Education January 2007)

areas where the ethnic composition is mixed, suffer labelling and discrimination that is severely compromising their idea of being British. They can feel beleaguered and marginalised, finding their own identities under threat. ... It makes no sense to focus on ethnic minority pupils without trying to address and understand the issues for white pupils ... white pupils are left feeling disenfranchised and resentful."[378] Iain Duncan Smith, the Conservative leader at that time, added, "For some white working class boys, it seems to them that everyone else has someone who worries about them. They feel they are at the bottom."[379] An analysis of GCSE results showed that, "Poor white boys are 'worst performers' at the age of 11. Working class white boys are officially the worst-performing group in English primary schools, official figures show. Fewer than half of white British boys from the poorest homes started secondary education with a decent grounding in the basics last summer. The disclosure comes amid fears that thousands of white British boys from deprived areas risk being turned into an educational underclass as they fall further behind their classmates."[380]

Shaun Bailey, a young black social worker who founded the charity MyGeneration and wrote the pamphlet *No Man's Land*[381], argued that Britain's sense of being a community is being weakened and its cultural heritage ignored. There is no patriotism and no commitment to the wider community. Instead of pride in being British, children take away a feeling of shame. Most of the youngsters in his area are West Indians with a Christian heritage and 73% of the population in the census of 2001 described themselves as Christian. Yet Bailey says schoolchildren learn more about Diwali than Christianity. I met a Jewish teacher who was indignant when she went into a school and found it given over to celebrating Diwali. She argued that the Jews have kept their own culture while accepting the majority culture.

Trevor Phillips, Chairman of the Commission for Racial Equality at the time, claimed that many white working class people, who vote for the BNP, sincerely believed that it is their colour that makes them poor, that their sons fail at school, or that the council gives everything to the Asians. He added that not all of this is imagined. He argued this could open social divisions and cause Britain to sleepwalk towards segregation. He criticised the constant emphasis on the worst possible interpretation of British history which would in the end lead to a society not merely of separate communities but of mutually hostile ghettos. On immigration Phillips commented, "For every professional woman who is able to go out to work because she has a Polish nanny, there is a young mother

[378] Ajegbo
[379] The Times January 24, 2007
[380] Daily Telegraph 19 Nov 2009
[381] Shaun Bailey *No Man's Land* (London Centre for Young Policy Studies, 2005)

who watches her child struggle in a classroom, where a harassed teacher faces too many children with too many languages between them."[382]

Eventually the Labour Party concluded multiculturalism was a mistake. Ruth Kelly, the Minister for Communities, declared in August 2006 that there were well-founded fears for the cohesion of society. She argued society was fragmenting into separate racial and cultural ghettos. Previously any questioning of multiculturalism had been ruthlessly suppressed. Rod Liddle in *The Sunday Times* observed, "Opponents of this corrosive and divisive creed of multiculturalism have been silenced by the accusation 'racist'."[383] In April 2011 the Labour leader Ed Milliband acknowledged that the issue of immigration had cost Labour votes and led to a decline in trust in the Labour Party. Lord Glasman, a Labour Party peer and strategist, commented in May 2011 "Labour lied to people about the extent of immigration and there's been a massive rupture of trust" ... "very, very hard rhetoric combined with a very loose policy" and "immigration and multiculturalism are the big monsters we don't like to talk about."[384]

John Sentamu, who was born in Uganda in 1949, was appointed Archbishop of York in 2005. In an interview with *The Times* just before he took up his post he said, "I speak as a foreigner really. The English are embarrassed by the good things they have done. They have done some terrible things, but not all the Empire was a bad idea. Because the Empire has gone there is almost a sense that there is not a big idea that drives the nation. ... Multiculturalism seems to imply, wrongly for me, let other cultures express themselves but do not let the majority culture tell of its glories, struggles, joys and pains." He said that he owed the British Empire a debt of gratitude and thanked the English teachers and missionaries who had worked in Africa. His words echoed those of the leading African American philosopher Thomas Sowell, who wrote, "What multiculturalism boils down to, is that you can praise any culture in the world except western culture - and you cannot blame any culture in the world, except western culture."[385]

The New East End

Simone Weil, described by T. S. Eliot as a 'woman of genius'[386] wrote of, "transforming society in such a way that the working classes may be given roots in it, or spreading to the whole of society the disease of uprootedness which has

---

[382] Report dated 20.4.08
[383] of 27th August 2006
[384] Lord Glasman in the May 2011 edition of Progress Magazine
[385] http://chicago-freedom-forum.blogspot.com/2009/06/great-quotes-from-thomas-sowell.html
[386] Simone Weill *The Need for Roots* (London Routledge 1952) p vi

been inflicted on the working classes."[387] *The New East End* which was published in 2005, chronicles the effects of mass immigration in the East End of London.[388] It is based on a survey of the views of local people in that area and is a sequel to a famous earlier book published in 1957 - *Family and Kinship in East London*. Trevor Philips - at the time Chair of the Commission for Racial Equality - in his review of *The New East End* wrote, "In a debate too often loud with the clash of uninformed opinion and smug-self-righteousness, *The New East End* offers a rather old fashioned contribution: evidence. The authors report what is actually happening in a community, based on what people say, and on hard measures."[389] Professor Bhikhu Parekh in his review referred to "an historically sensitive, sociologically perceptive and deeply moving analysis." Oona King, who was the black Labour MP for the area, wrote, "a beautiful journey ... as East End and world history collide" and Professor Peter Hennessy in his review of the book commented, "a fascinating and honest book".

What did the book say? The following are extracts: "It would be a misreading of the argument [of this book] to believe that giving voice to the feelings of dissatisfaction and resentment among some white Londoners we are presenting a justification of racist and retrograde ideas, as some may allege. Hostility to people seen as threatening whether as competition for scarce resources [like houses] or simply as incomprehensible strangers, must be better understood before it is written off as wicked or stupid."[390] And "There is a danger in accusing long-term residents of Britain of racism or xenophobia when they object to newcomers' speedy access to national resources. This seems to us not only to risk deepening existing divisions between cultural communities but to aggravate class antagonism too."[391] And "It is understandable that many old Bethnal Greeners felt cheated out of promised rewards for war service and unsurprising that some blamed immigration." [392] (The study had focussed on the Bethnal Green area of East London.) Lastly the authors stated, "The British administrative elite have promoted a swathe of policies that consolidate the rights of minorities, while multiplying the sanctions against indigenous whites. Working-class whites feel progressively disenfranchised."[393]

One of the main arguments of the book is that during World War Two the East End of London was heavily bombed by the Luftwaffe, resulting in massive destruction of houses and loss of life. As a result the populace was angry. The politicians promised that after the war new houses would be built for them. The

---

[387] Weill p. 72

[388] G. Dench, K. Gavron , M. Young *The New East End* (London Profile Books)

[389] Peter Willmott and Michael Young *Family and Kinship in East London*. (London Penguin Books 1957)

[390] G. Dench, K. Gavron , M. Young *The New East End* (London Profile Books) p. 8

[391] Dench, Gavron & Young p. 7

[392] Dench, Gavron & Young p. 5

[393] G. Dench, K. Gavron , M. Young *The New East End* (London Profile Books) p. 6

old system for the allocation of social housing was by people waiting for their turn on the waiting list. Over time this was replaced by the sole criterion of need. When the houses and flats were finally built in the 1960s large numbers of immigrants were arriving; they often gained preference over indigenous families because their families were larger, and so they were judged to be in greater need. This caused resentment, but when local people protested they were dismissed as racists.

In his novel *A Clergyman's Daughter* Orwell described the Eastenders as "the kind of people who are generally drunk on Saturday nights, and who tack a 'fucking' onto every noun, yet I have never seen anything that exceeded their kindness and delicacy".[394] His experiences in Lancashire and Yorkshire were set down in his book, *The Road to Wigan Pier*. These had shown him the decency of working-class life. He wrote, "In a working class home you breathe a warm, decent, deeply human atmosphere, which it is not so easy to find elsewhere. ...It falls more naturally into a sane and comely shape. I have often been struck by the peculiar easy completeness of the working-class interior at its best. Especially on winter evenings after tea, when the fire glows in the open range... It is a good place to be."[395] Orwell championed ordinary people, who are sneered at by some intellectuals as chavs. Michael Collins in *The Likes of Us* chronicled the demise of the white working class in London. William Woodruff wrote a best-seller called *The Road to Nab End* - an account of growing up in the Lancashire cotton town of Blackburn in the 1920s and the acute poverty in the Depression of the 1930s. He wrote, "There was a lot of pitching in, a lot of making do and a lot of pluck. Too little has been made of the working-class solidarity and community spirit. It wasn't the dole that saved Britain from revolution, it was the nature of the British working class."[396]

".... and some are more equal than others." (Orwell: Animal Farm)

George Orwell wrote, "Among the intelligentsia, colour feeling [prejudice] only occurs in the transposed form, that is, a belief in the innate superiority of the coloured races. ... Almost any English intellectual would be scandalized by the claim that the white races are superior to the coloured, whereas the opposite claim would seem to him unexceptional."[397] Julie Burchill, the columnist on *The Independent* newspaper had a working class upbringing and was surprised at university to discover that middle class left-wing students were operating what she called paint-box politics. Issues were judged by colour: white was bad, brown or black were good - an inverted racism was operating.[398]

---

[394] George Orwell *A Clergyman's Daughter*
[395] George Orwell *The Road to Wigan Pier* p. 117-8
[396] FT 4.10.08 Obituary quotation
[397] George Orwell *Essays* (London Penguin 1968) p. 311
[398] *The Independent,* 3.3.11.

John Gray maintains minorities have been given priority over the majority, "Not merely parity of treatment but a form of differential treatment, in which their group is accorded privileges over the majority."[399] *The Watford Observer* reported in 2007 that Alban Wood School in Watford divided children into two groups: dark skinned and white.[400] The dark-skinned children were given additional lessons regardless of need; and white children were given no additional lessons regardless of their needs. *The Watford Observer* campaigned for children to be treated equally.[401] The organisation "Black Boys Can" exists to help black boys with their education but turns away white boys. No "White Boys Can" exists to help white boys, because it would be deemed racist and so be illegal.

Rowan Williams, the Archbishop of Canterbury, acknowledged that in the past liberals played a positive role in combating racism, but he wrote, "To take a particularly painful example, it is quite often said by white liberals and radicals that there is no such thing as black racism … this is demonstrably untrue and carries overtones that the victimised group is incapable of the such violence."[402] He accused "white liberals" of inverting racism by giving black people a superior position to whites. He repudiated this approach and described them as "profoundly *un*hopeful"[403] (his italics). Williams wrote of their approach, "I atone for the primal sin of oppression by according a superior instead of an inferior place to my victims, placing a moral scourge in their hands to beat me as I once beat them; and this is a travesty of the process of human reconciliation and restoration."[404] What is particularly damaging, is that it harms those who were not involved in the original oppression. He continued, "They (the white liberals) invert the existing order, to create new victims out of old oppressors - or worse still, new victims out of neutrals."[405]

The point Williams makes about creating victims out of neutrals is worth exploring. Giving black people a superior position now, because they were victims of oppression in the past, makes little sense to the working class communities of Lancashire, where I was born and grew up. They would see their forebears as victims of the white ruling classes. In the eighteenth and nineteenth centuries, men, women and children worked 12-hour days in very unhealthy conditions amid dangerous machinery. The Factory Act of 1802 limited the number of hours a day that a child could work to twelve! However the Factory Acts were poorly enforced, so children continued to work longer hours. Arkwright, who built some of the early mills, employed children as

---

[399] John Gray *Enlightenment's Wake* (London Routledge 1995) p. 31

[400] The Watford Observer 31.10.2007

[401] The Watford Observer 31.10.2007

[402] Rowan Williams *Resurrection* (Darton Longman & Todd) London 2002) p.10

[403] Williams p.11

[404] Williams p.11

[405] Williams p.11

young as six, and two thirds of his 1,900 employees were children. In the early 19th century Richard Oastler campaigned for better conditions in the factories. He claimed that the conditions in the factories were worse than slavery, "It is the pride of Britain that a slave cannot exist on her soil. Yet thousands of our fellow-creatures .... are at this very moment existing in a state of slavery, more horrid than are the victims of that hellish system of colonial slavery."[406] He went on, "Thousands of little children, both male and female, but principally female, from seven to fourteen years of age are daily compelled to labour from six in the morning to seven in the evening, with only – Britons blush while you read – with only thirty minutes allowed for eating and recreation."[407] His campaign led to the Factory Act of 1847, which restricted the number of hours children could work in factories to a mere *ten* hours a day! Reports to the Children's Employment Commission in Queen Victoria's reign from Thomas Tancred state that young girls worked 24 hour shifts in bare feet to get orders out on time. The job of stove-girls at that time was to keep the stoves burning in temperatures of 110F (43c) degrees. Others hung up the wet goods to dry in conditions described by Tancred as "suffocating and oppressive". But the sufferings of the working classes have been largely ignored; the focus has been on the suffering of the slaves. It is true that slavery was wicked, cruel and degrading, but there was also great suffering nearer home which receives little attention.

An inconvenient truth?

Robert Putnam is one of America's best known social scientists courted by Presidents Clinton and Bush. He is Professor of Public Policy at Harvard University's Kennedy School of Government and a visiting Professor at Manchester University in the UK. He made his name with an analysis of the erosion of social capital in the USA. He later investigated the impact of ethnic diversity on societies. In a massive study based on over 30,000 interviews across 41 communities in the US he found - to his surprise and dismay - that nearly all the indicators of civic health are lower in diverse communities. In August 2007 The Boston Globe headed a report, "A Harvard political scientist finds that diversity hurts civic life. What happens when a liberal scholar unearths an inconvenient truth?"[408] Putnam's research into the effects of ethnic diversity led him to conclude that the more ethnically diverse a community was, the greater the isolation of individuals and the less social capital existed.[409] He claimed that in diverse communities there was a distrust of neighbours, regardless of race, and a withdrawal from close friendships. In general these

---

[406] Richard Oastler letter to the Leeds Mercury 29th September 1829
[407] Oastler letter to the Leeds Mercury 29th September 1829
[408] The Boston Globe Michael Jonas 5.8.2007
[409] Robert Putnam *Bowling Alone* (New York Simon & Schuster 2001)

people have less belief that they can make a contribution to society; they are less involved in politics and vote less; they expect the worst from society and its leaders; they give less to charity and volunteer less and work less on community projects; they appear to pull in like a turtle and huddle unhappily in front of the television resulting in a general malaise.

These research findings presented Putnam with an acute dilemma, because he was a liberal and had held pro-diversity views. He therefore spent several years checking his results - a process he called kicking the tyres. He tried over twenty alternative explanations: larger communities; wider range of income; more crime. He finally concluded, "It would be unfortunate if a politically correct progressivism were to deny the challenge to social solidarity posed by diversity."[410] He feared he would be pilloried as the bearer of an inconvenient truth. Putnam acknowledged an upside to diversity – people from different backgrounds can be more creative working together in - for instance - solving engineering problems. John Lloyd writing in *The Financial Times* reported that the British Home Office had independently confirmed Putnam's findings in Britain.[411]

In 2004 *The Guardian* published a series of articles entitled *The Discomfort of Strangers* by the founder and editor of *Prospect Magazine*, David Goodhart.[412] These stated that, "Too often the language of liberal universalism that dominates public debate, ignores the real affinities of place and people. These affinities are not obstacles to be overcome on the road to a good society, but its foundation stones."[413] Also "The left's recent love affair with diversity may come at the expense of values, and even people, it once championed."[414] The articles claimed that liberals think we are "equally obligated to all human beings from Bolton to Burundi"[415] and argued, "Diversity eats away at common culture and feelings of mutual obligation." Liberals face – what *The Guardian* called - the progressive dilemma: if a society opts for diversity, this will weaken the welfare state, because people will refuse to pay for people who are not like them. *The Guardian* articles maintained that welfare states were established when societies were ethnically homogeneous and warned, "High immigration can erode feelings of mutual obligation on which the welfare state depends."[416] According to *The Guardian* mass immigration, which had no democratic mandate, had led to "the erosion of feelings of mutuality among the white majority in Britain."[417]

---

[410] The Boston Globe Michael Jonas 5.8.2007
[411] John Lloyd *Study paints bleak picture of diversity* Financial Times 8.10.2006
[412] David Goodhart *The Discomfort of Strangers* The Guardian London 24 February 2004
[413] Goodhart
[414] Goodhart
[415] Goodhart
[416] Goodhart
[417] Goodhart

After the horrors of the 20th century many liberals believed the solution was to base society totally on internationalism, multiculturalism, cosmopolitanism and diversity. Clearly a move in this direction was needed. As a result liberals seek to weaken any sense of identity or loyalty to particular creeds and nations. So the ties that bind existing communities together have been loosened and social capital has become depleted. However others, including some on the left, think that multiculturalism has had the effect of fragmenting communities, and that a healthy society, while accepting a degree of diversity, needs also some cohesion and rootedness. They argue for a nuanced position. The liberal ideal of universal mankind and universal identity is a worthy one, but more local affinities and loyalties are beneficial in moderation in holding communities to-gather. Otherwise the price for creating a sense of universal humanity can be the unravelling of existing communities.

I fully acknowledge the positive contribution made by liberals in challenging the ugly racism of the past. My concern is that the pendulum has swung so far that instead of equality we have in some cases an inverted racism, and a politically correct culture which makes it impossible for such concerns to be raised or discussed in a fair and open manner. Too often liberals have dismissed legitimate anxieties of ordinary folk out of hand. In addition the media have been biased: the focus has been on the victims of racism in the ethnic communities, not among the white population. So the murder of Stephen Lawrence by a white gang received vastly more coverage, by the BBC and other media, than the murder of Ross Parker in Peterborough by an Asian gang in an unprovoked racist attack in 2001.

CHAPTER 10

The Liberal Delusions:
We are Shaped only by our Experiences and not by our Genes
(the Blank Slate Theory)

The following quotes are from Steven Pinker's book *The Blank Slate*:-

The Blank Slate theory is seldom articulated or overtly embraced
but lies at the heart of a vast number of beliefs and policies.[418]

The Blank Slate has become the secular religion of modern intellectual life. It is seen
as a source of values, the fact that it is based on a miracle – a complex mind arising
out of nothing – is not held against it.[419]

Challenges to the doctrine (Blank Slate) from sceptics and scientists have plunged
some believers into a crisis of faith and have lead others to mount the kinds of bitter
attacks ordinarily aimed at heretics and infidels. And just as many religious traditions
eventually reconciled themselves to apparent threats from science, so, I argue, our
values will survive the demise of the Blank Slate.[420]

The Blank Slate is a doctrine that is widely embraced as a rationale for meaning and
morality, and is under assault from science. As in the century after Galileo our moral
sensibilities will adjust to the biological facts, not only because facts are facts, but
because the credentials of the Blank Slate are spurious.[421]

Are parents to blame, if their children turn out badly?

A lady, who read a draft of this book, had two children of her own and
then adopted two. Her own children turned out well but the two she
adopted turned out badly. She had blamed herself and she found
Pinker's rejection of the theory that parents are entirely responsible for how their
children turn out immensely helpful. She wrote to me, "All four of my children
were bought up in the same way, with the same values. They have grown up to
have absolutely different values. In my opinion they have reverted to the way
they were born. They inherited certain traits that I just couldn't get rid of. I
spent a long time feeling I had failed. If it was all down to my bad parenting
skills, then all four children would be the same."[422] Lucy Wadham in her book,
The Secret Life of France comments that in France today professionals refuse to
accept that autism has a genetic cause. She wrote, "Long after autism was found
to be an organic disorder, triggered by genetic factors, French mothers were still

---

[418] Steven Pinker *The Blank Slate* (London Allen Lane 2002) p. 2
[419] Pinker p. 3
[420] Pinker p. 3
[421] Pinker p. 138
[422] Letter to the Author from RB 29.11.2011

being blamed for their 'failure to bond' with their child. ... the myth of the 'refrigerator mother' who causes autistic symptoms. ... Even today there are plenty of French analysts who refuse to accept the biological nature of autism, and continue to compound the anguish of families with autistic children, by apportioning blame."[423] Many sociologists assume that parenting is everything and ignore genes.

In his book *The Blank Slate*, Pinker argued that modern intellectual life is based on the Blank Slate theory: there is no inherited component in human nature; character and attributes can be explained by nurture alone. The book's subtitle is *The Modern Denial of Human Nature*. He claims the theory is all pervasive - influencing social policy, child-rearing, education, penal policy, economic planning, politics and morality. Our denial of the truth about human nature is, Pinker claims, like the Victorian attitude to sex. However, he asserts, scientific discoveries have undermined the Blank Slate: in particular, the discoveries of the Human Genome Project and evidence from the studies of twins. If he is right, many of our policies and practices, which are based on this mistaken dogma, will fail. A fundamental rethink is required. The consequences will be far-reaching. He likens us to card players - playing without a full deck.

These are bold claims. You would expect his book to receive a hostile reception. Surprisingly - it didn't ! John Morrish in *The Independent on Sunday* wrote: "It is unexpectedly bracing. It feels like being burgled. Pinker has stolen our illusions." Fay Weldon in *The Daily Telegraph* commented, "magnificent and timely." *The New Scientist*, "brilliant". "Required reading", said *The Literary Review*. "Startling – a breath of fresh air on a topic too long politicised", *The Economist*. "Another sizzling performance .... excellent" *The Spectator*. "The best book on human nature that I, or anyone else, will ever read. Truly magnificent", Matt Ridley in *The Sunday Telegraph*. "Sheer brilliance" wrote Helena Cronin, author of *The Ant and The Peacock*. Richard Dawkins wrote: "What a superb thinker he is .... and how courageous to buck the liberal trend in science." [Dawkins shares Pinker's views on the Blank Slate theory, but not on the Noble Savage.]

According to the Blank Slate theory, human beings at birth have minds like blank slates, on which societies and cultures may write whatever they want; or like a sheet of white paper on which anything may be written. To change the metaphor yet again, minds are like soft wax or 'silly putty', which can be moulded in any way society chooses. Pinker wrote, "The Blank Slate is the idea that the human mind has no inherent structure and can be inscribed at will by society or ourselves."[424] So there are no inherited characteristics and no influence from our genes. Pinker argues the theory is fundamental in the west, yet rarely acknowledged or discussed openly.[425] According to the theory, if a

---

[423] Lucy Wadham *The Secret Life of France* (London Faber and Faber 2009) p127
[424] Pinker p. 2
[425] Pinker p. 3

child has two parents, who are athletic, and then becomes athletic herself, this is explained only by nurturing. No genetic or hereditary explanation is allowed. Pinker claims that intellectuals believe it is morally wrong to think that the human mind has an inborn structure.[426]

Our intellectual mainstream is committed to the view that the human mind has no inherent structure and can be inscribed at will by society or ourselves. Pinker calls it a "poisoning of the intellectual atmosphere."[427] And there is now he maintains a "disconnect between intellectual life and common sense"[428] Many writers use extreme language to discredit the importance of genes. He notes the contempt of scholars for the concepts of truth, logic and evidence. "A hypocritical divide between what intellectuals say in public and what they say in private. ... The intellectual establishment has forfeited claims to credibility in the eyes of the public."[429]

Some may object: isn't this the age-old argument between nurture and nature? Haven't we all moved on, and recognised that it is a mixture of both? Steven Pinker argues that the part played by our genetic inheritance is largely ignored in the west, and those who have acknowledged the importance of genetic factors have been "picketed, shouted down and subjected to searing invective in the press."[430] He wrote, "To acknowledge human nature, many think, is to endorse racism, sexism, war, greed, genocide, nihilism, reactionary politics, and neglect of children and the disadvantaged. Any claim that the mind might have an innate organisation strikes people as an hypothesis that might be incorrect but as a thought it is immoral to think."[431] People think that the idea of an inborn human nature is dangerous. Pinker explains that he is not arguing that heredity is everything and culture nothing. What he finds puzzling is that the moderate position that nature and nurture play a part is regarded as extreme and that the extreme position that culture explains everything is regarded as a moderate one. Discoveries about human nature have been ignored. As Pinker noted, "The dogma that human nature does not exist, in the face of evidence from science and common sense that it does, is a corrupting influence."[432]

Of course in some situations nurture is the explanation e.g. which language you speak. What concerns Pinker, is that the idea that "culture is everything" dominates intellectual life, and the part played by our genes is denied. Today it seems that everything is a social construct. We have overestimated the importance of culture and society, and ignored inborn human nature. Differences between individuals and sexes are claimed to arise only

---

[426] Pinker p. viii

[427] Pinker p. x

[428] Pinker p. x

[429] Pinker p. x

[430] Pinker p. viii

[431] Pinker p. viii

[432] Pinker p. ix

from their varied life experiences. By changing these experiences, it is believed, you can change people's minds. It is claimed that boys are aggressive because of the way they were brought up. Parents are thought to be able to mould children any way they choose. If children are well behaved, confident and articulate, this is explained by good parenting, the genetic component ignored. Ashley Montagu, the American anthropologist even claimed that human beings had *no* instincts or drives - even a man's belief that orgasm was the object of sex was a social construct !

Many educationalists see a child's mind as putty in their hands. They seek to mould children: instilling politically correct views on the environment, gender, sexuality, ethnic diversity and aggression. They have tried to persuade parents and schools to make boys play with dolls, and banned guns, believing this would result in gentle, peaceable boys, incapable of aggression. However it has resulted in frustration. Pinker holds that it is better to acknowledge boys' aggression and channel it. The self-confidence of parents has been undermined, as they have been swamped with advice on child-rearing.

Downside of the Blank Slate theory

The idea that evil is caused by parents and society led to the belief that mankind could be "reshaped by massive social engineering projects and led to some of the greatest atrocities in history."[433] The historian Michael Burleigh commented on the practices of the Jacobins in the French Revolution, "Rejecting the Christian concept of original sin, the Jacobins subscribed to the infinite malleability of the human race. The new-born baby could be shaped this way or that, or as one Jacobin catechism had it: 'we think he is soft wax capable of receiving whatever imprint one wishes.'"[434] Burleigh explained that the aim of Jacobin education was to mould young minds with progressive ideas. Onto the soft wax of the child's mind the Jacobin social engineers were determined to stamp the imprint of atheism and egalitarianism. However this belief that mankind could be made anew by moulding and shaping according to Utopian ideals led to atrocities under the both Jacobins and communism.

The theory of the Blank Slate provided a theoretical basis for massive social engineering and some of the worst atrocities in human history: the Jacobin Reign of Terror, Stalin's Soviet Russia, Mao's China and Pol Pot's Cambodia.[435] Soviet Union undertook to reshape the thinking of tens of millions under its brutal Secularization Experiment. Those who refused were sent to the gulags where they nearly all perished in hunger and cold. Boris Pasternak, the author of *Doctor Zhivago* wrote, "When I hear of people reshaping life, it makes me lose all self-control and fall into despair. Reshaping life! People who say

---

[433] Pinker p. xi
[434] Michael Burleigh *Earthly Powers* (London Harper Collins 2005) p. 82
[435] Pinker p. xi

that have never understood the least thing about life."[436] The most determined effort at brain-washing young minds was carried out in the Soviet Union in the 1930s. Mao wrote: "It is on a blank sheet of paper that the most beautiful poems are written."[437]

Liberals tend to think that the Blank Slate theory is totally benign, and ideas of inherited characteristics intrinsically dangerous. Pinker rejects this analysis, pointing out that the belief that there are no inherited differences has had harmful consequences. For example it has led to the neglect of more able children, who are not well taught. The dogma that the mind is a blank slate has led to parenting policies that if children turn out badly it is the fault of the parents, causing them great anguish. The explanation that a child is happy and well-adjusted may be telling us something about his genes, rather than telling something about the parenting skills involved in his/her upbringing.

Why is the Blank Slate theory popular with liberals and intellectuals?

Pinker argues that the popularity of the theory with liberals and intellectuals is partly a reaction to Nazi ideology, which stressed the importance of genetic and racial differences.[438] Many intellectuals thought that the way to prevent any recurrence was to entrench the opposite belief - that genetics played no part. Pinker, who is Jewish, commented, "It is popular to say races do not exist, but are purely social constructs … but this is an overstatement."[439] He argued that our opposition to sexism and racism should be based on morals, and not on bad science. Pinker believes intellectuals are driven by a number of fears. They are afraid that if we acknowledge the importance of heredity and genes, then we cannot be held responsible for our actions. If no one is responsible for their actions, then chaos and anarchy will follow. Pinker's defence to this charge is that the science has been misunderstood. Those who stress the importance of genes are not arguing that human actions are totally predetermined. They hold that genes are probabilistic, but not totally predictive. However they do say that our behaviour is shaped more by genes, than is generally acknowledged.

The theory also appeals to liberals because it appears to guarantee both equality and freedom. If children are born with characteristics and qualities, then they are not free to choose to be anything they want - a first class footballer, mathematician or musician. The Blank Slate theory seems to guarantee freedom to choose to be whatever we wish because there is no genetic determinant. The second fear is that if human beings are different at birth, then

---

[436] Boris Pasternak quoted by Hadley Cantril *Soviet Leaders and the Mastery over Man* (USA NJ Rutgers University Press 1960) quoted by Froese p. 165
[437] Pinker p. 11
[438] Pinker p. 153
[439] Pinker p. 144

we are born unequal, and the drive for a more egalitarian society would be undermined. If the slate is blank, then we are all the same. The idea that inequality may be inborn is repugnant to those committed to equality, so they insist on sameness, regardless of the evidence. Egalitarians insist children are equal and so refuse to acknowledge any influence of heredity and inborn differences. They insist we inherit nothing - apart from morphology, like blue eyes - from our parents, so we are all equal, because we are all the same at birth. Differences between individuals are explained by varied life experiences, which alone determine outcomes. They also fear that if we are born different, this could justify discrimination. Lastly, liberals fear that if we acknowledge human nature has ugly aspects, which are inborn, then we may to some degree have provided a justification for them. So if we are greedy, selfish, cruel, ethnocentric and prone to violence, it is better to deny that these traits are inborn. Moreover if human nature is inherently flawed, then the dream of Utopia and the perfectibility of man are unachievable.

Scientific challenge to the Blank Slate

One of the first to challenge to the notion of the Blank Slate was Noam Chomsky. He pointed out that language was complex and yet mastered easily by children without them being taught it. So the brain must be hard-wired for language: the slate cannot be entirely blank. Pinker, who was formerly Director of the Centre for Cognitive Neuroscience at MIT, holds that advances in the understanding of the human brain – the cognitive revolution - have undermined the Blank Slate theory. In 2001 the sequencing of the Human Genome was completed, yielding more understanding of which genes are responsible for which characteristics.[440] The scientific evidence shows that a large part of our character and make-up comes from our genes.[441] Further evidence against the Blank Slate comes from studies of identical twins, which were separated at birth. According to the Blank Slate theory these children will turn out very different, because their cultural upbringing was different. In fact they turned out to be remarkably similar.[442] So genes, rather than nurture, determine outcomes. Also studies of virtual twins - children adopted at the same time from different parents – showed that genes were the key determinant. Having the same upbringing did not result in similar children. Genes are more important than parents, kin, culture or society. Pinker claims these scientific discoveries are

---

[440] Pinker p. 56.

[441] Pinker p. 44

[442] Mathew Taylor, who was the Liberal Democrat MP for Truro, was adopted at birth. He decided in his mid-forties to try to find his birth mother, even though his adoption had been happy. Eventually he traced her to New Zealand and met up with her. He was surprised to discover that his paternal grandfather had also been a Liberal MP; he was still alive, aged 102, and they were able to meet up.

causing many intellectuals a crisis of faith, and some have responded by launching fanatical attacks on doubters and heretics. It is ironic that the challenge to their faith comes from science. Furthermore the Blank Slate theory has a downside in that if people are all born the same, and then some do badly, they are partly to blame.

Liberal policies fail because they ignore human nature and this leads to weak policies on criminal justice and to the barbaric, where the state tries to coerce people into changing their nature. Taken to extremes the 'liberal' view of nurture being pre-eminent to nature results in extraordinarily intolerant policies, where deviation from what the state demands is considered unacceptable (e.g. the cultural revolution in China). A conservative belief in the importance of nature understands human foibles, accepts that we cannot be perfected and therefore is less vicious when we do not live up to expectations. The policies of the conservative minded work with human nature and recognise that people respond to incentives. We put ourselves and our families first, and we prefer institutions which are familiar and traditional over the abstract and 'logical'.

CHAPTER 11

The Dark Side of Liberalism:
Does liberalism harm the poor?

To their credit liberals seek greater social justice, but the effect of their policies has been to harm the very people they claim to want to help argues Shaun Bailey, a youth worker and pamphleteer. He was brought up by a single mum on a council estate in west London and co-founded and runs a community project, called MyGeneration. It helps disaffected, drug-addicted and unemployed young people in a deprived area of west London. His pamphlet *No Man's Land*[443] gives a graphic account of life on rundown estates and analyses what has gone wrong; it was reprinted in *The Sunday Times*. He wrote, "The liberal agenda hasn't benefited the working class" and "The more liberal we've become the more the poor have suffered." He added "All this over-caring liberalism is damaging." Liberals claim: "We understand your pain." He answers: "They are certainly not living the pain; they don't realise that individualism is causing others pain." He maintains liberals live in nice leafy suburbs miles away from the problems their polices have created.

Bailey maintains liberals have created a dysfunctional society – they promote a casual attitude to sex, undermine the family, erode discipline in schools and encourage drug-taking. In addition they devalue religion, marriage, notions of self-restraint and patriotism and while working class communities suffer from these policies, middle-class liberals live far away. He summed up his politics as: "A battle with liberal Britain." It is ironic that the kids he works with are damaged by the very people, who think they are helping.

My interview with Shaun Bailey[444]

JM   Shaun can you tell me something about your background and political views?
SB   Liberalism rose to prominence because we were too conservative, and this was linked to some of society's more unpleasant goings on. That's where liberalism gained some favour. There was some merit in it. It's not completely evil. But it definitely went too far. I'm a black man and we needed liberalism to deal with the ugly side of society. I grew up here and I had plenty of liberal views. But now liberalism is swinging all the way round to illiberalism. The key point about liberalism is that they made any language that was traditional, or normal, or useful seem right-wing, racist, sexist, homophobic, anti-this anti-

---

[443] Shaun Bailey *No Man's Land* (London Centre for Young Policy Studies, 2005)
[444] On 5th June 2009 I interviewed Shaun Bailey at the offices of MyGeneration.[444]

that and blah de blah. Public discourse is owned by the liberal intelligentsia. It is something that the public needs to take back.

The condition of families and children and the wider community in this country is dire because of liberalism. All the measures we've made are made ineffective and have been ineffective because of liberalism. I personally have an interest in children and families. What is really stunning to me is the liberal attack on marriage. Many liberals are married. But what the leaders have done is to deny to the followers in our society, the support and benefit of marriage, which they hold onto themselves. From the destruction of the core family all kinds of social evils sprang. Things they will never be subject to. When I say that I really loathe liberal politics, that's what I am talking about. I don't think people made the link. They don't really understand the impact this has had on society - particularly in poor areas. It is a set of selfish policies pushed on people by the liberal intelligentsia, who don't live in the world that they are trying to influence. They've been washing away the morals from people at the bottom of society, while people at the top hold onto theirs. We now have a sub-class that we've never had before. We've always had poor people, but now we have a sub-class who are not only poor but disconnected. It is devastating.

Liberal ideas have infiltrated the Labour Party and changed its views; the party now has policies that don't go down very well in their heartlands. Things like "You can't smack your children". Traditional Labour supporters are miles away from how liberals think. The Tony Blairs and Alistair Campbells of this world are very far away. Harriet Harman is miles away from what the Labour voting British voters are about. We kinda lost control of the Labour Party. You will probably find that people in Labour heartlands have conservative views. For me one of the key points is that liberals never take responsibility for these problems. They never own up to the damage they have caused society. Catholics have owned up and taken the rap for what went wrong in the Roman Catholic Church with paedophilia, but liberals never say sorry for the harm they have caused.

Education

SB   I think we will have to take a march back in the case of schools. Our schools fell apart. They absolutely fell apart. It is the do-gooders who are doing the damage. The teachers supported the liberals in the government, who removed competition and discipline. It was a disaster for the teachers. The schools that have made significant progress recently have removed that liberal atmosphere. The Government have been cowards. They have refused to face up to the fact that liberal policies have failed. Instead they have appointed an individual, who doesn't have a liberal view of how to run a school, and that person has been able to reverse some of the horrible results of liberal school policies. If you talk to teachers now, and generally they have been one of the most liberal professions going, you find a lot of disillusionment, particularly when discussing how to deal with the children. Their view of education has changed.

JM   So you think that teachers are recognising that we've become too liberal?

SB   Absolutely. Teachers suffer from it so much.

JM   It's taken them a long time to realise.

SB   Yes. I reckon they realised earlier but were embarrassed and afraid, and didn't know where to go with it.

JM   And education is controlled by the liberals.

SB   Absolutely. If you look at the teachers they have been a key group in handing over power to the children, but they have been the group that has suffered most. Thousands of teachers in the country would love to leave the profession in a heartbeat, just to get away from the children, who are the very reason they joined. They are no longer teachers, they are policemen, and they hate that. Power has been handed over to the children. We've gone so far down that route that children are immediately believed. Some of the best teachers in the country have had their careers blighted or ended because the liberals in the teaching profession believed the children. Obviously you should give children a fair hearing, but you need some balance and there has been none. Now teachers are looking and thinking 'Oh My God. What have we done'. They have to defeat the liberals within their own ranks because of what has happened.

Our children have been taught liberal policies. Where you have a society devoid of morals you're in real trouble. You're in absolute trouble. In fact our children are the unhappiest children in the world by their estimation and by many other people's. It's devastating for them. Children have grown up in that society and know nothing different. Our gang problem is escalating, while sexual activity among young people has absolutely mushroomed. We've just hidden the fact by giving them condoms. Take the morning after pill (MAP) which schools give out for free. For example a girl takes the pill. The next morning she doesn't want to go to school; but you as a parent don't know why. So the parent fights with the child, thinking she's had a late night, when actually she's had an abortion. If you don't deliver that child to school, then the school is onto you. But actually there's a root cause, which is being ignored.

Broadcasting

SB   Liberalism is damaging our children. I'll give you a classic example: we've liberalised broadcasting. We're against censorship because it's illiberal. With children you have to err on the side of caution everytime. I favour censorship of what our children watch, because parents don't have the time to censor their children's TV. When you're poor you are more exposed to these influences: your children spend less time with you, because you spend more time at work and you have less money. Your children definitely don't get the same academic, personal and social education that a child in a very good school would receive: and that education is the antidote to some of the things that are happening to our children and the wider community. Most of our social failings in this country in the last 25 years have been based on liberalism. But no-one from the liberal side takes responsibility. Liberalism has had very good PR .

JM   What is your view of the BBC?

SB   One of the first things a Conservative Government should do is to sort out the BBC, which sees itself as a propagandist for liberals values. I think the BBC have shot themselves in the foot. Their whole output is one-sided. The way they have behaved means that they won't be the power in the world that they were. I don't think the Conservative Party is afraid of them, because they've been against the Conservative Party for years. It's just part of the landscape. They are very rich because of the licence fee money, which should be divided up given to other broadcasters to provide alternative public service broadcasting. I think that's where we've got to go. If you'd made that suggestion 25 years ago, it would have been rejected out of hand. The BBC Trust was set up to control the BBC but it has been a failure. The output of the BBC is still biased.

JM   The BBC used to have a reputation for objectivity and truthfulness.

SB   Yes. I think that ultimately their position is unsustainable. It will come back to bite them. Sky News is now much more even-handed, which is a shock, because Sky is a commercial broadcaster.

Other topics

SB   Also the liberals have turned in on themselves, at a recent National Union of Teachers conference they were talking about banning all religious schools. But religious schools - generally speaking - do far better than secular schools.

JM   And parents want them.

SB   That's right. I know a Jewish couple who send their child to a Roman Catholic school. And I said, 'Is that a problem?' They said, 'No. He's a Jew. We're happy for him to be around other religious people, because they don't prevent him from engaging in his own religion. They engage in theirs, but they don't prevent him in engaging in his.' That's the difference from a secular school. Everyone can engage with their religion. Liberalism has set itself up as secularism to attack religion of all shades. But real liberalism should say that you are allowed to be religious. They are being what they claim not to be. People who think they are liberal should take a real look at themselves.

JM   I find that Christians are often liberal. Do you agree?

SB   Yes, because it suits people. If you write one thing about me, it is this: liberalism is selfish. People talk about Thatcher and all that, and about the rise in selfishness and individualism. Liberalism is the cause of that. We are more selfish now than the Thatcher era ever was. Nobody acts unselfishly now. As we became rich, we became selfish. You have more money to spend on yourself. And we're still looking for ways that allow us to have no collective responsibility; and yet have all our personal freedoms. It's impossible.

JM   Is the Conservative Party receptive to what you are saying?

SB   I think one of the best things that David Cameron did was when he started talking about marriage. He began to draw a line in the sand. I would say that Cameron and the Conservative Party are about a journey. I am fairly sure we won't become more liberal. There is a good long journey back to the centre because obviously swinging right back is not particularly useful. One thing about my time in politics – win, lose or draw – I have been able to challenge people's liberal views.

JM   What are you views on race?

SB   What liberals are in effect saying to members of the ethnic minorities, like me, is this, "You are welcome to come to this country, but part of the bargain is that you sign up for liberal values. So you must give up your conservative attitudes on the family, marriage and sex, the discipline of children and the importance of religion." Liberals do not respect the values of the ethnic minorities. However we can see the damage that liberal policies are doing to our societies: the emphasis on the rights of children, not on their duties, obligations and responsibilities; the teenage mothers and fatherless children, the binge drinking and drug taking. Liberals expected immigrants to adopt liberal values. It is a shock to them that this is not happening, and they have become intolerant. Their attitude is patronising and racist. Because I am black I can play the race card against them. I say to them, that they are being racist, by being intolerant of the values of black people like me. They created this weapon - the race card - to silence opponents and close down arguments, but when it is used against them, they have no answer.

JM   Thank you very much.

Shaun Bailey makes the case against liberalism

The quotes are taken from his pamphlet *No Man's Land* unless otherwise indicated. Many of the young people he deals with are – like himself - descended from West Indian families that came to Britain in the 1950s and 1960s. Some of them brought a traditional family structure and Christianity. But, he says, in the 1960s it became acceptable for young girls to get pregnant and bring up children on their own. Many of the young mums of to-day are themselves the children of single mothers. He argues that within the black community marriage has almost died out and with each generation things get worse; girls' attitudes to sex becomes ever more casual. They think it normal to be shared by boys. The pressure to have casual sex becomes greater: notions of self-control, self-restraint and abstinence have disappeared. Young people feel under pressure to have sex by their schools, by pop culture and by the media. The sex education they receive is merely a 'how to do it' course: this is how a condom works. When he was speaking to ninety girls in a school, only three had even heard of abstinence. Instead children are told where they can get free condoms and morning-after pills, and abortions can be arranged without the knowledge of their parent(s). All this weakens the family unit. As a further encouragement to have sex, the state rewards pregnancy by giving flats and welfare benefits. He says that young people openly discuss: "How to screw the most out of the welfare system". Some couples split up to maximise their welfare benefits, further undermining families. Partly because of the disappearance of the traditional family, and because they give a sense of belonging, gangs have developed.

He claims many youngsters are hooked on drugs, violence and crime. A quarter of them smoke cannabis, but crack and heroin are becoming more common. He wrote: "The liberal intelligentsia relaxed the drug rules for themselves, not for the poor or the working classes." And "By decriminalising drug-taking, we are criminalising the kids." In addition multiculturalism, Bailey argued, is destroying Britain's sense of being a community - its own cultural heritage was ignored. He says children in schools learn more about Diwali than Christianity. Yet for many West Indians Christianity is part of their heritage, and 73% of the British population in the last census in 2001 described themselves as Christian. There is no patriotism and no commitment to the wider community. "There are so many things about being British that are positive. Those values have been eroded in the poorer classes."[445] Instead of pride in being British, they take away a feeling of shame.

According to Bailey the result of liberalism is a downward spiral into violence, crime and social chaos. The violence is escalating with guns and knives being used more. The number who avoid getting caught up in crime is shrinking. The age at which they get involved in serious crime is falling. They talk constantly of "f**king people up", stabbing people and blowing their heads off. They have no social skills, nor any idea of resolving conflicts peacefully. They think that if you ask a question, you are not showing them respect. All they can say is "What d'ya want. What d'ya want?" He believes the schools attended by their grandparents back in the West Indies did set boundaries; but in British schools today there is often disorder and lack of respect.

Bailey describes the children he comes across as preoccupied with money and status - the celebrity culture. They are not helped by a media focussed on sex, violence and celebrity. They are obsessed with getting money and flaunting it. They see no connection between getting money and working. The very antithesis of the Protestant work ethic. Their way to wealth is through drugs and crime. They have totally unrealistic expectations of wealth, fed by the rap music and videos they watch. The films and TV they watch feature violence and sex. However censorship would be deemed illiberal. Freedom of expression has a

---

[445] The Guardian interview 2.5.07

value, but Bailey argues, if rap music encourages violence, the gun culture, greedy materialism and treatment of women as mere sex slaves for men, then its freedom should be curtailed. In America President Obama has spoken of the evil influence of rap music on young kids. However liberals would oppose any attempt to restrict freedom of expression.

Following a spate of teenage murders in London in 2007, Bailey wrote an article for the *Sunday Telegraph*[446] claiming we are failing to teach our children any sense of right and wrong. He argued that there has been a dramatic increase in teenage violence, more out-of-control kids, who are prepared to use guns and knives. He goes into schools and speaks against violence to women and girlfriends: but now the response he gets is one of surprise. "Why not?" they say. He says he's regarded as coming from another planet. They learn early on that they can get away with violence which escalates: first knives, then guns. He argues that our society places too much stress on the rights of children with little attempt to discipline them. He wrote: "Liberal toleration means adults have abdicated responsibility for educating children emotionally." Teachers are afraid to teach basic values like honesty, politeness and respect for others. And how does the government respond? He says that after the murder of Damilola Taylor in Peckham, the government spent millions of pounds physically rebuilding the area, but that it has done nothing to change attitudes. So the government cares, but responds in inappropriate ways. Meanwhile government ministers and Labour MPs make sure their own children grow up miles away from such anarchy. Bailey recently had a group of children come over from Brazil on an exchange. They were shocked at the behaviour of the British children. One said to him: "I'm glad we're not allowed to behave like that." He believes that the problem in Britain is the liberal agenda, which results in us being "So busy telling children of their rights, that we do not tell them of their responsibilities."[447]

Bailey maintains that another problem is that liberals want to keep people dependent on them. He wrote, "Liberals like to keep their people. They tell them to hang around and they will sort out things for them."[448] They keep people in a state of dependency, which undermines the willingness of the community to take responsibility and tackle things themselves. So although they mean well, they harm the people they say they want to help. He is scathing of the welfare state: "It is horrible. It traps the poor."[449] And speaking of black communities, "Well-meaning people try to help them, but they rob them of the will and skill to look after themselves. They say that they will do it for us."[450] The charity *Habitat for Humanity* which builds affordable social housing

---

[446] Dated 11.02.07
[447] The Guardian interview 2.5.07
[448] The Guardian interview 2.5.07
[449] The Guardian interview 2.5.07
[450] The Guardian interview 2.5.07

throughout the world, has identified the problem of creating dependency, and describes its policy of one of hand-ups but not hand-outs.[451] Their aim is to make people independent so that they stand on their own feet. Bailey condemns the dependency culture, "The key wickedness is the idea the government can pay for everything. If you continually give people things, and ask for nothing back, you rob them of their will. People have to be involved in their own redemption. There are people sitting at home now, who don't work, because it's not worth their while to do it under the benefits system. That is wrong."[452]

In an interview with the American magazine 'World' he maintained "Well-meaning white people have hurt us, and we've been self-indulgent. . . . They remove religion from schools but give out condoms, and girls end up with lone parenting their only career choice. They talk about rights but not responsibilities, as if blokes are incapable. . . . Add to that school failure, some children are not going to be academically sharp, yet school doesn't teach them any vocational skills. . . . The government sucks in all the pounds and wastes them."[453] Some parents with a West Indian or West African background are so dismayed by British education that they send their children back to their countries of origin, so that they will receive a more traditional and disciplined upbringing. There they are taught moral values and respect for others. Bailey maintains religion provides a moral compass; but most liberals are secular and strive to reduce the influence of religion. Schools don't "do" religion or morality. Children on the estates receive little or no discipline from family, school or church.

The Sunday Times reported in 2007 that scores of parents of Ghanaian origin with children in Britain were sending them back to Ghana because of their fears that the British education system would damage them.[454] According to the report, "They exchange truancy and gang culture for traditional teaching and strong discipline." Abena, a 16 year old from Hackney said, "When I was in London I was bad basically. I stopped going to school and in my head I was thinking money, money, money." Sieman aged 17 from North London said, "When your friends know you are going to Ghana they know that you're going to get straightened up. I used to be really bad." He mentioned gangs and playground violence. The head of one of the Ghanaian schools Oswald Amoo-Gottfried said the key to success was discipline and that he used the cane. The report said the atmosphere at the school was quiet and studious. Sieman admitted he had been caned and said it had worked to some extent for him. Isaac from Norwood had become involved in gangs and stealing from his parents. Now he is softly spoken and articulate. A girl called Asante said that at her British school there was a lot of fighting. British children at the Ghanaian

---

[451] Financial Times 5.5.07
[452] Interview Daily Telegraph 30.9.2008
[453] *World Magazine* dated 12.8. 2007
[454] *The Sunday Times* 4.11.2007

schools agreed that the discipline was tough but that their lives had changed for the better under the strict Ghanaian school system. James from Edmonton said that "What gets you respect in England, is a disgrace over here."

CHAPTER 12

The Dark Side of Liberalism:
The Dictatorship of the Intelligentsia

Not a few contemporary liberals have gone through a peculiar evolution
- so strange a reversal. From the free individual following his inner light ...
to an authoritarian state obedient to the directives of an elite. [455]
Sir Isaiah Berlin

The grand delusion of contemporary liberals is that they have both the right and the
ability to move their fellow creatures around like blocks of wood.[456]
Thomas Sowell the leading African-American philosopher

Those with special wisdom and virtue convey this wisdom and virtue to others -
through articulation, where that is deemed effective, and through coercive power
where it is not.[457]
Thomas Sowell

The intellectuals are more totalitarian than the common people. ...
Most of them are perfectly ready for dictatorial methods, secret police, systematic
falsification of history, etc as long as they feel that it is on 'our' side.[458]
George Orwell

Liberals aim to create a 'new liberal man' not so different from the goal of the Soviet
education system to create a 'new socialist man' and this seems to violate the essence
of liberalism.[459]
Michael Walzer, Professor of Social Science at Princeton

Liberal individuality is invariably a prescription for abject conformity
to prevailing *bien-pensant* opinion.[460]
John Gray, Professor of European Thought at the London School of Economics

The Enlightenment throughout the liberal period has always sympathised with social
coercion. [461]
M. Horkheimer and T. Adorno: The Dialectic of Enlightenment

---

[455] Isaiah Berlin *The Two Concepts of Liberty* in *Liberty* edited by Henry Hardy (Oxford University Press 1969) p 198
[456] Cited by Robert Conquest in *Dragons of Expectation* (London Duckworth 2005) p. 19
[457] Thomas Sowell *A Conflict of Visions* (USA Basic Books 2002) p 164
[458] Orwell *The Collected Essays Etc* ed S Orwell & I Angus (USA New Hampshire Nonpareil 2000) Vol 3 *As I Please* p 150
[459] R Dworkin, M Lilla & R B Silvers *The Legacy of Isaiah Berlin* (USA New York Review of Books 2001) p 176
[460] John Gray *Enlightenment's Wake* (London Routledge 2007) p. 193
[461] M Horkheimer and T Adorno *Dialectic of Enlightenment* (California Stanford University Press 2002) p 9

Liberals hate to admit it, and indeed do not believe it - but their creed rests upon coercion, and to be preserved must continue to be so. [462]
John Lloyd, a former editor of the *New Statesman*.

Liberals "tell people to ignore their own experience and to think only in approved ways."[463]

John Lloyd

According to Sir Isaiah Berlin, Britain's leading historian of ideas of the last 50 years, liberals have gone from a belief in freedom, to an intolerant mindset that seeks to coerce others – "from a doctrine of individual responsibility to ... an authoritarian state obedient to the directive of an elite."[464] Liberals think they are morally and intellectually superior to ordinary people and this gives them the right to impose their views by coercion if necessary. Berlin described this 'peculiar evolution' in a famous essay he wrote, called *The Two Concepts of Liberty*. He argued there are two strands of liberalism, which he called the negative and positive concepts of liberty. The negative concept is the removal of obstacles to freedom - a policy of non-interference and leaving people alone. The second strand, the positive concept of liberty, arises where people think they are superior to ordinary folk. Berlin gave an example of the way liberals think and how they justify the bullying and coercion of others. "I try to educate you. But I am responsible for public welfare. I cannot wait until all men are wholly rational. .... If you fail to discipline yourself, I must do it for you; and you cannot complain about the lack of freedom. ... like a child, a savage, an idiot you are not ripe for self-direction."[465] So those who are enlightened and superior must dictate and force the ordinary people to do what the elite knows is best for them. We will force you to be really free. Berlin explains liberals' thinking, "I conceive of myself coercing others for their own sake, in their not my interest. I am claiming that I know what they truly need better than they know it themselves."[466]

Liberals claim to know what is best for people, better than they know themselves. Berlin calls this a monstrous impersonation.[467] It equates what X wants, with what the elite say he really wants. For liberals ordinary folk "are uneducated and irrational and need to be coerced... The uneducated cannot be expected to understand or co-operate with the purposes of their educators."[468] And

---

[462] FT Magazine 2.9.2006
[463] FT Magazine An insult to Reason: Liberal posturing when truths are unpalatable should offend us all. 21.10.2006
[464] Isaiah Berlin *The Two Concepts of Liberty* in *Liberty* edited by Henry Hardy (Oxford University Press 1969) p 198
[465] Berlin p. 199
[466] Berlin p. 179
[467] Berlin p. 180
[468] Berlin p. 195

"I cannot be expected to consult you, or abide by your wishes. In the end I must force you. The sage knows you better than you know yourself."[469] The suffering and oppression of the masses does not matter, because they need to be raised to a higher level. So it is necessary to violate their freedom and force them to be free. This shabby argument is used by dictators, bullies and the deluded idealists of communism. Berlin wrote: "The immature and untutored must be forced to say: 'The only way I can learn the truth is by doing blindly what you coerce me to do.'"[470] However, "Once I take this view, I am in a position to ignore the wishes of men or societies, to bully, to oppress, to torture them in the name, and on behalf of their 'real' selves."[471] This opens the door to tyranny, totalitarianism and political correctness. It explains the behaviour of the elite in the Reign of Terror during the French Revolution, the Paris commune of 1871 and under the communism. In Britain this tendency manifested itself in the Labour Government (1997-2010), which constantly tried to shape and mould the way people think and behave by legislation, and by a media - such as the BBC - which has a covert mission to impose liberal values on the country, and sees its role as 'educating' people into accept its superior values.

Berlin gave an interview to Prospect Magazine in September 1997, in which he wondered whether left-wing politics were finished. The Prime Minister Tony Blair responded by writing to Berlin and challenging his view. Blair argued there was a value in the positive concept of liberty, although he admitted that it had failed in countries like the Soviet Union. Blair wrote to Berlin, "The positive concept of liberty is valid, despite the depredations of the Soviet model."[472] It was an early indication of New Labour's top-down approach. For them democracy is the imposition of the ideas of the liberal elite on an unenlightened populace. Sadly, Berlin died shortly after receiving Blair's letter. It would have been an interesting correspondence.

George Orwell and *Nineteen Eighty-four*

In 1948 George Orwell wrote the novel *Nineteen Eighty-four* - a forewarning of the dangers of totalitarianism. It portrayed Britain under the control of a political party known as 'Big Brother'. The party believed that, "He who controls the past controls the future. He who controls the present controls the past." The Party's aim was to change people's sense of identity by cutting them off from their past, so they had no knowledge of their own history. Children would be taught the party line in schools and the state broadcaster would promote the same lies through TV soaps and documentaries. The message was that the past was terrible and that they were lucky to be living in the present, because things were so

---

[469] Berlin p. 196
[470] Berlin p. 198
[471] Berlin p. 180
[472] M. Ignatieff: *A Life: Isaiah Berlin* (London Chatto & Windus 1998) p. 298

much better now. Winston Smith - the hero of the novel - came to believe it was all lies. He worked at the Ministry of Truth, which fabricated lies, and falsified history by portraying the past as dreadful. Orwell modelled the Ministry of Truth on the BBC, where he had worked. Malcolm Muggeridge, a friend of Orwell's, observed, "It was not by chance that Orwell took the BBC as his model for the Ministry of Truth."[473] Winston Smith came to realise that life was better in the past and this knowledge survived among the working classes. The Party believed that the working classes had a false consciousness, which could be corrected by brainwashing in schools. Another of the aims of the Party was to destroy the traditional family, which was seen as conservative and obsolete and which encouraged loyalty to a small unit. Thought police monitored independently minded people closely and silenced them. This could be done by interrogating them; sometimes torture was necessary, sometimes the only solution was death. The Party believed that by controlling history and language, opinions contrary to theirs would become die out.

Orwell was also convinced that the intellectuals had become totalitarian. He wrote, "most of them are perfectly ready for dictatorial methods, secret police, systematic falsification of history etc. so long as they feel it is on 'our' side."[474] He asserted, "Totalitarian ideas have taken root in the minds of intellectuals."[475] and described intellectuals variously as – shallow, spreading a narrow selfish outlook, doing nothing but harm, damaging Britain, being a disaster and having their heads screwed on backwards. In the Preface to *Animal Farm* he wrote, "One cannot expect intelligent criticism or even plain honesty from liberal writers and journalists who are under no direct pressure to falsify their opinions."[476] He complained it was impossible to get a fair hearing. Are things different to-day? Robin Aitkin, who worked for the BBC in current affairs departments for 25 years, says that any conservative viewpoint is dismissed in the BBC as mad or bad.[477] Orwell himself wrote, "History is not being written in terms of what happened. ... the very concept of objective truth is fading out of the world."[478]

Do thought police operate? Are people afraid to say what they think? In 1999 during the run-up to the European Elections George Staunton, a 78 year old pensioner was arrested and charged with "racially aggravated criminal damage" for writing "Free Speech for England" and "Remember World War Two" on a wall in Toxteth in Liverpool. Mr Staunton, who served in the Merchant Navy during the Second World War, said, "I don't see the problem. My slogans are not hurting anyone, and they're not racist. I just believe in free speech and the right for

---

[473] Malcolm Muggerdidge *The Green Stick* p. 304

[474] Bernard Crick *George Orwell* (London Penguin Books 1980) p. 448

[475] George Orwell *Collected Essays* etc Vol IV p. 502

[476] Preface to Animal Farm by George Orwell published later as an Essay *The Freedom of the Press*

[477] Robin Aitkin *Can We Trust the BBC?*(London Continuum 2007)

[478] George Orwell Essay *Looking back on the Spanish War* (New Road Anthology)

the UK to rule itself. With all the crime in this area, I couldn't believe they nicked me for writing on a building that's being pulled down anyway. They arrested me on June 9th - election day. I didn't even get the chance to vote, because they banged me up for supporting democracy." Mr Staunton added, "You can't say anything now, because people will point their finger and cry 'harassment'."[479]

Of course it is right that homosexuality has been decriminalised and that homosexuals are not victimised or persecuted. Rightly we are a more tolerant society. However in 2005 the author Lynette Burrows was interviewed on BBC Radio Five Live; she expressed the view that children ideally need a male and female parent, so she questioned the wisdom of gay adoption. The following day she was phoned by the police; they said that a homophobic incident had been logged against her name. She asked if she had committed a crime. "No, but it will be logged against you, as a homophobic incident" was the chilling reply. In 2003 Peter Forster, the Bishop of Chester, said, "Some people who are primarily homosexual can re-orientate themselves." Two uniformed policemen went round to his home and interrogated him; they sent a report to the Crown Prosecution Service recommending that he be prosecuted. The Chief Constable of Cheshire publicly warned the bishop to stop expressing such views. The Bishop never repeated them. The solution here is obvious: clergy must remember to submit their sermons to the local police for clearance beforehand. Writing in *The Times* in 2006 the homosexual journalist Matthew Parris wrote: "I think sexuality is a supple as well as a subtle thing, and can sometimes be influenced, even promoted; I think that in some people some drives can be discouraged and others encouraged; I think some people can choose." [480] So the Bishop's view, that some people have an element of choice in sexual orientation, has support from within the gay community.

Political Correctness

Lenin coined the term 'political correctness' in 1922.[481] He wrote, "The fundamental idea is clear: to bring forward a politically correct statute, which sets out the essence and justification of terror." Political correctness meant not deviating from the party line. It was enforced by terror. Anyone not following the party could be denounced as an enemy of the people. Language became a weapon in the imposition of communist views. The politically incorrect were horrifically tortured and worked to death in appalling conditions. Lenin aimed to make his opponents too frightened to express any contrary views. The historian Robert Conquest described the Stalinist terror as driven by "a determination to break the idea of truth, to impose on everyone the acceptance of official falsehood."[482] In

---

[479] Daily Telegraph July 10th 1999
[480] The Times 5.8/06
[481] Frank Ellis *Political Correctness* letter to Kursii dated 17th May 1922
[482] Robert Conquest (Oxford University Press, 1990) p. 131

Pasternak's novel *Doctor Zhivago* one of the characters speculates that the Communist Party resorted to thought control to stop people speaking about the tens of millions, who had died in the state created famines and the death camps.[483] China under communism experienced similar methods. One Maoist pamphlet said, "China needs unifying thought, revolutionary thought, correct thought. That is Mao Tse-tung thought."[484] The Chinese gulag was used to "educate" people with incorrect views, destroying them mentally by threatening them with violence.

Political correctness is used to control our language just as in Orwell's *Nineteen Eighty-four*. The guidance given to public services on communication has been revealed. Banned words include 'morning' 'evening' 'afternoon' 'child' 'businessman' 'youth' 'youngster' 'homosexual' and 'heterosexual'. Worcestershire Police have a pamphlet for employees called *Communication: Some Do's and Don'ts*. It says when communicating with ethnic minorities, "Don't assume that words for the time of day have the same meaning." A spokesman explained that terms such as 'afternoon' and 'evening' are somewhat subjective in meaning and can vary according to a person's culture and we need to be aware of it. So PC Plod must ensure that he is fully aware of all the subtle linguistic nuances of all the cultures of the world, and then adapt his own language to ensure that it fits in with other people's understanding of the word 'morning' or whatever. Perhaps we should take this further, there may also be a subjective element in the use of the words – 'tree' or 'dog' or 'green'. The Essex Police and the Northern Ireland Fire Service issued a booklet, which instructs employees to avoid words such as "child, youth or youngster" because these may have "connotations of inexperience, impetuosity, and unreliability, even dishonesty". It advised that the words 'boy' and 'girl' may cause offence and banned words including: 'manning the phones' 'fireman' 'taxman' 'layman's terms' etc.

Terence Blacker, a columnist on *The Independent*, wrote "for too long the liberal establishment has been talking and listening only to itself … all the right prejudices are played back to us by those, who share the same general view in the media. There is no room here for argument. Those outside the bubble are rarely heard, hardly ever taken seriously. A mindless almost fundamentalist form of rejection is taking place, one that brooks no disagreement, that responds to alien political or religious positions with an unthinking contempt." He described how liberals enforce their hegemony, "Those who disagree are shifted out to the margins and ignored. Columnists who break the consensus are forced to apologise. Politicians who let slip inappropriate views are vilified. Anyone who unbalances decent liberalism is quietly excluded from the debate."[485] In the 1990s Peter Jenkins, the former associate editor of *The Independent*, forewarned Britain of the dangers of political correctness. He described the PC movement as "disturbing and

---

[483] Boris Pasternak *Dr. Zhivago* (Milan Feltrinelli 1957) p. 519
[484] Documents on the great Proletarian Cultural Revolution in China. Foreign Language Press Peking 1970 p. 240
[485] The Independent 10th November 2004

a threat to freedom and cultural traditions".[486] The PC codes adopted by American universities were incompatible with free speech. He claimed, "The second prong of the PC movement is more sinister". The great names Plato, Chaucer, Shakespeare, Milton, Goethe and Voltaire are dismissed as DWEMs (Dead White European Males). He wrote, "The thrust of the PC movement is towards the repudiation of the whole Western cultural tradition." He wrote, "multiculturalism is being promoted as a dogma" - reading lists are purged, free speech is suppressed and non PC teachers are persecuted. "The intolerant zeal of the extreme multiculturalists invites comparison with the McCarthyism of the 1950s. Its innate silliness encourages the hope it will blow itself out, but for the moment it is subverting the cultural foundations of the US, and we should be on our guard against its contagions".[487] His forewarnings were ignored.

In the past people used to say "Britain is a free country". No longer. A Yougov poll showed that only one third of people believe there is freedom of speech in Britain and only 20% said they felt free to say what they thought on a sensitive subject .[488] Political correctness also prevents discussion of problems such as world population growth. David Attenborough, who heads the Optimum Population Trust, has described a 'curious taboo' which prevents the discussion of world population growth. By 2050 it will have increased to 10,000,000,000 an increase of 3,000,000,000. This could easily lead to wars for scarce resources, such as water, and condemn billions of people to poverty. However political correctness prevents discussion, lest it should seem that the West is saying that people in the third world are having too many babies. In Britain on present trends according to the Office for National Statistics (ONS) population is expected to grow by nearly 17 million to 77.2 million by 2050. The projected figure for 2076 is 84 million. An opinion poll found that a third of the British public regard population growth as our most serious problem, but political parties shy away from dealing with it. [489] A study published by *Migrationwatch* in 2011 found that immigration was responsible for almost 40% of the growth in households between 2001 and 2008.[490] It stated, "Looking ahead, 36% of new households will, according to official projections, be a result of immigration so we will have to build, on average, 200 homes a day for the next 25 years just to house the extra population arising from immigration. Even if house building were to increase by 25% over the current level to 200,000 a year, there would be a shortage of around 800,000 homes by 2033 - equivalent to the number of homes in Leeds, Manchester, Newcastle and Nottingham combined." Sir Andrew Green, Chairman of Migrationwatch UK, commented "Political correctness has dictated that the construction and planning industry should not refer to the massive impact of

---

[486] Peter Jenkins *The Independent* 10th November 2004
[487] Peter Jenkins *The Independent* 10th November 2004
[488] Survey for 'Friction TV' cited by James Delingpole in his book *How to be Right*
[489] Ipsos-Mori poll, August 2006
[490] Migrationwatch (Briefing Paper No 7.13) September 1st 2011

immigration on housing."[491] In September 2011 the Royal Institute of British Architects reported, "Many new houses are shameful shoeboxes which are too small for family life. This squeeze on size is depriving thousands of families the space needed for children to do homework, adults to work from home, guests to stay and for members of the household to relax together."[492]

So Orwell was right to forewarn us: Britain has become more totalitarian. The police do attempt to silence those with politically incorrect views. There is an orthodoxy which cannot be questioned. The opposite approach is summed up in the remark attributed to Voltaire, "I may disagree with what you say, but I will defend to the death your right to say it." He stands for an older tolerant form of liberalism, that believed in freedom, including freedom of speech (the negative concept of liberty). However modern liberals feel justified in taking away freedom of speech and browbeating and coercing others (the positive concept of liberty). What we have now is: illiberal liberalism, intolerance in the name of tolerance, and tyranny masquerading as virtue.

"Liberalism is totalitarianism with a human face."[493]
Thomas Sowell

"I believe that totalitarian ideas have taken root in the minds of intellectuals everywhere."[494]
George Orwell

---

[491] Migrationwatch website September 13th 2011
[492] Royal Institute of British Architects Report 14th September 2011
[493] Thomas Sowell attributed but unsourced
[494] George Orwell *The Prevention of Literature* in *The Collected Essays Etc* ed S Orwell & I Angus (London Secker & Warburg 1968) Vol IV p. 502

CHAPTER 13

The Dark Side of Liberalism:
Atrocities by Secularists and Rationalists

Were atheistic regimes the most evil in history?

The French Revolution was the first occasion in history when an 'anti-clerical' and self-styled 'non-religious' state embarked on mass murder that anticipated many twentieth century horrors. The secular state was capable of unimaginable barbarity... in what was tantamount to genocide. [495]

Michael Burleigh in *Earthly Powers*

There are dark eras in the history of European rationalism including one genocide committed in the name of Reason.[496]

Michael Burleigh

Carrier came down to the Loire and slew,
Till all the ways and the waves waxed red:
Bound and drowned, slaying two by two,
Maidens and young men, naked and wed.[497]
Swinburne (*Les Noyades*)

The Nazi holocaust was not the only ideologically inspired holocaust in the twentieth century, and intellectuals are only beginning to assimilate the lessons of the others: the mass killings in the Soviet Union, China, Cambodia and other totalitarian states carried out in the name of Marxism.[498]

Steven Pinker

Asked to name the most evil man of the 20th century most would answer Hitler. But there are other candidates – Stalin and Mao. This does not detract from the wickedness of Hitler and the Nazis. It merely points out that for brutality and mass killings they can match Hitler corpse for corpse; and some leading historians - Robert Conquest, Roy Medvedev of Russia and Norman Davies - estimate Stalin was responsible 51 million deaths in peacetime in the USSR. (A breakdown of these figures is at the end of the chapter.) In Stalin's state-planned terror-famine in the Ukraine 6,500,000 died and in the death camps of the gulag an estimated 17,000,000 lost their lives. So why is one evil monster well known and the others largely ignored? The answer is liberal bias. Pinker, who is Jewish, points out that intellectuals are now debating, "Whether the atrocities (of the communists) were worse than the Nazi

---

[495] Michael Burleigh *Earthly Powers* (HarperCollins London 2005) p. 97
[496] Burleigh p. xi
[497] Swinburne *Les Noyades*
[498] Steven Pinker *The Blank Slate* (London Allen Lane 2002) p.155

Holocaust, or only equivalent."[499] Altogether atheistic communist regimes have a death toll of approximately 121,000,000. Some atheists claim that they are morally superior to theists. But the historical evidence shows that atheistic regimes have been amongst the most evil in history - if not the most evil.

I start with events during the atheistic phase of the French Revolution. The ideals of the Enlightenment - reason, science, secularism, freedom, equality, tolerance and brotherly love - were forged in France into a powerful weapon against the ancien regime and contributed to the French Revolution of 1789. The Enlightenment had taken an atheistic turn in France because much of the French Catholic Church had become rich and powerful. There was no equivalent anti-Christian feeling in Protestant areas like Germany, the United States, Britain and the Netherlands. Before the Revolution there had been 40,000 parishes in France, by 1794 only 150 still celebrated the mass. So did the Revolution bring about reason, brotherly love and tolerance? Or were the idealists, who preached brotherhood and a godless Utopia, and yearned for a perfect society, among the most brutal, bigoted and barbaric in history?

In 1789 the Rights of Man were declared; history and tradition were rejected; a new calendar was created - starting again at year one and eliminating all Christian festivals and Sundays. Simon Shama in *Citizens,* his masterly account of the French Revolution, records that in the September Massacres of 1792 two thousand were slaughtered in cold blood, including three bishops and over two hundred priests. At Bicêtre there occurred the "systematic butchering of adolescent boys"[500] some as young as twelve and thirteen. At Abbaye twenty-four priests were hacked to death. He concluded, "The massacres reveal the true nature of the Revolution: its dependence on organised killing."[501] The Jacobins, who seized power in 1793 attempted to eliminate religion by violence. They rejected the notion of sin and thought people's natural goodness would emerge once oppression had ended. They believed science would replace religion. Their catechism stated "A child is like soft wax capable of receiving any imprint one wishes."[502] The imprint in their case was atheism.

They attempted to dechristianise France; churches were ransacked, stripped of all Christian iconography and in many cases closed; priests were murdered and crucifixes smashed; the Catholic mass was forbidden[503]; and Christians subjected to abuse. Many churches were 'debaptised' in secular ceremonies and turned into 'Temples of Reason'. Chaumette devised secular services for the worship of Reason: songs were sung praising Reason; officials bent the knee to a figure representing Reason. Nôtre Dame in Paris on 10th

---

[499] Pinker p.155

[500] Simon Schama *Citizens* (Penguin Books London 1989) p. 634

[501] Schama p. 637

[502] The Jacobin catechism is quoted in Michael Burleigh *Earthly Powers* (HarperCollins London 2005) p. 82

[503] In May 1793 and again by the law of 24 November 1794

November 1793 was the setting for 'La Fête de la Liberté', where an actress sitting on a pile of papier-mâché represented 'Reason'. The Jacobins went on to inaugurate in 1793 the Reign of Terror in which over 55,000 died, most at the guillotine after perfunctory trials. People were arrested on mere suspicion - often from informers, who had their own axes to grind. Schama described the Jacobins as in favour of "unrelenting surveillance, indictment, humiliation and death."[504] One Jacobin, Claude Javogues in the Loire, promised, "One day blood will flow down these streets like water after a downpour" and said "I will relish the pleasure of having all these buggers guillotined."[505] The Jacobins were zealots for both the Reign of Terror and for atheism. Simon Schama maintains the French Revolution's unconscionable slaughters cannot be justified.[506] He describes the Reign of Terror and the killings as a "human catastrophe of colossal propositions" carried out by "enthusiastic Terror-ists (sic) and dechristianisers."[507]

The revolt against state imposed atheism

In poor communities many parish clergy had performed a valued role and here the attack on Christianity was strongly resisted. Republicans had toured the countryside burning down churches, smashing religious symbols like crucifixes and killing priests. In March 1793 under the banner of "For God and the King" a rebellion broke out in the Vendée in the west of France. The rebels' manifesto declared, "You have introduced atheism in the place of religion, anarchy in place of the law, men who are tyrants in the place of the King. You reproach us with religious fanaticism, you whose pretensions to freedom have led to extreme penalties." On 1st August 1793 the French Convention responded by voting for the destruction of the Vendée and the extermination of its inhabitants: *"Soldats de la liberté, it fault que les brigands de la Vendée soient exterminés."* (Soldiers of freedom it is necessary to exterminate the brigands of the Vendée)[508] After some initial success the rebels were defeated and large numbers were taken prisoner.

Extermination camps were set up at Noirmoutier and elsewhere. Troops were ordered, "to burn down everything and to spear with your bayonets all the inhabitants you meet. We must sacrifice all and burn all the towns and villages."[509] General Turreau instructed his soldiers to kill women and children as a priority. He promised to turn the Vendée into a cemetery. Justice was abandoned: there were no trials of the accused. Various methods of mass killing

---

[504] Schama p. 806
[505] Schama p. 767
[506] Schama p. 791
[507] Schama p. 839
[508] *Le Livre Noir de la Revolution Francaise* (Cerf Paris 2008) p. 232
[509] *Le Livre Noir de la Revolution Francaise* p. 232

were tried: children and women were thrown into red hot ovens; water and bread were poisoned; mass shootings and later mass drownings took place; thousands of prisoners were lined up in fields and shot by firing squads. 'Infernal columns' - marauding bands of soldiers – killed, raped, pillaged, razed churches to the ground and burned people to death in barns and churches. At Gonnard two hundred old people, plus mothers and children were forced to dig a large pit, then kneel down in front of it, so when they were shot, they fell into the pit: thirty children and two women were buried alive. Beaudesson reported seeing fathers, mothers and children of all ages naked and swimming in blood. The generals in charge promised to make the land a desert: they burnt crops and farms, slaughtered herds and razed villages to the ground. Gracchus Babeuf, writing at the time, coined a new word – populicide. We call it genocide. In the words of Simon Schama, "Every atrocity the time could imagine was meted out to the defenceless population. Women were routinely raped, children killed, both mutilated."[510]

The father of Victor Hugo, Joseph Hugo, acting on instructions, massacred whole villages and church congregations. He wrote, "Wherever we go we bring flames and death. Neither do we respect age or sex. A soldier kills three women with his bare hands. It's horrific. We shoot everyone. Everywhere are bodies and flames."[511] Men were castrated and their testicles worn as earrings.[512] In the case of women the order was, "*Faire exploser des cartouches dans l'appareil génital des femmes*"[513](Explode your cartridges in women's genitals). Mass shootings took place in Angers and Laval. Children were not spared because they were deemed to be "brigands to be". Even loyal Republicans were shocked. Men like Mariteau, the mayor of Fontenay-le-Comte, wrote, "It was a scene of horror - no-one was spared men, women, children, babies feeding at the breast, pregnant women, all perished. They burnt the wheat in the fields and the grain in the barns; all the animals were slaughtered. The orders were to massacre, shoot and burn everything they found."[514]

General Westermann reported to the Committee of Public Safety in Paris as follows, "There is no more Vendée. It died with its wives and its children by our free sabres. I have just buried it in the woods and the swamps. According to the orders that you gave me, I crushed the children under the feet of the horses, massacred the women, who at least will not give birth to any more brigands. I do not have a single prisoner to reproach me. I have exterminated them all. The roads are sown with corpses. At Savenay, brigands are arriving all the time

---

[510] Schama p. 791
[511] Burleigh p. 100
[512] *Le Livre Noir de la Revolution Francaise* p 233
[513] *Le Livre Noir de la Revolution Francaise* p 233
[514] *Le Livre Noir de la Revolution Francaise* p 234

wanting to surrender. We shoot them all. Mercy is not a revolutionary sentiment."[515]

Jean-Baptiste Carrier, in overall charge of suppressing the revolt, stated on 23rd February 1794, "The Vendéens will all be exterminated."[516] He invented the 'Bagnoire Nationale' - stripping men and women naked; tying a man and a women back to back, leaving them shivering in the cold for hours; then throwing them into the river to drown. For added merriment a monk and a nun were tied together. Nantes on the River Loire had a wide river and a plentiful supply of shallow bottomed boats. Carrier devised a system for mass drownings called 'noyades'. Boats were crammed full of prisoners and the hatches were closed. Then the boats were sunk. Once the captives had all drowned, the boats were refloated and taken back to the river bank, ready for the next batch. Anyone who tried to clamber out had their hands hacked off. At Bourgneuf and Nantes special drownings were organised for children.[517] The boatloads of prisoners drowned were called 'cargoes' – the same word was used by the Nazis in their genocide, according to Michael Burleigh.[518]

It is estimated that the total death toll was around 250,000. Historians Simon Schama, Michael Burleigh and Norman Davies all see a parallel between these mass killings and those of the Nazis. For Norman Davies the 'Noyades' foreshadow the Nazi extermination of Jews, Slavs, gypsies and other 'undesirables'. Both Nazis and secularists wanted to kill large numbers of people quickly. The Nazis chose gas chambers, the secularists drownings and shootings.[519] For Simon Schama they are "a sinister anticipation of the technological killing of the twentieth century"[520] and for Michael Burleigh a genocide committed in the name of Reason.[521] In the short-lived Paris Commune of 1870 Jacobin ideas resurfaced and again led to bloodshed. The Archbishop of Paris and seventy clergy were bayoneted or shot. Half of Paris's churches were turned into stores or rooms for political debates. Dostoevsky following events from Russia wrote, "It's the same old Rousseau and the dream of recreating the world anew through reason and knowledge. They chop off heads – why? Because that's the easiest of all. They wish for the happiness of man ... that is a fantasy. That madness doesn't seem to them a monstrosity."[522]

---

[515] Schama p. 788
[516] Le Livre Noir de la Revolution Francaise p. 234
[517] Le Livre Noir de la Revolution Francaise p. 232
[518] Burleigh p. 101
[519] Norman Davies Europe (Pimlico London 1997) p. 706
[520] Schama p. 789
[521] Burleigh p. xi
[522] Fyodor Dostoyevsky Complete Letters ed. And trans. David Lowe (Ann Arbor 1989) Vol 3, nr 428 p. 360

Atheistic Communism

Communist values derive from the Enlightenment: science, rationalism, secularism, progress, equality and the belief that human nature is malleable and perfectible; plus the method of the Jacobins – violence. As the philosopher John Gray observed, "Soviet communism was an Enlightenment ideology."[523] Communists thought they could create a perfect society. They were atheists who sought to eliminate religion, which was seen as unscientific and backward. Lenin attacked religion as vile, abominable and filthy.

Before the Revolution in October 1917 there had been 100 million Orthodox believers in Russia, 54,450 churches and 57,100 priests and 94,000 monks and nuns.[524] After the revolution priests were declared class enemies; their children banned from schools; religious instruction forbidden; almost all monasteries closed; cathedrals turned into anti-God museums, or defaced or demolished. Education promoted the new state religion of 'scientific atheism'. Every subject taught was slanted against religion and in favour of atheism. "The League of the Militant Godless" was established to eradicate religion. In 1922 Patriarch Tiklon protested to Lenin that thousands of clergy and over 100,000 believers had been killed. Many killings were gruesome. Aleksandr Yakovlev, an advisor to Gorbachev, researched previously secret documents and recorded that "bishops were mutilated, castrated, frozen to death by being doused with freezing cold water, strapped to the paddlewheel of a steamboat, buried alive, crucified and burned."[525]

It is sometimes claimed that communism had an initial benign phase and later went off the rails. However from the beginning Lenin favoured the use of terror. In 1917 he called for a "war to the death against the rich, idlers and parasites."[526] Orlando Figes' history of the Russian Revolution called, *A People's Tragedy* described Lenin as an advocate of mass terror. Figes wrote, "Lenin always stressed that communism was a system of organised violence."[527] Some of this violence was directed against religion. Figes again, "From 1921 the war against religion moved from words and rituals to the closure of churches and shooting priests. Lenin instigated a totally gratuitous Reign of Terror."[528] On 26th February 1922 Lenin ordered that all valuables, including those used in worship were to be seized. Battles were fought between troops with machine-guns and women and men with pitch-forks and rusty rifles. 7,100

---

[523] John Gray *Enlightenment's Wake* (Routledge London 2007) p. 48
[524] Robert Conquest in *The Harvest of Sorrows* (London Pimlico 2002) p. 200
[525] Aleksandr Yakovlev *A Century of Violence in Soviet Russia* 2002 Paul Froese *The Plot to Kill God* (USA University of California Press) p. 49
[526] V I Lenin *How to Organise Competition* December 1917 cited by Orlando Figes *A People's Tragedy* (Pimlico London 1997) p. 524
[527] Orlando Figes *A People's Tragedy* (Pimlico London 1997) p. 525
[528] Figes p. 748

religious people were killed, of whom 3,500 were nuns. In March 1922 Lenin issued a secret order that the clergy were to be exterminated. He wrote, "I have come to the unequivocal conclusion that we must now wage the most decisive and merciless war against the clergy and suppress resistance with such cruelty that they will not forget it for years to come... The more members of the reactionary bourgeoisie and clergy we manage to shoot the better."[529] This secret order, first published in 1990, reveals in the words of Figes, "The cruel streak in Lenin's nature. It undermines the 'soft' image of Lenin previously favoured by left-wing historians who would have us believe that the 1920s were a hopeful period before the onset of Stalinism."[530] The historian Robert Conquest claims there is now plenty of evidence that Lenin insisted on mass shootings and hangings. All this makes a nonsense of Richard Dawkins' claim that when atheists carry out atrocities they are not motivated by atheism. The atheists targeted and killed people because they were religious, and they did so on a massive scale.

Lesley Chamberlain in her book *The Philosophy Steamer* recorded that in 1922 the secret police rounded up intellectuals and sent them into exile. Maxim Gorky, a leader of the Revolution, protested to Lenin, "Scholars should be treated with care and respect. We are decapitating the people, destroying our own brain."[531] Lenin replied, "Intellectuals are shit."[532] She commented, "One of the key aims of communism was to destroy religion in Russia.... Marxists objected to faith because it sanctioned an inner life, which allowed freedom of thought. Soviet totalitarianism meant denying individuals an inner life."[533] Lenin devised political correctness which forbade any views other than the state's. Opponents ceased to be human beings and became 'capitalists', 'enemies of the people', 'bloodsuckers', 'parasites' and 'lice'. Once they had been dehumanised they could be eliminated. Gorky, observed in 1918, "We are destroying the spiritual capital of the Russian people...We are breeding a new crop of brutal and corrupt bureaucrats and a terrible new generation of youth, who laugh at daily bloody scenes of beatings, shootings, cripplings and killings."[534] Lenin was wholly indifferent to human suffering. His comment on the Russian famine of 1891-2 was, "This talk of feeding the starving masses is nothing but the expression of saccharine sweet sentimentality characteristic of

---

[529] Figes p. 749

[530] Figes p. 749

[531] Quoted in Arkadi Vaksberg, *Le Mystere Gorki* (Paris: Albin Michel, 1997) p 111 Quoted in Stephane Courtois ed *Black Book of Communism: Crimes Terror and Repression* (Cambridge USA Harvard University Press 1999) p. 737

[532] Quoted in Stephane Courtois ed *Black Book of Communism* (Cambridge USA Harvard University Press 1999) p. 737

[533] Lesley Chamberlain *The Philosophy Steamer* (Atlantic Books London 2006) p. 61

[534] Bertram Wolfe *The Bridge and The Abyss The Troubled Friendship of Gorky and Lenin* (London 1967) p. 67

the intelligentsia."[535] According to Gorky "Lenin had no pity for the mass of the people" and "the working classes are to Lenin, what metals are to a metallurgist".[536]

The terror famine

If you had been wandering around the Russian countryside in the 1920s and 1930s you would have been shocked by the poverty - peasants eking out a meagre living. Communist theory divides these people into two groups - the bourgeoisie (owners of capital) and the proletariat (workers without capital). Some by hard work had improved their lot slightly – maybe buying a horse or hiring a man to help with harvest. But that could be a fatal mistake - literally fatal - because to the communist by buying a horse or hiring labour, you moved from the proletariat to the bourgeoisie, and became a class enemy - a kulak. These absurd communist distinctions led to the deaths of millions.

In the Ukraine Stalin eliminated the kulaks by starvation, because he wanted to establish collective farms to comply with socialist ideology, and to gain greater control of agriculture. By setting unreasonably high quotas of grain, which the peasants had to hand over to the state, they were left without enough to eat. Over six million starved to death. The borders of the Ukraine were guarded to prevent any food entering. Those caught trying to smuggle food in were severely punished. This proves that it was the intention to starve people to death. While peasants starved to death, the communists feasted before their eyes, and refused to allow the peasants to take from the huge mountains of grain, which were allowed to rot. Mothers were shot for gleaning a few grains of wheat to feed their starving children, after their husbands had been sent to the Arctic gulags. Why was the Ukraine targeted? Both Marx and Engels had racist attitudes towards the Ukrainians. Karl Marx wrote, "Except for the Poles, the Russians and at the best the Slavs in Turkey, no Slavic people has a future"[537] and Engels, "I have damned little sympathy for the small Slavic peoples."[538] The Ukraine was ethnically and culturally different from Russia. Stalin feared that it would break away and become a separate country. It is that now.

A young communist called Kopelev gave this account of his part in the terror famine, "I heard the children choking, coughing with screams... I saw the men frightened, pleading, impassive. I explained to myself that I was realising an historical necessity. Our goal was the triumph of communism and everything was permitted – to lie, to steal, to destroy hundreds of thousands and even

---

[535] quoted by Robert Conquest *Dragons of Expectation* (London Gerald Duckworth 2005) p. 93

[536] Conquest p. 93

[537] Karl Marx *Democratic Panslavism* Neue Rheinische Zeitung February 1849

[538] Friedrch Engels letter to Karl Kautsky 7th February 1882 Marx and Engels Collected Works, New York 1973 v 10, p. 393

millions of people, anyone who stood in our way. We mercilessly stripped the peasants of their grain, deaf to children's cries and women's wails. We knew better than the peasants how they should live. I did not curse those who had sent me to take away the peasants' grain and force skeleton-thin people to go into the fields to achieve the communist sowing plan. I did not lose my faith. I wanted to believe."[539]

In 1932 *The Manchester Guardian* sent Malcolm Muggeridge to Moscow as its correspondent. Like many intellectuals he was originally besotted with communism, but he soon became disillusioned. Others turned a blind eye to the cruelty, injustice and barbarity, and continued to praise the USSR. He reported on the famine: the hunger, the hopelessness, the loading of peasants at gun-point onto cattle-trucks at dawn, to be sent to some Arctic gulag, from which few if any returned. He described it thus, "This particular famine was planned and deliberate; not due to a natural catastrophe like failure of rain. An administrative famine brought about by the forced collectivisation of agriculture."[540] Of the western liberals visiting the Ukraine he wrote, "Travelling with radiant optimism through a famished countryside, wandering in happy bands about squalid overcrowded towns, listening with unshakeable faith to the fatuous patter of carefully indoctrinated guides, repeating the bogus statistics and mindless slogans – all chanting the praises of Stalin and the Dictatorship of the Proletariat."[541] He concluded that people's credulity is unshakeable. They want to believe everyone is nice. He recorded how almost all the luminaries of the liberal-left were in denial - Beatrice and Sidney Webb, G.B. Shaw, H. G. Wells, Harold Laski and Julian Huxley. The American journalist Lincoln Steffens on his return from Russia in 1921 remarked, "I have seen the future, and it works." Muggeridge described them: "All resolved, come what may, to believe anything, however preposterous, to overlook anything, however villainous, to approve anything however brutally authoritarian, in order to preserve intact the confident expectation, that one of the most thorough-going, ruthless and bloody tyrannies, could be relied on to champion human freedom, the brotherhood of man, and all other good liberal causes to which they had dedicated their lives."[542] He recounted that in despair he turned for solace to Dostoevsky, who had "so brilliantly and devastatingly exposed the vain hopes and destructive purposes of the liberal mind."[543]

---

[539] Kopelev pp 11-12 cited by Robert Conquest in *The Harvest of Sorrows* (London Pimlico 2002) p. 233
[540] Malcolm Muggeridge *Chronicles of Wasted Time Vol:1 The Green Stick* (Fontana Glasgow 1975) p. 286
[541] Muggeridge p. 272
[542] Muggeridge p. 307
[543] Muggeridge p. 296

The Soviet Terror

In addition to the millions of deaths in the famines, millions more were sent to horrific prison camps in Siberia and the Arctic regions and never heard of again. They were transported in cattle trucks – for days, sometimes for weeks - with no heating, no food, no sanitation and in some cases no water. Seventeen million died from starvation, cold, hunger and disease. In the frozen north they were underfed and worked to death. It is estimated that over 90% died in these harsh conditions, in what were in effect death camps. Sometimes the trains carrying the prisoners stopped in the middle of a frozen wasteland. The prisoners were ordered off the train and told to build a camp where they were. They complained there was no food; a truck arrived with flour which it dumped; but they had neither ovens nor yeast, and so could not even bake bread. So they mixed a paste of flour and water, which was polluted, resulting in widespread sickness and death. Other prisoners were killed by drowning, reminiscent of the French Revolution. The brutality and inhumanity cannot be overstated.[544] The poet Irina Ratushinskaya described her life in prison tortured by hunger and cold and saw herself as "a victim of those who are full of hatred of God."[545] In the persecution of 1937-41 thousands of clergy plus hundreds of thousands of individual believers were killed. 97% of Russian churches, which had been functioning in 1916, were closed by 1940. In total it is estimated that 40,000 priests as well as 40,000 monks and nuns were killed.[546]

In 1936 Stalin began what came to be known as 'The Great Terror'. There would be a knock on the door in the middle of the night. The person arrested would be taken away to the Lubyanka or some other prison. Terrible beatings would begin – sadistic and brutal. Stalin's instructions were to beat and beat and beat again. Any sign of unwillingness to beat viciously and you could become a victim yourself. Fists, boots and table legs were used to beat prisoners senseless. People emerged unable to walk without help, with broken backbones, broken limbs, broken ribs and broken wrists. Sometimes they would urinate blood for a week afterwards. Wives were brought in to witness their husbands' beatings; and the daughters of those being interrogated were brutally raped in front of them. Prisoners were held in special hot and cold cells. In the hot cells prisoners would swelter, and in the cold ones they shivered all the time. Some cells were flooded with water, so prisoners' feet were always wet. On top of all this prisoners were not given enough food or clothing. The overcrowding in the cells was chronic - in some cases the prisoners had to stand all the time for lack of space.

---

[544] Paul Froese *The Plot to Kill God* (California University of California Press) p. 50
[545] Irana Ratushinskaya cited by Paul Froese *The Plot to Kill God* p 8
[546] Diarmaid MacCulloch BBC TV Programme *A History of Christianity* :Programme on Orthodoxy 2010

Prisoners were subjected to relentless interrogation for days on end - known as the conveyor. Interrogators operated in shifts, while those interrogated were denied sleep, food and daylight. Denial of sleep took various forms - including being woken up every 10 minutes. Some were made to stand for hours on tip-toe, or seated on chairs from which the seat had been removed. A torture called 'The swallow' was used: arms and legs were tied together behind the back, and then the prisoner was hoisted in the air and left for hours or days. The relentless questioning, accompanied by lack of sleep and food, led to confessions to crimes they had not committed. They were promised that if they confessed, they would be shown mercy. At their trials they pleaded guilty, thinking they would be spared. They were all shot. Western observers at the trials were easily duped into thinking that the due process of law had taken place - blithely ignorant of the means by which the confessions had been obtained. In total over one million died. As a result everyone lived in great fear. At a diplomatic party in Moscow Muggeridge asked an officer in the secret police why they arrested innocent people. He laughed. They wanted everyone to be frightened. If they arrested and tortured only the guilty, the innocent would not feel afraid. In his book *The Whisperers* Orlando Figes chronicled a society where people would only whisper the truth to their closest kin and friends.

China and elsewhere

Jung Chang's bestselling book *Wild Swans* gave an account of life during the cultural revolution in China and became an international best-seller. Now with her husband, the British historian Jon Halliday, she has written a biography of Mao called: *Mao: The Unknown Story*. It is a tale of brutality, inhumanity, mass murder, the destruction of traditional culture, and attacks on religion in the name of 'scientific atheism'. I have used their book as my main source. Their well documented assertion is that Mao was responsible for the deaths of over 70 million Chinese: 38 million by starvation and 27 million in the Chinese gulags where prisoners were underfed, overworked, worked to death, executed, tortured or committed suicide as a result of tortures.[547] In addition tens of millions were put under surveillance and lived in dread of arrest and being sent to the gulag.

The authors conclude that Mao enjoyed killing people - especially slowly, so they suffered more. Mao rejected traditional ideas on: marriage, property and religion. He declared, "The country must be destroyed and reformed."[548] and "We have no duty to other people."[549] He learnt from Stalin the use of terror and violence to control a population and would complain to his subordinates,

---

[547] J Chang and J Halliday *Mao The Unknown Story* (London Jonathan Cape 2005) p. 338
[548] J Chang and J Halliday p. 15
[549] J Chang and J Halliday p. 13

"You're not killing enough people."[550] Like Stalin, Mao began a war against the peasants. Collective farms were established, which conformed to Marxist ideology and gave him greater control. Unreasonable food quotas were set and the peasants were forced to yield up grain, so he could sell it to the Soviet Union and buy weapons. The resulting shortages led to starvation and terrible beatings of the peasants. There were over 250,000 suicides. But Mao was not content. He urged greater brutality saying, "We must kill, and say it is good to kill."[551] and "We must arrest 1.5 million."[552] If the starving peasants tried to hide some of the grain and were caught they were executed, sometimes by being buried alive. Some were strangled to death; or had their noses cut off; one small boy tried to take a scrap of unripe fruit and had four fingers chopped off. Often the food expropriated from the peasants rotted in large granaries. Yet Mao insisted that no grain be given to the peasants, even if they were starving to death, "Absolutely no opening of the granaries even if the people are starving."[553] He declared, "We are willing to sacrifice 300 million Chinese for the victory of world revolution,"[554] and "Half of China may have to die."[555] Mao even set quotas of between 1% and 10% for the number of peasants to be killed in each province. Meanwhile he lived in great luxury with numerous villas and servants.

In 1950 Mao set about 'liberating' Tibet from religion, by invading it and imposing 'scientific atheism'. After the conquest the Tibetans were brutally beaten and murdered. The Buddhist religion was central to the lives of Tibetans. One of its leaders, the Panchen Lama wrote, "People were beaten till they bled from their eyes, ears, mouths, noses; they passed out, their arms and legs broken... others died on the spot."[556] He added that of 2,500 monasteries in 1950 only 70 were left by 1961, and over the same period the numbers of monks and nuns reduced from 110,000 to 7,000. Mao in 1959 declared to the Dalai Lama "Religion is poison. It has two great defects: it undermines the race ... and retards the progress of the country. Tibet and Mongolia have both been poisoned by it."[557] Celibate monks and nuns were forced to marry; their holy scriptures were used for manure; pictures of the Buddha were abused; monasteries destroyed; and statues of the Buddha smashed. Suicide became common for the first time in Tibet. Between 15% and 20% of all Tibetans and half of adult males were thrown into prison and worked to death.[558] They were

---

[550] J Chang and J Halliday p. 337
[551] J Chang and J Halliday p. 434
[552] J Chang and J Halliday p. 411
[553] J Chang and J Halliday p. 456
[554] J Chang and J Halliday p. 457
[555] J Chang and J Halliday p. 457
[556] J Chang and J Halliday p. 476
[557] Mao in conversation with the Dalai Lama in 1959
[558] J Chang and J Halliday p. 476

flogged with wire whips while pulling heavy ploughs. Mao also attacked religion in China: he ordered the destruction of the house in which Confucius had lived. Hundreds of Roman Catholic priests were executed, beaten, and suffered endless interrogations leading to many suicides.

Another of Mao's objectives was the destruction of traditional Chinese culture. In the Cultural Revolution which began in 1966, Mao incited pupils against their teachers and gave strong support to violence. Mao's henchman Lin Boa urged the Red Guards to "smash the old culture" and "don't be bound by moral rules from the past."[559] The Red Guards responded with slogans such as, "We will be brutal" and "We will strike you to the ground and trample on you." Books were burned; teachers denounced and deported to gulags, abused, manacled, their faces blackened; and women sexually molested. Some were beaten and forced to licked their blood off the ground; some tortured to death; some beaten to death and some executed. It is estimated that 11 million pupils went to Peking to be 'inspired' by Mao. Not a single school escaped the Red Guards and Cultural Revolution. The army was told not to intervene to restore law and order. It was openly admitted that the government policy was brainwashing. Chen Yi, a Foreign Minister of China, described the China of the Cultural Revolution as "one big torture chamber."[560]

Other communist countries suffered similar fates. In Cambodia Pol Pot and the Khmer Rouge were responsible for the deaths of two million by gruesome sadistic tortures, executions and starvation. Religion was forbidden; Buddhist temples destroyed; people caught praying were killed; the Roman Catholic cathedral was razed; Christian clergy and Muslim imams executed. In Mongolia 35,000 Buddhists were killed. In Albania article 37 of the constitution of 1976 stated, "The state supports atheistic propaganda in order to implant a scientific materialistic worldview on its people."[561] Religion was banned; all churches and mosques closed; museums of atheism established. The regime was repressive, cruel and tyrannical with no freedom of speech. In North Korea, modelled on the USSR of Stalin, an estimated 2 million died; it is still repressive, totalitarian and atheistic. Atheists who claim that atheism is superior to theism should try living in North Korea.

Have liberal historians distorted history?

According to Simon Schama liberal historians have turned a blind eye to atrocities when carried out by those they consider progressives e.g. in the French Revolution. He wrote, "Historians tend to avert their eyes ... the Anglophone tradition this century has a particularly egregious record of silent

---

[559] J Chang and J Halliday p. 540
[560] J Chang and J Halliday p. 546
[561] Albanian Constitution of 1976 Article 37

embarrassment."[562] He added that the atrocities and genocide were subject to "selective forgetfulness practised in the interests of scholarly decorum."[563] He added, "It does historians no credit to look aside,"[564] and "avert their gaze from these atrocities."[565] He regards the liberal account of the September Massacres by French historian Pierre Carron as a whitewash: "the scholarly normalisation of evil."[566] The French historian Reynard Sécher calls the events in the Vendée - genocide followed by memoricide. Mass murder followed by the killing of the memory. The British historian Norman Davies noted, "It has taken the best part of 200 years for France to come to terms with this terrible story of *populicide, of genocide franco-français*".[567]

Liberal historians focused on the horrors of the Nazis, while similar atrocities carried out by 'progressive' regimes were ignored. Stéphane Courtois, the editor of the Black Book of Communism, claims the "single-minded focus on the Jewish genocide is an attempt to characterise the holocaust as a unique event, and has prevented an assessment of other episodes of comparable magnitude in the communist world."[568] And "Hitler and Nazism are now a constant presence in Western print and television, whereas Stalin and communism materialise only sporadically."[569] He argues liberals have double standards: no Gulag camps have been turned into museums; no memorials for the millions who died under communism. Liberals give communism an easy ride. Courtois maintains "Western societies have refused to face the reality of communism."[570] Michael Burleigh commented "Critics, being on the liberal left, feel that their subscription to progressive ideals is sullied whenever communism, an offshoot of the Enlightenment and the French Revolution, is associated with nihilism of National Socialism."[571] Lesley Chamberlain, the author of *The Philosophy Steamer* (see above) admits historians ignored these atrocities by communists, because their sympathies were with them; she admitted, "As a secularist myself I have a great deal of sympathy with the historians."[572]

Steven Pinker rejects the approach of many historians which focuses on Nazis atrocities and ignores those of the communists. He sees Marxism and Nazism as remarkably similar. Both shared a vision of reshaping mankind through violent means, and saw history as a conflict between different groups:

---

[562] Schama p. 631
[563] Schama p. 632
[564] Schama p. 792
[565] Schama p. 631
[566] Schama p. 631
[567] Davies p. 707
[568] Courtois p. 23
[569] Courtois p. xiii
[570] Courtois p. 26
[571] Burleigh p. 2
[572] Chamberlain p. 8

for the Marxists these were based on class, for the Nazis race. The goal was the same - the transformation of society and the culmination of history; their means were violent conflict and mass murder. Liberals reserve their outrage for the mass murder on the grounds of race, while ignoring mass murder on the grounds of class. Pinker argues that liberal historians are now being forced to rethink their accounts, as more and more evidence becomes available of the cruelty and genocide of communist regimes in the Soviet Union, China, Cambodia and elsewhere. This re-evaluation is according to Pinker a wrenching experience for those who thought the Nazis were uniquely evil. The debate now is 'how many millions died under communism - over a hundred million or less'? Pinker commented, "The conviction that humanity could be reshaped by massive social engineering projects led to some of the greatest atrocities in history."[573] The rationalists' and atheists' claim to the moral high ground is based on ignorance of history. The hallmarks of atheistic regimes were persecution, oppression, brutality, cruelty and mass killings. Atheistic regimes *from the start* embarked on violence and have been amongst the most evil and bloodthirsty in all human history. The motivation of many of the killings was a hatred of religion. Totals of deaths under Soviet Communism excluding World War Two (see below) was compiled by historians Robert Conquest and Roy Medvedev and included in Norman Davies' book *Europe: A History*.[574]

DEATH TOLL IN SOVIET RUSSIA/ SOVIET UNION 1917-1953
EXCLUDING WORLD WAR TWO

Civil War and Volga Famine 1918-1922	4,000,000
Political repression 1920s	50,000
Forced collectivisation/"dekulakisation" after 1929	12,000,000
Ukrainian terror famine 1932-3	6,500,000
The Great Terror (1934-9) and purges	1,000,000
Deportations to the gulag to 1937	10,000,000
Shootings and random executions, 1937-9	1,000,000
Deportations Poland, Baltic States Romania, 1939-40	2,000,000
Foreign POWs: Poles, Finns, Romanians, Japanese	1,000,000
Deportations to the Gulag, 1939-1945	7,000,000
Deportations of nationalities: Germans, Chechens, etc	1,000,000
Post-war screening of repatriates etc	5,500,000
GROSS TOTAL (MEDIAN ESTIMATE)	**51,050,000**

---

[573] Pinker p. xi

[574] Totals compiled by Robert Conquest and Roy Medvedev and cited in in Professor Norman Davies' book *Europe: A History* (London Pimlico 1997) Appendix III Section 5 p. 1329

CHAPTER 14

The Dark Side of Liberalism:
Liberalism and Truth

A message to English left-wing journalists and intellectuals generally: 'Do remember that dishonesty and cowardice always have to be paid for. ...
Once a whore, always a whore.[575]

George Orwell

There is a contempt among many scholars for the concepts of truth, logic and evidence. A hypocritical divide between what intellectuals say in public and what they really believe.[576]

Steven Pinker

How did the mental distortions arise? How did the aversion to and alienation from reality come about? How did the destructive intellectual epidemic strike?[577]

Robert Conquest

The BBC is not impartial or neutral. It's a publicly funded, urban organisation with an abnormally large number of young people, ethnic minorities and gay people. It has a liberal bias not so much a party-political bias. It is better expressed as a cultural liberal bias.[578]

The BBC's *Andrew Marr*

George Orwell

The repeated rejection for publication of his novel *Animal Farm* led George Orwell to write a hard-hitting Preface to that novel, in which he gave vent to his anger against the liberals and intellectuals, who were preventing the book's publication. Liberals objected to *Animal Farm* because it was an attack on communism rather than on totalitarianism in general.[579] Orwell complained that there was no freedom of thought or freedom of expression, because the right-thinking elite exerted a censorship on opinions which challenged theirs. In the Preface he denounced intellectuals and liberals for telling deliberate lies, falsifying history and cowardice. It has been largely ignored by the same people. It was too outspoken and did not appear until 1972, years after his death, as the essay *The Freedom of the Press*. This is an extract –

---

[575] George Orwell *The Collected Essays Etc* ed S Orwell & I Angus (USA New Hampshire 2000) Vol 3 *As I Please* p. 227
[576] Steven Pinker *The Blank Slate* (London Allen Lane 2002) p. x
[577] Robert Conquest *The Dragons of Expectation* (London Gerald Duckworth 2005) p.46
[578] Andrew Marr *Daily Mail* Oct 21st, 2006
[579] Orwell acknowledged this in the Preface to the Ukrainian edition (See London Penguin 2000 edition)

"One cannot expect intelligent criticism or even, in many cases, plain honesty from liberal writers and journalists. ... The English intelligentsia feel that to cast any doubt on the wisdom of Stalin is blasphemy. ...uncritical loyalty to the USSR is the current orthodoxy, and ... they are willing to tolerate not only censorship but the deliberate falsification of history ... and plain dishonesty.

The servility with which the greater part of the English intelligentsia have swallowed and repeated Russian propaganda from 1941 onwards would be quite astounding, were it not that they have behaved similarly on several earlier occasions. On one controversial issue after another the Russian viewpoint has been accepted without examination and then publicised with complete disregard to historical truth or intellectual decency. To name only one instance, the BBC celebrated the twenty-fifth anniversary of the Red Army without mentioning Trotsky. This was about as accurate as commemorating the battle of Trafalgar without mentioning Nelson, but it evoked no protest from the English intelligentsia, who had developed a nationalistic loyalty towards the USSR, and in their hearts they felt that to cast any doubt on the wisdom of Stalin was a kind of blasphemy. Events in Russia and events elsewhere were to be judged by different standards. The endless executions in the purges of 1936-8 were applauded by life-long opponents of capital punishment, and it was considered equally proper to publicise famines when they happened in India, and to conceal them when they happened in the Ukraine. ... Anyone who challenges the prevailing orthodoxy finds himself silenced with surprising effectiveness. A genuinely unfashionable opinion is almost never given a fair hearing."[580]

It is ironic that the Enlightenment project, which began as an assertion of the right to think for yourself (Aude sapere), has ended as the opposite. On the subject of 'democracy' under Stalin - one man, one vote, one candidate - Orwell wrote that if from time to time you express a mild distaste for slave-labour camps, or one-candidate elections, you are deemed either insane or actuated by the worst motives. He called the intellectuals 'renegade liberals', who believed in "destroying all independence of thought."[581] They had allowed their commitment to what they saw as progressive forces - i.e. Stalin and communism - to blind them to truth, and to justify intolerance of other views and the silencing of opponents. Orwell believed that truth and objectivity were being lost. In his essay *The Prevention of Literature* he wrote, "On the long view the enemies of truthfulness, and hence of freedom of thought in England are the intellectuals themselves."[582]

---

[580] George Orwell *The Freedom of the Press* originally drafted as a Preface to *Animal Farm* included in Penguin edition of 2000

581 Orwell, *The Freedom of The Press*.

[582] George Orwell *The Prevention of Literature* in *The Collected Essays Etc* ed S Orwell & I Angus Vol IV p. 64

Liberalism has become intolerant of other views. In Orwell's time - as today - speaking the truth is fraught with difficulty. A nuanced position is not allowed. Everything is black and white. There are no subtle shades of grey. All must abide by the norms set by the elite. In his autobiography, Malcolm Muggeridge recounted his talks with Orwell, "We often discussed how difficult it is, in an ideologically polarised society like ours, to take up any position without being assumed to hold all the views of and attitudes associated with it. ... Thus to attack the Soviet Union or the Spanish Republicans was to support the Nazis or Fascists; to expose the fatuities of the liberal mind, to commend the authoritarian one."[583] Our society remains polarised. There is little freedom to accept in part and reject in part, no subtlety, no freedom of thought. If you criticise any aspect of liberalism, you are deemed to be opposed to everything liberals stand for. You must accept their position 100%. You must not think for yourself. As Muggeridge put it, you have to 'vote the ticket' not pick and choose on an individual basis. This hinders a grown-up debate and rational discussion. Furthermore liberals, Orwell claimed, turned a blind eye to atrocities when carried out by those on the left, but were outraged by those of a right-wing regime. It is the same to-day. The media focus on Nazi atrocities, while those of Stalin, Mao, Pol Pot and other communists are largely ignored.

Steven Pinker

Steven Pinker, Professor of Psychology at Harvard, accused liberal intellectuals of dishonesty. He maintained they have ignored scientific discoveries about human nature and silenced and abused opponents. They disregard the facts and opponents who are telling the truth are silenced. Bullying and oppression are allowed, so long as 'progressive' views prevail. He claims they are intolerant - resorting to personal abuse, vilification and ostracism of anyone who challenges their views; and those who have challenged the liberal orthodoxy, have been, "picketed, shouted down, subjected to searing invective in the press and even been denounced in the US Congress."[584] Others have been assaulted, censored and threatened with prosecution. He went on, "The analysis of ideas is commonly replaced by political smears and personal attacks. This poisoning of the intellectual atmosphere has left us unequipped to analyse pressing issues about human nature just as new scientific discoveries are making them acute." [and led to] "a disconnect between intellectual life and common sense. ... This is the mentality of a cult in which fantastical beliefs are flaunted as proof of one's piety. That mentality cannot co-exist with an esteem for truth, and I believe it is responsible for some of the unfortunate trends in modern intellectual life. ... The intellectual establishment has forfeited claims to credibility in the eyes of the

---

[583] Malcolm Muggeridge *Chronicles of Wasted Time* (London Fontana 1972) Vol 1 p. 304
[584] Steven Pinker *The Blank Slate* p. x

public."[585] Moreover the social engineering based on their progressive ideas led to some of the worst atrocities in history in the Soviet Union and China.[586]

Robert Conquest

The distinguished historian Robert Conquest made his name with two groundbreaking books: *The Harvest of Sorrows* and *The Great Terror*. These chronicled for the first time the true scale of the horrors of communism under Stalin - especially the state-planned famine in the Ukraine, the gulags and the purges. As a result he was abused and vilified. Over time however he has not merely been vindicated, but even been shown to have underestimated the true scale of the atrocities. Conquest held that liberals defended communist regimes, which were marked by mass murder, oppression, terror, tyranny and economic failure. The British intelligentsia kept their faith in communism by ignoring the facts. Reflecting on today's divide between intellectuals and reality, he commented, "They are fact-proof and argument-proof today, as was the case with their grandparents on the Soviet Union."[587] He added, "One would think that the purpose of education was to get people to listen to the argument and the evidence. ... What one finds too often is an 'educated' class, particularly in Europe, which is not aware of any general attitudes but its own ... [and which] speaks as if no alternative opinion is possible."[588] Those who challenge the prevailing orthodoxy are silenced. We have today, "an increasingly irrational conformism, often no longer open to, or even cognisant of argument."[589] Worse still there is a "strong tendency to silence those, who disagree with the accepted beliefs, so those unwilling to face all the abuse and fuss can hardly even raise their objections."[590] Conquest likens today's oppression by liberals to totalitarianism: people with a progressive set of ideas use state institutions to impose their ideas. He wrote, "the power, the conformism, the mind blockages are to be found, not merely in the bureaucracy but also in the education system and the organised media such as the BBC."[591] Like Orwell, Conquest maintained there is a split in British society between the intellectuals and the working classes, who have been demonised and are dismissed as chavs.[592]

Evidence of the distortion of history by liberals was given in the chapter *The Dark Side of Liberalism;* historians Simon Schama, Norman Davies, Michael Burleigh, Lesley Chamberlain and Reynald Secher of France all acknowledged

---

[585] Steven Pinker *The Blank Slate* p. x
[586] Steven Pinker *The Blank Slate* p. x
[587] Conquest p. 51
[588] Conquest p. 48
[589] Conquest p. 45
[590] Conquest p. 50
[591] Conquest p. 79
[592] Conquest p. 47

that there has been a liberal bias in history. A blind eye has been turned to evil when carried out by rationalists and secularists. Michael Burleigh, one of the our most distinguished historians with books such as *The Third Reich* and *Earthly Powers*, wrote "Academics perpetuate their cosy left-liberal view of the world ... in their histories of fascism, Nazism and the Holocaust. Publishers collude, content in the certainty that they can sell a ton of books decorated with a swastika. Television producers, who uniformly share the same left-liberal outlook, cater for this insatiable market because it chimes in so well with the liberal-left's high-minded view of itself. Meanwhile the crimes of communism are swept under the carpet. The devastating *Black Book of Communism* which chronicled how Marxist regimes killed 120,000,000 people in the 20th century failed to find a British publisher."[593]

Liberalism and the Media

BBC's Director General Mark Thompson commented in September 2010, "In the BBC I joined 30 years ago there was, in much of current affairs, in terms of people's personal politics, which were quite vocal, a massive bias to the left. The organisation did struggle then with impartiality. Staff were quite mystified by the early years of Thatcher. There is less overt tribalism now. The BBC is like the *New Statesman* used to be, with various shades of hard and soft left."[594] In 2012 he explained that the BBC was sensitive to faiths which were associated with ethnic minorities, but not to Christianity.[595] As part of its anti-Christian agenda, Christians have been removed from the BBC's *Songs of Praise*: the producer is a Sikh, the Head of Religious Broadcasting, a Muslim. A recent programme was based on the Titanic with few Christian elements.[596] Andrew Marr, the BBC's political editor, confirmed that the BBC has a liberal bias (see quote at start of chapter).

Antony Jay is best known for the long-running BBC comedy *Yes Minister* which he co-wrote. Before that he worked in the BBC Current Affairs department for nine years. In 2007 he wrote an article called *The Confessions of a BBC liberal*.[597] According to Jay, BBC current affairs programmes are biased: the topics chosen, the questions asked, and the pitting of a strong exponent of the case the BBC supports against a weak opponent, are all part of its hidden agenda. BBC staff belong, to what Jay calls, the metropolitan arts graduate tribe. He wrote, "We saw ourselves as part of the intellectual elite, full of ideas about how the country

---

[593] Michael Burleigh *Don't let the Nazis occupy Your Mind* The Sunday Times 15th December 2002
[594] Mark Thompson interview in the New Statesman September 2nd 2010.
[595] Mark Thompson posted online in the Free Speech debate, a research project at Oxford University reported in The Telegraph 2.3.12
[596] BBC1 *Songs of Praise* 11th March 2012
[597] Antony Jay *Confessions of a BBC Liberal* The Times August 12th 2007

should be run. Being naive in the way institutions actually work, we were convinced that Britain's problems were the result of the stupidity of the people in charge of the country. This ignorance of the realities of government and management enabled us to occupy the moral high ground. We saw ourselves as clever people in a stupid world, upright people in a corrupt world, compassionate people in a brutal world, libertarian people in an authoritarian world." And "We had an almost complete ignorance of market economics. That ignorance is still there .... It was an ideology based not on observation, but on faith and doctrine. We were weak on facts and shied away from arguments. If defeated we did not change our beliefs." Ignorance and arrogance. He lists BBC prejudices as anti-industry, anti-capitalism, anti-advertising, anti-selling, anti-profit, anti-patriotism, anti-monarchy, anti-police, anti-armed forces and anti-authority. Jay argues these values are also widespread in: the Church of England, academia, *The Guardian*, Channel 4 and show-business. They form a liberal metropolitan consensus, which he dubs 'media liberalism'. Furthermore, he asserts, the BBC News and Current Affairs focuses exclusively on bad news stories with the aim of making British people feel bad about themselves. Martyn Lewis, a former BBC newsreader, confirmed BBC News never gives any good news about Britain.

Peter Sissons worked for 20 years in BBC News; he was a newsreader and a presenter of BBC1's *Question Time* programme. In his autobiography *When One Door Closes* he asked, "Is the BBC biased?" His answer: "At the core of the BBC is a way of thinking that is firmly of the left. ... I was in no doubt that the majority of BBC staff vote for parties of the left. By far the most popular and widely read newspapers at the BBC are *The Guardian* and *The Independent.*"[598] He added, if there are any conservatives at the BBC they would be well advised to keep it hidden, because the one thing that could seriously blight your career at the BBC, is the knowledge that you are a conservative. He claims that far from being impartial the BBC has views on everything. According to Sissons the personnel department at the BBC discriminates against whites, and promotions favour ethnic minorities. Sissons lists BBC characteristics: anti-Christian, but respectful of Islam; anti-monarchy (until 2012?); hatred of Mrs Thatcher; arrogance, dismissive of any complaints, their attitude to those who complain is 'get lost'. The BBC poses as a champion of diversity, but its staff overwhelmingly share a liberal outlook and damage their career prospects if they do not sign up to it. Sissons describes the BBC style of interviewing as full of "acrimony, cynicism, point-scoring ... confrontational and aggressive."[599] Michael Parkinson, who used to present an interview show, says the BBC no longer wants the sort of serious intelligent interview programmes he used to make. Instead we are treated to celebrity tittle-tattle and sexual innuendoes on chat shows. Another distinguished broadcaster Michael Buerk, in his review of Sisson's book wrote, " What the BBC

---

[598] Peter Sissons *When One Door Closes* (London Biteback Publishing 2011) p. 321
[599] Peter Sissons p. 307 f

sees as normal or extreme is conditioned by the common set of assumptions held by the people who work for it, often notably adrift from national sentiment". He described BBC staff as having an ill-disguised contempt for business, industry, the countryside, traditions and politicians. "The Guardian is their Bible and political correctness their creed. In the Corporation's eyes Tony Benn is a lovable national treasure and Melanie Phillips a swivel-eyed fanatic."[600]

Robin Aitken worked at the BBC for 25 years in its News and Current Affairs departments. In 2007 he published a book called *Can We Trust the BBC?* in which he argued that the BBC's reputation for honesty, integrity and fairness, built up before the 1960s, was now undeserved. When he joined the News Department at the start of his BBC career there was a fastidious obsession with the truth and being even-handed. The BBC in those days was rightly seen as trustworthy. According to Aitken it has been taken over by liberals, who slant programmes to advance a 'progressive' agenda. He wrote, "for the last 40 years the BBC has been surreptitiously promoting a set of liberal values at odds with traditional morality."[601] His description of BBC News: "The pretence was that our analyses were objective. In truth they were merely the ones we favoured. Analyses which ran counter to our interpretation were discarded. We were just as opinionated as any commentary in *The Guardian* or *The Independent*. The system ensured that heavily opinionated versions of 'the truth' were broadcast masquerading as objective impartial journalism."[602] The British public have been hoodwinked. This breach of trust is contrary to the BBC Charter, which requires the broadcaster to be fair and impartial. Aitken worked on *The Money Programme* in the 1980s and described it as follows, "The staff were almost without exception of the centre-left.... Our films attempted to undermine the right-wing economic agenda – looking back it is extraordinary how wrong-headed they were."[603] And "It was arrogant journalism: the message was that no-one in government had a clue; our superior intellects had worked out the answers."[604] Aitkin also worked for BBC Scotland where the programmes were slanted to show the economy doing badly: decline was covered, but new industries and economic growth were ignored.

According to Aitken the BBC went from being proud to be British, to guilt-ridden and self-loathing, from a champion of Christianity to secular humanism, which aims to undermine religious belief. Its prejudices are pro-multiculturalism, pro-immigration, republican, anti-Unionist in Northern Ireland and anti-British. The Ulster Unionists fell foul of the BBC on a number of scores: they were patriotic, religious, family orientated, loyal to the British crown and opposed to homosexuality. As a result news reports on Northern Ireland were

---

[600] Michael Buerk *Blowing the BBC's Gaff* Standpoint April 2011
[601] Robin Aitken *Can We Trust the BBC?* (London Continuum 2007) p. 143
[602] Aitken p. 24
[603] Aitken p. 25
[604] Aitken p. 26

heavily slanted against them. He maintains the BBC undermines British institutions: the crown, Parliament, the Church of England, the armed forces, the police and the political process. It has contempt for politicians and depicts them all as corrupt. Aitken concluded, "The BBC is not impartial. It covertly promotes its own agenda, excluding voices it does not like, it becomes a hidden persuader."[605] It holds other institutions to account, but no-one holds the BBC to account. He accuses Conservative politicians of cowardice for failing to challenge the BBC.

On the BBC show *Have I Got News For You?* the 'comedian' Richard Blackwood described the Queen as a "bitch". The BBC defended the use of the word saying, "Richard Blackwood was using the term as it is used in rap music, to mean 'woman', not as a term of abuse." Following complaints to The Broadcasting Standards Authority, it defended Blackwood's use of the word "bitch" to describe The Queen as "acceptable street slang."[606] The former BBC Business Editor, Jeff Randall, wrote of the BBC, "It's not a conspiracy. It's visceral. They think they are on the middle ground."[607] They dismiss anything outside their mindset as extreme. In his book *Scrap the BBC!* Richard North complained that the BBC annual reports are full of conceit: "The BBC rose magnificently to the occasion." and "The BBC covered the story with impeccable judgement."[608] John Lloyd, a former editor of the *New Statesman*, opined that cynical journalists are destroying public faith in the democratic process.[609] The masters of the news universe inflict damage with impunity. When interviewing politicians they adopt a 'how can you be so stupid ' attitude, which fails to acknowledge the difficulties of government.

Anglophobia and the BBC

According to Orwell British intellectuals have become anti-British. He called their attitude "Anglophobia: within the intelligentsia a derisive and mildly hostile attitude to Britain is more or less compulsory. During the war it manifested in the defeatism of the intelligentsia... many were undisguisedly pleased when Singapore fell or when the British were driven out of Greece, and there was a remarkable unwillingness to believe in good news e.g. El Alamein or the number of German planes shot down in the Battle of Britain. English left-wing journalists did not of course want the Germans or Japanese to win the war, but many of them could not help getting a kick out of seeing their own country humiliated."[610]

Two examples of this Anglophobia cropped up while I was writing this book and show that what Orwell wrote is still true. A BBC TV programme entitled

---

[605] Aitken p. 26
[606] The Times 28.2.2001
[607] The Observer, Jan 15th, 2006.
[608] Richard North *Scrap the BB!C* (London The Social Affairs Unit 2007) p. 23
[609] John Lloyd *What the Media are doing to our Politics* (London Constable and Robinson 2000)
[610] George Orwell *Essays* (London Penguin 2000) p. 313

After Rome dealt with the so-called Dark Ages.[611] The presenter described life in England as barbaric: people lived in wattle and daub houses; Oxford was merely the place where an ox forded the river. By contrast Muslim civilisation was described as splendid, fizzing with intellectual excitement. He told us, "There were thousands of libraries in Cordoba." However Bede in Jarrow had a well-stocked library, which enabled him to write his *Church History of the English People* and 40 other books in the early 8th century. The Lindisfarne Gospels, created around 700 A.D., were described by Kenneth Clark in his TV programme *Civilisation*, as "pages of pure ornament, almost the richest and most complicated pieces of abstract ornament ever produced, more sophisticated and refined and elaborate than anything in Islamic art."[612] When Charlemagne wished to educate the Holy Roman Empire he turned to an Englishman - Alcuin of York. It is true there was a flourishing culture in Muslim Spain, but this was exaggerated, and England denigrated. I complained to the BBC and received a reply saying that the comment about "thousands of libraries in Cordoba" was "off the cuff" and "of course a slip of the tongue, which was corrected when the presenter said that there were thousands of volumes in the libraries."[613] How does that correct it? If they knew it was wrong, why not do a retake? It was not a live broadcast. It is part of a consistent BBC pattern to denigrate the English and airbrush out the Anglo-Saxons.

In 2012, when the book was almost finished, the BBC broadcast a series called *How God made the English*. It was another great outpouring of bile against the English. We were told that "England was the least tolerant country in the world." Its history was "a discreditable tale." We were informed that the English are only 5% Anglo-Saxon; strange then that they speak the language derived from the Anglo-Saxons; and we were told the English are in fact Spanish! So the Germans must be Spanish as well! There were also numerous sideswipes against Christianity, showing yet another well-known BBC prejudice - anti-Christian. We were told that Christianity was all about "blood for blood"; there were "fanatical Christian missionaries" organising "wholesale Christian genocide" and believing in a "bloody violent vengeful God". The programmes claimed that the problem with the English is that they suffer from a massive superiority complex; they "think they are God's chosen people." It was Bede's fault because he invented the English and then gave them a complex. If it hadn't been for Bede the English would not exist and there would have been no empire! In fact in 573 almost 200 years before Bede wrote, Gregory a cardinal-deacon, later Pope Gregory the Great, asked a seller of slaves in Rome, who the slaves were and was told they were Angli.[614] The Pope replied Non Angli sed Angeli, (not English but angels) on

---

[611] BBC Series *After Rome* presented by Boris Johnson 2009

[612] Kenneth Clark (later Lord Clark) *Civilisation* (London BBC 1969) p.11

[613] email from the BBC to the author dated 20.3.09

[614] E. Cobham Brewer *Dictionary of Phrase and Fable*. 1898.

account of their fair hair and blue eyes. The mission he sent to the Angli arrived in Kent home of the Jutes and surrounded by Saxons, so 'Angli' didn't mean the Angles, but the English. Bede didn't invent the English at all.

On the tin of the BBC it says, fair, impartial, objective and trustworthy. The evidence from George Orwell, Mark Thompson, Antony Jay, Peter Sissons, Michael Buerk, Jeff Randall, Andrew Marr and Robin Aitkin - all of whom worked for the BBC - is that the BBC is untrustworthy and one-sided. A brilliant coup by liberals: to take over an institution with a reputation for fairness and impartiality, and to use it as a propaganda vehicle for 'progressive' ideas, while never admitting the change. What's more, the propaganda can be subliminal e.g. soaps like Eastenders can promote and influence people's thinking without the viewers being aware. Is it really too much to ask for a BBC which does not discriminate against the English, Christians, conservatives, heterosexuals and whites?

PROGRAMMES YOU WON'T SEE ON THE BBC:
The achievements of Anglo-Saxon civilisation
How Christianity transformed the Roman Empire and saved
    western civilisation
The world's worst atheistic regimes
The horrors of Stalin's purges
Mao's death toll of 70 million in China
The growth of Christianity in China

CHAPTER 15

The Dark Side of Liberalism:
The Attack on the Family and the Growth of Crime

Social affairs intellectuals routinely attack marriage and the traditional family as instruments of male domination. They seek to debunk what they see as the myth that the traditional family of the past was a stable, emotionally satisfying and well-functioning institution. Their arguments are asserted without evidence, but have become widely held.[615]

Peter Saunders, Professor of Sociology at Sussex University

The conventional wisdom of the social affairs intelligentsia ignored the importance of marriage.[616]

Norman Dennis and *George Erdos*, sociologists from Newcastle University

This marks the end of the liberal social consensus on law and order. ... People have had enough of this part of the 1960s consensus. ... A society of different lifestyles has spawned a group of young people who were brought up without parental discipline, without proper role models and without any sense of responsibility to or for others.... People want a society of respect, of responsibility; they want the law-abiding majority back in charge.[617]

Tony Blair in 2004 announcing the government's crime strategy.

Working class parents who occasionally smack their children have been stigmatised by the middle classes.... Parents feel anxious about imposing discipline on their children... People in constituencies like mine who are often poor, often in deprived areas, fear the social services knocking at the door. That is the reality. And there's another group of people who never come into contact with social services in their lives ... Smacking is a last resort, but it must be left to the parents. The liberal elite often have the means to help their kids understand that there are boundaries.[618]

David Lammy MP

In the 1960s liberal values of freedom and equality led to women's liberation and feminism. Liberals fought to end discrimination by gender and aimed to empower women, so they could become free and self-governing, no longer bound in male-centred, patriarchal, repressive and authoritarian structures. The traditional family was debunked and weakened. Marriage was seen as bondage, slavery and servitude. Feminists urged women to reject marriage and the traditional role of wife. For existentialists like Simone de Beauvoir marriage was inauthentic and a sign of bad faith; for Marxists it was bourgeois. They preferred cohabitation or open marriages. Many progressives held that children were

---

[615] Peter Saunders in the Afterword to Norman Dennis and George Erdos *Families without Fatherhood* (London Institute for the Study of Civil Society 2000)
[616] N. Dennis and G. Erdos *Cultures and Crimes* (London Civitas 2005) p. xxviii
[617] Tony Blair Announcing the Labour Government's Crime Strategy 19.7.2004 BBC News
[618] David Lammy 29.1.12 Daily Mail

harmed by the traditional family, which was a bad place to bring up children, because it prevented freedom and authentic self-expression. The focus on freedom, the decline in commitment to others, the weakening of marriage, the emphasis on rights rather than duties and obligations, have all had an adverse impact on families. Divorce, separation, births outside marriage, one-parent families, cohabitation and sex outside marriage have all increased. Policymakers have tried to erode the difference between married and cohabitees. For thousands of years families have cared for their members across the generations, but these social values are being eroded. Single parenthood had not been socially acceptable in the late 19th and early 20th century and those who transgressed were treated harshly, but the purpose was to discourage others, so that there were fewer fatherless children.

One of the pathfinders for the sexual revolution and feminism was Germaine Greer, who in 1970 published *The Female Eunuch,* a bestseller, described by *The Listener* as "a brilliant attack on the family." She saw the nuclear family as a short-lived experiment which had failed and wrote, "The mother is the dead heart of the family"[619] and "My duty is to myself."[620] Greer argued that women's freedom is curtailed by marriage and it is ridiculous for girls to pledge themselves in marriage for life, declaring, "Marriage is an impossible set-up."[621] Instead a woman's duty is to have fun and liberate herself. This overrides any duty to husband or children. If a woman is married, she should leave her husband, taking their children with her. Women, she argued, had been "brainwashed into deluding themselves that their monotonous and unremitting drudgery in the home is doing some good."[622] She wrote "Men are the enemy"[623] and "Women have very little idea how much men hate them."[624] By her own account the family in which she grew up was dysfunctional; so she concluded that all families are dysfunctional; all marriages are a disaster and sex is disgusting. She seems not to have noticed any happy marriages. She described married life as one of impotence and hatred masquerading as love, and claimed mother-child relations are full of conflict, and bringing up children is not a real job. Children are ungrateful hooligans, who grow up, leave home and reject their mothers. She claimed that men also have a jaundiced view of marriage, "Sooner or later you find yourself screwed permanently, working in a dead-end job to keep a fading woman and her noisy children in inadequate accommodation in a dull town for the term of your natural life."[625] She promoted self-fulfilment;

---

[619] Germaine Greer *The Female Eunuch* (London Granada 1981) p. 263
[620] Greer p. 25
[621] Greer p. 378
[622] Greer p. 327
[623] Greer p. 350
[624] Greer p. 293
[625] Greer p. 294

children were regarded as a nuisance who interfered with the pleasures of adults, so increasingly they are sent to their bedrooms and forgotten.

These ideas have been influential. My aunt taught in the 1970s in a primary school in Blackpool, after 20 years she went back and visited her old classroom and the age-group she had taught. The present teacher told her that of the 30 children in the classroom, only one lived with both its natural parents. In addition welfare benefits were structured to disadvantage couples, who receive more benefits if they live apart; so some couples split up to maximise their benefits.

In Defence of the Family

Eventually there was a fight back against these liberal ideas. A. H. Halsey, Emeritus Professor of Sociology at Oxford and a leading socialist, attacked the notion that if everyone behaves selfishly we can all benefit. He argued that excessive individualism was damaging to society - we are all interconnected; and he accused the intelligentsia of damaging society.[626] He recognised that children learn how to behave socially in a small environment, and can then apply those lessons to the wider community. They learn how to share and behave less selfishly. It is the failure of some families to socialise their children that causes many of society's ills. In his view families are crucial for the well-being of society. The stability known by earlier generations is being lost; children need a stable environment if they are to mature into self-confident young people capable of taking on the responsibilities of adulthood. Short-term relationships do not nurture mature personalities. Today there are increasing signs of distress among our young people: the increase in self-harm and eating disorders.

"The success of the attack on the family was astonishing"[627] wrote two British sociologists, Norman Dennis and George Erdos in 2000. It ran counter to common sense and there is a mass of evidence showing that children of single mothers, or those who live in step or blended families, fare less well than those brought up in traditional families. They argued for a strengthening of the family, so reversing existing policy. This is in no way a criticism of the many single parents who, often through no fault of their own, find themselves in that position and who do a magnificent job in difficult circumstances. Dennis and Erdos maintained children suffer if their natural father is not committed to their upbringing, and where their parents do not follow the traditional pattern: they die earlier; have more illness; achieve less at school; have poorer nutrition and more unemployment; are more prone to deviance and crime and tend to repeat the pattern of unstable parenting. They criticised the BBC which had upheld

---

[626] Halsey wrote the Foreword to Norman Dennis and George Erdos *Families without Fatherhood* (London Institute for the Study of Civil Society 2000)
[627] Dennis and Erdos p. 24

traditional values until the 1960s; they gave as an example Radio 4's *Woman's Hour* which had been a stalwart defender of marriage, but after the liberal take-over marriage was described as an "insult" and "Women shouldn't touch it."[628]

The authors claim intellectuals were intolerant of the respectable working class, dismissing them as 'bourgeois' - using a Marxist analysis; they sneered at their values of loyalty, commitment, thrift, prudence, sex within marriage and hard work. The Labour Party no longer defends the values of these people; instead it now stresses freedom in personal lifestyle and social matters - everyone should be free to do whatever they want and the state will pick up the pieces. Cohesive societies with a strong sense of community and mutual support have been undermined. Traditional working-class values have been weakened by the progressive middle classes. Halsey and Dennis described the respectable working classes as, "based on solid family life, the devotion of parents to their children, hard work, honesty and consideration for neighbours. The Labour Party was once the party of such decent, straightforward men and women, but today it has been captured by middle-class intellectuals, whose values are very different."[629] They claim many intellectuals have "a wanton ignorance or open hostility to the known facts"[630] and relentlessly attack family life.

Research shows that 70% of children admitted to local authority care are from single parent households and two thirds of homeless youths had experienced family breakdown.[631] Young males with stepparents are three times more likely to run away from home. The absence of the father is a significant factor in delinquency. Children who experience divorce or separation are two or three times more likely to be suspended or expelled from school. Divorce is a risk factor for children in health problems, depression and underachievement at school, and can lead to psychological problems in adult life. Children living with a stepfather are thirty-three times more likely to suffer abuse than those living with their natural father.[632] Unmarried couples with children are five times more likely to split up than married couples. The evidence shows that cohabiting couples are less happy, have poorer relationships and are twice as likely to suffer domestic violence. According to a Government Report, only 2% of children are brought up in Local Authority care, but they comprise 25% of prison population. In 2002 149,335 children experienced their parents' divorce. In 1951 3% of marriages ended in divorce within 10 years, in 1991 the figure was 41%.[633] Yet public opinion - influenced by the media - thinks cohabiting is as good for children as the traditional family, a view now at odds with most social science

---

[628] Dennis and Erdos p. 30

[629] David Green Editor's Foreword to 1993 edition of *Families Without Fathers*. p. ix
Halsey and Dennis's book is called *English Ethical Socialism.*

[630] Dennis and Erdos p. 90

[631] Patricia Morgan *Farewell to the Family* (London Institute of Economic Affairs 1999)

[632] Dennis and Erdos p. 96

[633] *Confident families in a Secure Britain* Government White Paper HMSO 2008

research. The public has been given a misleading picture of the effects of single parenthood and cohabiting.

A liberal approach to discipline and morality

As well as changes to the family over the last 60 years we have seen a remarkable change in attitudes to discipline and child-rearing. In part it is a reaction against the harsh and stern discipline in the past. It is true that some children were punished too much and their wills broken. There was too much beating of children. I remember as a new history teacher in a well-known public school in the 1970s, saying to a housemaster that one of the boys in his house had not done his homework. His response was, "I'll beat him." So there was a need to be softer to some extent, but it has been taken it too far.

In the past children learnt moral values by internalising those of their society; this created self-controlled individuals guided by conscience. Family, kin, neighbours, and teachers helped to control behaviour informally by reproving wrongdoing. Anti-social behaviour of various sorts can be curtailed in this way. But by stressing the rights of the child this approach has been undermined and no support is given to those who do make a stand. Also multiculturalism has weakened any consensus on what is right and wrong; it is easier to enforce rules, to encourage benign influences and suppress bad ones where there is a common set of values, shared history, traditions and culture.

From the 1960s onwards the socialisation of the child by family, church and school was successfully opposed. The outcome is that schools no longer aim to produce law-abiding citizens and no longer teach morality. Each child must find out for himself what is right and wrong. Some educationalists went further and proposed: no discipline, no authority, no respect for authority and no punishments. The headmaster A. S. Neill declared that it was his policy never to punish a child and claimed all punishment was a mistake. He rejected any idea that schools should attempt to socialise children. The liberals' fear of socialisation stems in part from the experience of Germany in the 1930s under the National Socialists, where the German population was socialised to such an extent that authority was not questioned, even the orders of a Hitler. The liberal response has been to conclude that all socialisation must be bad. However *'abusus non usus tollit'* – the abuse does not remove the use. There needs to be a middle way between extreme socialisation and no socialisation; the latter is a prescription for anarchy at worst or at least anti-social behaviour.

The failure to discipline children

In August 2011 many English cities erupted in riots, looting and vandalism. David Lammy, the Labour MP for Tottenham in north London, where extensive riots took place, has now written a book seeking to understand what happened.[634] One of the causes of the riots, he argues, lies in the inability of parents to discipline their own children, following the curtailment by the Labour Government of a parent's right to smack her/his child. Despite Tony Blair's fine words in 2004, it was his government that changed the law on smacking, restricting parents freedom to discipline in this way. Under the new rules a smack must not lead to any reddening of the skin. Lammy points out this is meaningless to him and many of his constituents because their skin is black; it reveals an out of touch white middle-class liberal elite. Previously the law had allowed 'reasonable chastisement' which included smacking. Judges had decided what was reasonable, but now social workers decide, and have the power to take children away from their parents. According to Lammy "Parents are no longer sovereign in their own homes, and live in constant fear that social workers will take away their children if they chastise them."[635] He argues that in working class homes a smack is a traditional and effective way of administering justice, but the Labour Party imposes middle class values, and has become divorced from the working class communities it claims to represent. He thanked his own mother for giving him firm discipline, including being smacked, and he said that he does smack his own children on occasion. Lammy also rejects the liberal explanation of the riots: arguing they were not a rational response to deprivation but an outbreak of nihilism and hedonism.

In 2012 *French Children Don't Throw Food* by Pamela Druckermann was published.[636] The author was an American mother who had been living in France for five years. Staying for a week in a hotel with her children she noticed that her children were misbehaving and throwing food, unlike the French families. She wondered why. Her conclusion was that French parents are strict with their children, and don't think the relationship should be one of equality. Setting clear rules is seen as a way of helping the child develop. They say to their children, *'C'est moi qui decide'* (I'm in charge) and French children are taught to say *'bonjour' 'au revoir' 's'il vous plaît'* and *'merci'*. Parents insist on politeness from an early age. Children are forced to engage respectfully with adults, and are not allowed to stay in their little bubble, glued to their Gameboy consoles. Both these books - in their different ways - point to our failure to discipline children.

Was there less crime in the past?

In the past life was a struggle for many, yet Charles Booth's book *Life and Labour of the People of London,* based on a study of the East End of London portrayed working class lives as decent with enough food and

---

[634] David Lammy *Out of the Ashes: Britain after the Riots* (London Guardian Books 2011)
[635] David Lammy 29.1.12 Daily Mail
[636] Pamela Druckermann *French Children Don't Throw Food* (London Transworld Publishers) 2012

clothing.[637] He wrote, "I can only speak as I have found: wholesome pleasant family life, very simple food, very regular habits. Healthy bodies, and healthy minds, affectionate relationships of husbands and wives, mothers and sons, elders and children and of friend with friend."[638] Robert Roberts' book, *The Classic Slum: Salford Life in the First Quarter of the Century* noted, "Parents brought up their children to be decent, kindly and honourable. Slum life was not mindless and uncouth as later claimed."[639] He painted a picture of happy family life. Some intellectuals have tried to explain away the increase in crime by suggesting that in the past there was a large amount of unrecorded domestic violence. An accusation usually made by those who are anti-marriage. There is no contemporary evidence to support this.

Police records of crime show that England enjoyed low levels of crime in the late 19th and early 20th centuries. Henry Mayhew's book, *London Labour and the London Poor,* which appeared in 1851, described life in Victorian London, including the costermongers - sellers of fruit and vegetables - who used to leave their stalls unattended without any loss by theft, even overnight. Some stored their fruit and vegetables in stables, which did not even have a latch, let alone a lock, but their goods were never stolen. At their dances they were well-behaved and their women were not brazen. Few formal marriages took place, but mostly couples stayed together and were faithful to each other. It was unusual to find a child unacknowledged by a father. He described their hallmarks as fairplay, decency, self-control and honour. Liberals would have predicted a high crime rate, because of the deprivation and poverty.

A dramatic increase in crime occurred in the second half of the 20th century. Between 1951 and 2001 the population grew 19% but the number of crimes increased by 881% - 46 times faster. From 1857 – 1914 there were never more than 100,000 crimes a year; the average being 90,000 crimes. Whereas in 2001 there were over 1,000,000 in London alone. Crime is very high by historical standards. In 1893 there were 400 robberies in the whole of the country. Now in Lambeth alone robberies are running at around 500 a month. In addition the detection rates for crime have fallen; in Lambeth, the 18,000 robberies from 1999 to 2003 had a clear up rate of 7%.[640] Dennis and Erdos cite the following figures from police records:

	Population	Crimes
1861	20,000,000	88,000
1907	34,000,000	100,000
1951	44,000,000	520,000

---

[637] Charles Booth *Life and Labour of the People of London* (appeared in 17 volumes between 1891 and 1903).

[638] Charles Booth, *Life and Labour of the People of London.*

[639] Dennis and Erdos p. 37

[640] Dennis and Erdos p. 21

| 2001 | 52,000,000 | 5,100,000 |

Crimes of Violence

| 1906 | 228 |
| 1997 | 256,000 |

Does deprivation cause crime?

Liberal attitudes to crime, discipline and behaviour flow in part from their belief that mankind is naturally good. There is nothing wicked or evil that is inborn, so no-one would naturally choose to commit a crime. Therefore any wrong-doing is a result of the warping of inborn goodness by society and parents. Liberals believe people are driven to commit crimes because of their circumstances - crime is caused by deprivation, inequality, colour prejudice, lack of constructive opportunities, poor housing, unemployment and poverty; the criminal is a victim. It follows, on this theory, that as deprivation, discrimination and other forms of inequality decrease, crime will also decrease. Opponents of liberalism reject the notion of inborn goodness and see human nature as basically self-centred, so crime is no surprise and a strong set of moral values should be inculcated.

Today's living standards are much higher than 60 years ago. So if crime is caused by deprivation, then we should now have much lower levels of crime than in the 1950s. In 1951 52% of British homes had no piped water; 1,800,000 million shared a tap; 740,000 (13%) shared a WC, many outside; and 37% had no fixed bath – only a tin bath. There was also much overcrowding. However by 2001 only 104,000 shared a WC or lacked a bath; many consumer durables were widely owed: 98% had a TV, 94% a phone, 88% gas central heating, 87% a fridge. Educational opportunities are much greater now; the number of university students has increased dramatically. Yet crime is now ten times greater - less deprivation has been accompanied by greater crime. It is clearly false to claim that poverty, poor housing and lack of educational opportunities are the causes of crime.

Norman Dennis grew up in working class neighbourhoods of Sunderland in 1930s and 1940s. These were noteworthy for their social cohesion and lack of crime even during the great Depression of the 1930s. He and Erdos maintain England has historically been socially harmonious with low levels of crime, but the social affairs intelligentsia no longer value the achievement of English cultural institutions in producing a law-abiding citizens and see instead the stunted growth of individuals. Many intellectuals ignored the growth of crime, "Almost universally dismissed by England's public intellectuals as a false alarm ..... created by ill-informed people in the throes of a moral panic."[641] Dennis and

---

[641] Erdos and Dennis p. xi

Erdos's thesis is that the increase in crime is caused by social and family breakdown. The state destroyed society's moral and institutional capital by dismembering families based on lifelong monogamy for the procreation and raising up of children.

"Make your school rules strict, then your criminal laws can be gentle: but if you give youth its freedom, you will have to keep on building prisons."[642]
Michel de Montaigne

---

[642] Michel de Montaigne *Essais*

Afterword

In the 1960s a high tide of liberalism swept all before it. British institutions - academia, the media including the BBC, the civil service, the judiciary and the churches were taken over by 'progressive' thinking. Despite some real gains for which liberalism deserves credit: more equality, greater social justice, less class division and better treatment of sexual and ethnic minorities, there has been a downside which has been largely overlooked. I believe we urgently need to understand how liberalism has also harmed society. I recap some of the key points of the book below. (For references please refer back to the original chapters).

The roots of liberalism lie in The Enlightenment which turned traditional ideas of human nature upside down. The Biblical view of human nature as sinful was rejected and replaced with THE BIG LIE of liberalism - we are born good and rational and later corrupted by parents and society; so children are morally superior to their parents - truly a leap of faith! The bedrock of Judeo-Christian cultures for thousands of years was overturned. Children have been empowered and their rights asserted, while parental authority has been weakened. Many parents now hesitate to discipline their own children; and the ability of schools to discipline pupils was whittled away until very recently. The liberal approach is mistaken: children need to be disciplined where necessary and given clear boundaries. The belief that we are essentially good but corrupted by society influenced penal policy. Liberals see criminals as victims, not as wrongdoers; because surely no-one would choose to do something wrong. Society is to blame. So prisons are made as pleasant as possible and the life inside soft and easy. Liberals struggle with concepts like justice and punishment.

This belief in human goodness is now being challenged by science. Steven Pinker, Professor of Psychology at Harvard and author of *The Blank Slate,* maintains scientific discoveries in the fields of the mind, the brain, genetics including the Human Genome Project, and evolutionary psychology have all undermined it. It is ironic that liberalism has been undermined by science. History provides ample evidence of human violence, cruelty, greed and selfishness. Anthropologists have found that many primitive societies are violent - the peace-loving Noble Savage turns out to be a rarity. Freud and Jung had no illusions about human goodness. Despite all this the belief in human goodness persists, because it has an emotional appeal. People want to believe that everyone is nice; like Richard Dawkins who calls himself 'Pollyanna'.

If we are good we can jettison the restrictions of the past. We can abandon morality, religion and customs, and maximize freedom. Liberalism's aim is self-governing individuals, free from external coercion; many aspects of life have been liberalised - sexual behaviour, alcohol consumption, censorship, gambling, divorce laws and economic activity. Self-discipline, self-restraint and self-sacrifice have become alien concepts. The upshot is a society suffering from an excess of freedom: ever earlier sexual intercourse, promiscuity, pornography, a great increase in sexually transmitted diseases, lack of commitment, unlimited drinking hours, with some supermarkets selling below-cost alcohol. The outcome is binge-drinking, drunkenness and a dramatic increase in liver failure. Liberal divorce laws are one factor in the increase in marital breakdown. The gambling laws have been liberalised leading to a significant increase in gambling. The abolition of censorship has led to ever more violent and sexually explicit TV, films and video games. Economic liberals thought free markets were rational and good - a laissez-faire approach of minimal government interference and light-touch regulations. This led to the credit crunch and the greatest financial crisis since World War Two. So in some areas freedom needs to be curbed and we need greater self-discipline.

Our society is marked by a loss of morality - the tabloid newspapers which carried out phone hacking; the MPs who fiddled their expenses; the company directors who are motivated by personal greed rather than the well-being of their companies and workforces; the TV executives whose only concern is their ratings, regardless of the impact of their programmes; plus a decline in honesty and trust. Morality has been a casualty of liberalism for a number of reasons: firstly, if we are good, we have no need of rules to restrain us; and morality is seen as an unwarranted restriction on our freedom. Liberals are also suspicious of morality because it lacks a scientific basis; because it comes from the past, which they see as tainted; and because it often has a religious basis, which they regard as suspect. They maintain all moral values are equal; so no-one should try to impose his/her values on others; children should make up their own set of values with no adult input. The outcome is moral disorder; the weakening of the traditional family. Many fathers have little sense of commitment to their children; in these situations it is right to be judgmental. Society has been demoralized in both meanings - removing morality and leaving us degenerate and depressed.

The liberal focus is on individual freedom, not on obligations to others. They start from the premise that society is formed from individuals with rights and prioritize the individual over society. My duty is to myself, to fulfill myself; consequently society has become increasingly selfish and individualistic. A world far removed from the self-sacrifice and fraternity shown during World War Two. It has not brought happiness but rather more isolated individuals. Moreover if it is my right then there is no place for gratitude.

There is certainly a good side to the liberals' desire for social justice and greater equality, although they have no monopoly of caring. I believe the gap between the rich and the poor is too wide; this increases social disharmony and is unjust. Despite these positive aspects, egalitarianism in some of its guises has been harmful and detrimental. In education an 'all must have prizes' approach has led to a dumbing down of standards, easier exams and grade inflation. The outcome is that Britain has fallen in the world rankings for education. The goal of equality of opportunity was replaced by equality of outcome, thereby hindering bright children. Comprehensive schools - some with no setting by ability - have reduced social mobility. The insistence of liberals that all family arrangements are of equal worth for the upbringing of children, disregards the overwhelming evidence that children fare best when brought up by their biological parents, who are committed to each other in marriage. A misguided egalitarianism sees all works of art and literature as equal; nothing is better than anything else. So an unmade bed and a dead sheep (entries for the Turner Prize) are treated as significant works of art.

Other aspects of a liberal worldview that can be traced back to the Enlightenment include: the importance of science and reason, secularism, downplaying history, universalism and multiculturalism, and lastly the belief that we are shaped by our experiences not by our genes. The Enlightenment put its faith in science, believing it to be certain and benign. Despite the great achievements of science and technology, mustard gas and nuclear bombs have shown its dark side. Moreover the truths of science are provisional - even the theories of Newton were qualified by Einstein. Chaos theory showed that we will never gain sufficient knowledge of the world to be able to predict the future with certainty; and Heisenberg's Uncertainty Principle belongs to the strange unpredictable world of Quantum Mechanics. The success of science and technology bred arrogance - science has all the answers. The vast cosmos is reduced to numbers and formulae, which give an illusion of mastery with little sense of awe and mystery. The west is dominated by a materialist worldview - the universe is nothing but matter; an assumption without a scientific basis. This has fostered an attitude that the earth is there to be exploited by technology.

Materialism rejects anything spiritual or divine. Richard Dawkins claims Einstein was an atheist and cites as his authority Max Jammer's book *'Einstein and Religion'*. Yet Jammer comes to the opposite conclusion, and produces many quotations which show Einstein did believe in a transcendent God, albeit not a personal God. Other scientists, like the cosmologist Paul Davies, maintain the universe is not just a meaningless accident and argue the universe is fine tuned for life, which points to the existence of God. The notion that science and religion are in conflict has been debunked by John Hedley Brooke, Professor of the History of Science at Oxford, who holds that science and religion have been overwhelmingly in harmony. As Wittgenstein said, when science has answered all its questions the mystical ones remain unanswered.

Freedom for self-governing individuals can include a wish to be free from the past, its traditions, customs and values. A liberal worldview devalues the importance of history and tradition. However history gives us our identity and without it our lives lack meaning. History in schools has been whittled away;

many children leave school largely ignorant of it. What little survives tends to focus on the Nazis and slavery. Liberals are also committed to universal mankind - they seek to obliterate distinctions of race, creed and class. So they champion multiculturalism and promote diversity. This partly explains why they can be anti-Christian and anti-British. After the awfulness of World Wars One and Two, it is understandable and right that a move in that direction was made. However to remove all creeds and sense of national belonging loosens social bonds and leaves people rootless; and the Archbishop of Canterbury, Rowan Williams, accused white liberals of inverted racism.

Most liberals also believe that we are shaped by our experiences, not by our genes, sometimes called The Blank Slate theory i.e. at birth we are like soft putty which can be molded any way we choose. This stresses the importance of upbringing and ignores heredity. It appeals to liberals, because it seems to guarantee both freedom and equality. They think we can be anything we like, because we are not determined by our genetic inheritance, and we are all equal because at birth there are no differences between us - except morphology, like fair hair. However Pinker argues that the scientific evidence, from the Human Genome Project and the study of twins who are separated after birth, shows that our genetic inheritance is fundamental in shaping us.

The Dark Side of Liberalism

While there have been some positive aspects to liberalism in the past, there is also a dark side which has been largely overlooked. Shaun Bailey, the youth worker and social commentator, argues liberalism harms poor communities. He was raised in inner-city London by a single mother on a council estate; he co-founded the charity MyGeneration and wrote the pamphlet *No Man's Land,* according to which the more liberal we have become the more the poor have suffered. He accuses middle class liberals from leafy suburbs of undermining marriage, weakening discipline in schools, eroding parental authority, encouraging promiscuity and giving value-free sex education in schools. He claims the history taught in schools has an anti-British bias; and those with a West Indian background find their Christian heritage devalued. He also accuses liberals of an overcaring approach which fosters dependency.

Sir Isaiah Berlin, the historian of ideas, in a famous essay *The Two Concepts of Liberty* charts what he calls the 'peculiar evolution' of liberal ideas, from a belief in freedom to something sinister: forcing people to be free: an elite, convinced of its moral and intellectual superiority, thinks it has the right to impose its views on ordinary people. The maxim here is: we know what is best for you, better than you do yourselves. This can be found in an extreme form in communist regimes and to a lesser degree in political correctness. In addition, regimes founded on the principles of rationalism, science, secularism and equality have been among the most bigoted, bloody and barbaric in history e.g.

the Reign of Terror in the French Revolution and communism. George Orwell recorded how liberals tried to stop the publication of *Animal Farm* and accused them of being totalitarian and dishonest. The charge of dishonesty is also levelled against liberals by Steven Pinker, Sir Isaiah Berlin, Rowan Williams Archbishop of Canterbury, and historians Simon Schama, Robert Conquest and Michael Burleigh.

Many Christians think their faith and liberalism go hand in hand. Yet it all depends what you mean by the word 'liberal' - if you mean a concern for social justice they are right; but there is a fundamental disagreement between liberals and Christians over human nature: liberals maintain human goodness, while Christianity holds human nature to be fallen. Liberals promote freedom, while many Christians believe we are suffering from excessive freedom, sexual promiscuity and drunkenness, with too much selfishness and individualism and loss of morality. The leading Anglican theologian, and former bishop of Durham, Tom Wright, claims liberals have a lot to answer for and refers to the culpable arrogance of the inheritors of the Enlightenment, and Rowan Williams described the liberal state as vacuous.

The BBC - not what it says on the tin

On the tin of the BBC it says: impartial, trustworthy and honest. George Orwell accused intellectuals of Anglophobia, "Within the intelligentsia, a derisive and mildly hostile attitude to Britain is more or less compulsory."[643] He criticised their falsification of history to fit a liberal agenda; he cited the BBC as an example. In the 1960s the liberals gained a total ascendancy at the BBC. It went from being pro-Christian to anti-Christian, from patriotic to anti-British, from pro-marriage to anti-marriage. Its covert objective was, and is, to change Britain by imposing a liberal set of values, while maintaining the pretence of being even-handed and unbiased. The British public has been hoodwinked; programmes, news bulletins and soaps are cleverly slanted. The BBC needs to become transparent and own up to the particular worldview it seeks to impose. The current Director General of the BBC Mark Thompson has spoken of the BBC with a massive and vocal bias to the left, struggling with impartiality, whose staff are all hard or soft left. Andrew Marr described the BBC as a culturally liberal organization with an abnormally large number of ethnic minorities and homosexuals. Peter Sissons described the BBC as firmly of the left, always with its axes to grind and with promotions rigged against whites. Michael Buerk agreed that *The Guardian* is their Bible and political correctness their creed. Antony Jay, best known for *Yes Minister*, worked in the BBC Current Affairs department for nine years. BBC programmes are biased, he

---

[643] George Orwell Essay *Notes on Nationalism from Decline of the English Murder and Other Essays (*London Penguin 1965) p. 155

argues: the topics chosen, the questions asked, and the pitting of a strong exponent of the case the BBC supports, against a weak opponent. Some think the BBC is fair, because they aren't well informed enough to spot these dirty tricks. It seems too much to ask for, a BBC that does not discriminate against conservatives, Christians, whites, and heterosexuals? There is a need for a powerful independent body to audit the BBC for fairness and impartiality.

Have things got better or worse since the 1950s?

There is a waxing recognition - including those on the left - that we have been on the wrong track. Will Hutton's article in *The Observer* in 2010 entitled, WE HAD IT ALL - SEX, FREEDOM, MONEY. DID WE THROW IT ALL AWAY? chronicled how babyboomers, like himself, embraced liberal values and left us with "flux, uncertainty and a lack of social and cultural anchors ... the cornerstones of British life have been shattered."[644] The world of the 1950s, where you could rely on the stability of marriage, the trustworthiness of companies and banks, where people gained a sense of belonging from their British identity, from churches and trade unions, has gone. Hutton rues our wanton destruction of a society that functioned well, writing, "We have lost our capacity to think straight. We pulled down one culture with its rules and imagined that another would spontaneously take its place. How could we have been so destructive?" He maintains the debate now is about how far we need to row back and reintroduce restraints. As a babyboomer myself I echo Hutton's description of the 1950s which I remember as a lad growing up in north Lancashire. There was a great sense of optimism, decency, trustworthiness, loyalty, patriotism, a strong sense of belonging and pride in being British, borne in part by the fraternity shown in World War Two.

There have been two well-known studies of the East End: *Family and Kinship in East London* (1957) and its sequel *The New East End* (2006). Trevor Philips, then Chair of The Commission for Racial Equality, reviewing the latter wrote, "The public debate is full of smug self-righteousness.... This book makes an old fashioned contribution - evidence, the authors report what is actually happening." In other words: arrogance and ignorance. Michael Young, one of the authors, commented that the power of fraternity shown during the war was wiped out after the war. The East End communities, whose bravery and resilience had been valued in wartime, were soon forgotten by royalty and others after it. One of the authors commented, "The world described in *Family and Kinship* was one of a richly shared communal life, through families into streets and neighbourhoods. ... Family reciprocity across the generations was at the heart of local community life.... But all this could easily be blown away."[645]

---

[644] Will Hutton *We had it all sex, freedom, money. Did we throw it all away?* The Observer 22.08.2010

[645] G. Dench, K. Gavron , M. Young *The New East End* (London Profile Books) p. 12

It was all blown away; blown away by progressive middle-class policy-makers, who cared little for long-established communities: multiculturalism destroyed their culture, their sense of belonging and identity; tower blocks instead of terraced houses destroyed their communities; undermining the family weakened their social bonds; giving housing to immigrants on arrival in Britain, contravened their sense of fair play and their moral code of opposing freeloaders. Their protests were dismissed. According to the authors of *The New East End*, "Working-class people no longer see the state as on their side... The middle classes are seen as favouring newcomers, changing the welfare state to suit their needs, and labelling as racist any member of the white working classes who object."[646] The understanding between the classes made in the 1940s and early 1950s, which the authors see as an era of optimism and solidarity, has been broken, mistrust and sullen resentment prevail. Trevor Phillips described the book as "One of the most important books I've read in a long time."[647] Shaun Bailey and David Lammy also bore witness to the sense of alienation and fragmentation of society, which was laid bare by the widespread riots in English towns in August 2011.

Liberals like to think of themselves as morally and intellectually superior; they claim a monopoly of virtue and think others don't care. Jonathan Haidt, a self-confessed liberal and Professor of Psychology (University of Virginia), maintains liberals dismiss conservatives as irrational and stupid, but he has now come to the conclusion that liberals are in fact blind to what is going on.[648] According to Haidt liberals only have two values: 1) to protect the weak and 2) to prevent suffering. He argues that conservatives share these beliefs, but have additional values: the importance of loyalty to a group, rewarding effort and valuing religion. He claims liberals think that concern for the well-being of long-established communities and respect for the spiritual are irrational and a hindrance to the quest for greater freedom and equality. Haidt shares the liberal concern for the poor, outsiders, women and minorities, but he now argues that liberals are making a big mistake when they dismantle communities that give meaning to people's lives and curb natural selfishness. He argues Edmund Burke and conservatives are right to value the cohesion of communities, and to recognize their fragility; whereas liberals value diversity, difference and novelty. Most people need to feel they belong to something greater than themselves. Liberals think that their version of a rational secular society should appeal to everyone and that people will behave well once oppression is ended and equality achieved. He warns that liberals may end up destroying social order and moral values in their pursuit of individual freedom.

---

[646] G. Dench, K. Gavron , M. Young p. 5
[647] G. Dench, K. Gavron , M. Young See front cover of the paperback edition of the book
[648] Jonathan Haidt *The Righteous Mind: Why Good People Are Divided by Politics and Religion* (London Allen Lane 2012)

To sum up: in the past there were positive aspects to liberalism, but at its core lies a deeply flawed attempt to impose a romantic, but unrealistic, view of human nature on society. Because it is fundamentally untrue, lies, bullying and coercion are needed to impose it, and opponents must be silenced. Because its view of mankind is idealistic, its devotees think it must be true, and are strongly committed to it. It is congenial to people who are well-meaning and who have a naïve rose-tinted view of the world, which avoids dwelling too much on the ugly side of life, like the single mum in a tower block in Tottenham, trying to keep her children safe and worrying about gangs and knife-crime. It is in denial of the fact that many aspects of life are worse today than in the past. Liberals cling to their views, ignoring the evidence of science, psychology, anthropology, history and of social workers. It is a blind faith in a Utopian project, which blithely dismisses reality and regards its opponents as prejudiced. There is nothing to discuss because we are right. Ignorance and arrogance are its hallmarks. Sadly for its devotees, truth will out in the end. The experiment was foredoomed from the start.

Index

A

Sowell, Thomas 14, 18, 21, 35, 99, 122, 129
Soviet Union 12, 16, 81, 84, 90, 92, 96, 109-10, 124, 130, 141, 147-8
Summerhill School 14, 19, 30

T

Taylor, Charles 49, 51, 66
Theism 71, 74, 76, 77, 142

V

Victorian 17, 18, 30, 32, 46-8, 59, 103, 107, 161
Voltaire 63, 128, 129

W

Williams, Rowan 12, 21, 42, 52, 83, 86-7, 90, 102
Wittgenstein, Ludwig 62, 166
Wright, Tom 85-6, 168
Wordsworth, William 11, 30

Other thought-provoking titles from Arena Books –

The Future of Politics
with the demise of the left/right confrontational system

by Robert Corfe

The old left/right confrontational system, which has served as the linchpin of the democratic process for 200 years, is now coming to the end of its useful purpose. This is not only reflected in the collapse of party memberships worldwide, but in the tendency of legislation and the executive to compound rather than resolve the issues of our age.

Meanwhile, a new class is emerging in advanced industrial societies which the author describes as the 90% middle-middle majority, whose underlying economic needs are not represented by any parliamentary groups, left, right or centre. The old parties are trapped in the time-warp of the past from which they cannot escape, and our most cognisant politicians are fully aware of this fact. The age-old political ideologies have become meaningless.

Over the past 60 years society and the world of work have been transformed out of all recognition, and new ideas and systems of democracy are needed if a free, just, and equitable basis is to be built for the future of humanity. But to achieve this, unifying ideas founded on an understanding of our present financial-industrial system are needed in repudiating the fallacies of the past and in constructing the future. In promoting the concept of *personal* property, the author is as critical of mis-named 'privatisation' as he is of the collectivism of the left.

ISBN 978-1-906791-46-9   **£12.99 / US$ 20.99**

Swiss Democracy
a model for Britain

by Kenrick Jones

This is a timely and important work in presenting pointers which could be significant in helping regenerate the sad state of British politics. British politics is in the doldrums. Until the 2001 General Election voter turn-out since the Second World War averaged 77%. However in 2001 it fell to 59%, and in 2005 it was a mere 61%.

This book demonstrates that one European country, viz., Switzerland, has a direct citizen-based democratic structure which could at least in part be beneficially incorporated into our representative parliamentary system. The ideas of the author are motivated by his own patriotism linked to a broader understanding of international institutions, and his proposals are designed to strengthen our democracy and not to denigrate it.

The book compares the relative significance of local government in both Britain and Switzerland. There are practical examples of how everyday issues are dealt with in both nations. Participating in the democratic process of our country, and seeking tangible results from our votes is the only sensible response in the face of national disillusionment.

ISBN 978-1-906791-43-8   **£14.99 / US$ 32.99**

Lightning Source UK Ltd.
Milton Keynes UK
UKOW05f1954180117
292387UK00008B/394/P